THE MASONIC THREAD IN MOZART

THE MASONIC THREAD IN MOZART

by
KATHARINE THOMSON

1977
LAWRENCE AND WISHART
LONDON

Lawrence and Wishart Ltd
39 Museum Street
London WC1

First published 1977
Copyright © Katharine Thomson 1977
SBN 85315 381 7

to

G.T. and F.K.

Printed in Great Britain by
The Camelot Press Ltd, Southampton

CONTENTS

PREFACE

Mozart was a man of deep convictions and, like many other classical composers, sought to express his outlook on life through music. This we know of him, not only from his letters and from what his contemporaries said about him, but also from the fact that he was an active member of the Order of Freemasons. In his time, the Masons were a secret society, regarded with suspicion by the government authorities and later banned, with definite views on social, ethical and even political questions – and also on the function of art. Music was valued largely for its moral influence, and certain motifs were associated with specific Masonic ideas.

Mozart wrote a number of works for the Order, including songs and cantatas, and an opera, *The Magic Flute*, which is a Masonic allegory. The connections between Masonic ideas and the musical motifs in these compositions have been identified by scholars such as Paul Nettl and Jacques Chailley. There remain, however, a number of instrumental works in which similar motifs occur. The aim of this book is to explore this wider field and to examine the significance of Masonic ideas in Mozart's instrumental compositions by comparing them with vocal works in which the same themes are to be found.

Some understanding of what these Masonic ideas were, of what they meant to Mozart, and of how they are expressed musically, must surely be relevant to our interpretation of his music as a whole. No singer would think of singing in a foreign language without knowing what the song was about, and an adequate performance of "programme music" must entail some knowledge of the content of the "programme". All this is generally accepted; yet in the field of what is usually known as "abstract music", it is sometimes assumed that we cannot attach to the music any significance which is not purely aesthetic, without somehow debasing it.

All his life Mozart loved riddles and mysteries. For several years he and his father used a secret code in their correspondence, for fear it should fall into the hands of the Archbishop of Salzburg. It is easy to see how he became interested in the musical code of the Freemasons, which he expanded and developed, and we should use our knowledge of this code to deepen our understanding of his music.

The book opens with a general account of eighteenth-century Freemasonry in Central Europe. There follows an outline of Mozart's life, with extracts from his correspondence and from contemporary documents, selected so as to throw light on the development of his ideas on society and on music. No attempt is made to give a comprehensive account of his compositions or a formal analysis of the music, since there are many books on this subject. But certain works in which Masonic ideas appear to find expression are examined in some detail, with musical illustrations.

A good deal of work has been done by continental scholars on the history of eighteenth-century Freemasonry. But comparatively little of it is available in English, and there still remains the task of relating it to Mozart. In the present book the results of previous research are brought to bear more closely on his life and thought, and a new interpretation is offered of certain instrumental works, including the "Jupiter" Symphony and some of the piano concertos.

The book is intended for the general reader, but it is assumed that he will have some knowledge of musical terminology. A glossary is provided for his assistance, and some of the technical explanations have been relegated to an appendix. In general, the stories of operas are not given here, since they are readily available elsewhere. But in view of the importance of *The Magic Flute* in a study of Mozart's Masonic music, a synopsis of that opera is provided in an appendix. The extract from Meggenhofen's Letter to Weishaupt (Appendix II) has not previously been published in English.

Some of the material in this book appeared in my article "Mozart and Freemasonry" in *Music and Letters*, January 1976.

Translations of the German words are mostly given in literal prose, but titles of songs are quoted in familiar versions.

I wish to thank Alan Bush, Maurice Cornforth, Brenda Griffith, Frida Knight and Roy Pascal for their advice and helpful suggestions during the preparation of this book. I am indebted to Georg Knepler for showing me a chapter from his forthcoming book, and to Richard van Dülmen for information contained in his book on the Illuminati, which was unfortunately not available in time for me to consult.

I am also grateful to Bernard Williams and Christopher Raeburn for permission to quote from their talks on Radio 3, to Brian Humphries for advice in compiling the List of Recordings, to Eric Ashcroft for copying the music, to Sylva FitzGerald and Margaret Alexiou for their careful reading of the typescript, and to many friends for their help and encouragement.

I owe a special debt to Martin and Elsie Marshall, of the Birmingham Clarion Singers, whose interpretation of the parts of Figaro and Susanna led me to a better understanding of Mozart.

K. T.
Birmingham, 1976.

1

FREEMASONRY IN THE EIGHTEENTH CENTURY

"He was a diligent member of our Order: brotherly love, a peaceable disposition, advocacy of a good cause, beneficence, a true, sincere sense of pleasure whenever he could help one of the Brethren with his talents: these were his chief characteristics."[1]

These words are from a Masonic Oration delivered in Mozart's memory shortly after his death. He had been initiated in the small Viennese lodge *Beneficence* on 14 December 1784, when he was nearly twenty-nine years old. Two months later he recruited his friend Joseph Haydn and his father Leopold to the Brotherhood. He attended meetings regularly and wrote a number of works for ceremonies in the lodges. In the last year of his life he wrote an opera which is a Masonic allegory, *The Magic Flute*.

The great Mozartean scholar Alfred Einstein has written that "the consciousness of his membership in the Order [of Freemasons] permeates his entire work. Not only *Die Zauberflöte* [*The Magic Flute*] but many others of his works are Masonic, even though they reveal nothing of this quality to the uninitiated."[2]

What did it mean to be a Freemason in Vienna at the end of the eighteenth century? To answer this question we must find out something about the history of the Order, remembering that in those days it differed considerably from the institution as we know it in England today. In this country Freemasons are usually regarded as a highly respectable body of men, whose pursuits are mainly charitable. But in Central Europe in the eighteenth century their activities were often considered to be dangerous and subversive. After the French Revolution of 1789, rumours circulated that the Freemasons were actually responsible for the Revolution, and in several countries the Order was banned. It is of course untrue that the organisation itself was revolutionary, although individual Freemasons, such as Mirabeau, were active supporters of the Revolution, and the slogans "Liberty, Equality and Fraternity" were basic principles in some forms of Freemasonry.

The development of the movement varied considerably in different countries. In general, Freemasonry represented the outlook of the new bourgeoisie – merchants, manufacturers and professional men, as opposed to the old landed aristocracy, whose privileges were based on rights of birth.

The first Grand Lodge was established in England in 1717. The society was secret, with an elaborate ritual derived partly from the old Craft, or Operative Masonry, and partly from the ancient mysteries of Egypt and Eleusis. Lodges were run on egalitarian principles, as written into Anderson's Constitutions in 1723: "To be the means of conciliating true friendship among persons who must otherwise have remained at a perpetual distance."[3]

Religious tolerance was supported, but Masons were not atheists; in fact they stated that "a Mason . . . will never be a stupid Atheist, nor an irreligious Libertine."[4] Political discussion was prohibited in the lodges: "We . . . are resolved against all Politicks, as what never yet conducted to the welfare of the *Lodge*, nor ever will."[5]

The movement never became a political force in England, where the transition from medieval to modern society had begun much earlier than in the rest of Europe. But it had the support of many industrialists and scientists of the time.

Freemasonry is thought to have been introduced into France by Jacobite exiles in 1725. Among its leading members was a Scot, Andrew Ramsay (later known as "Knight Ramsay"), a colourful figure who had been tutor to the children of the Old Pretender in Rome. In a famous speech he set out the aims of the Order, one of which was "to make men lovable men, good citizens, good subjects, inviolable in their promises, faithful adorers of the God of Love, lovers of virtue rather than reward".[6]

French Freemasonry was at first neither anti-clerical nor atheistic; it had the support of several members of the privileged classes, including royalty; it even became something of a fashionable cult. Later, dissensions arose between two sections, described by a contemporary as "freemaçons catoliques, royalistes et jacobites", and "freemaçons hérétiques apostats et républicains."[7] In 1773 the Grand Orient Lodge of France was founded, with the aim of uniting the different sections; its Grand Master was the Duke of Orleans (later known as "Philippe Égalité"). It has been estimated that on the eve of the Revolution there were at least 100,000 Freemasons in France. Among them were such men as Condorcet, Voltaire and d'Alembert. One of their declared aims was that "all brothers in every country are to unite in collecting materials for a Universal Dictionary of liberal arts and useful sciences (excluding politics and religion)".[8] Thus their ideas were clearly related to those of the Encyclopaedists and of the Enlightenment.

Freemasonry was introduced into Germany in the 1730s. One of the first lodges was established in the Free City of Hamburg, an important commercial centre, where Freemasons later acquired considerable influence.

Eighteenth-century Germany was divided into a number of small states, many of which were governed by absolute princes, and free cities. The country was economically and politically backward, especially the Catholic south, like Bavaria, where education was entirely in the hands of the Church, and the population as a whole was ignorant and superstitious.

The culture of the aristocracy was trivial and conventional, dominated by the influence of the French court. Strict censorship was enforced, and there was virtually no way in which criticism of the existing social order could be expressed. When the ideas of the Enlightenment reached Germany, they were eagerly welcomed, especially in the Protestant states. Lessing was one of the first to express these ideas, and later the revolt of writers and artists exploded in the literary movement known as "Sturm und Drang", of which Goethe, Schiller and Herder were the best-known representatives.

There was thus a basis for Masonic ideas of equality and fraternity, and the movement found ready support in Germany; among those who joined the Order were Goethe, Herder and Lessing. The aims of Masonry were defined by Lessing in his *Masonic Dialogues*: "By the exercise of Brotherly Love we are taught to regard the whole human species as one family, the high and the low, the rich and the poor, created by one Almighty Being, and sent into the world for the aid, support and protection of each other."[9]

Masonry was brought to Austria by Maria Theresia's husband, Francis I, who had been a zealous Mason in his native France, and who founded the first Masonic lodge in Vienna in 1731. The movement spread rapidly, both in the Habsburg dominions and in the rest of Germany. Most of its support came from the bourgeoisie, but members of the nobility and of the army joined the Order, and even some of the clergy, in spite of the edict issued by Pope Clement XII in 1738 forbidding Catholics to be Freemasons. This ban was not observed in Austria until after the death of Francis I, when Maria Theresia, a bigoted Catholic, banned the Order and persecuted the Freemasons. Her more enlightened son Joseph II, who succeeded her, introduced various reforms; he lifted the ban on Freemasons and even showed them some favour.

By the middle of the eighteenth century Freemasonry in Germany was divided into different groups, with varying aims and forms of ritual. Although certain features were common to all these groups, it is important to distinguish between them, since they were often strongly opposed to each other. Among the most significant were the Rosicrucians and the Illuminati.

The Order of Rosicrucians, based on a seventeenth-century group, and originally separate from orthodox Freemasonry, was mainly concerned with mysticism and magic. One of its adherents was Dr. Mesmer, exponent of the theory of "animal magnetism", who became famous as a hypnotist.

The Illuminati, whose Order was also at first outside Freemasonry, were opposed to the Rosicrucians; their aims were rationalist and ethical. (It has been said that the Rosicrucians represented the right wing and the Illuminati the left wing of Freemasonry.) Since this group was particularly strong in southern Germany and in Austria, it is worth examining its history and aims in greater detail.

The founder of the Illuminati was Adam Weishaupt, a professor of canon law at the university of Ingolstadt in Bavaria. He had been educated in a Jesuit seminary, and, although strongly opposed to the philosophy of the Jesuits, he was influenced by their methods of organisation. In 1776 he formed a secret society called a "League against the enemies of Reason and Humanity", based on the ideas of Rousseau and Diderot. He believed that liberty and equality were the inalienable rights of man, and that it was possible to abolish oppression and to achieve universal happiness by means of moral perfection and of reason, based on the study of nature. (By "nature" he meant the whole field of human nature in relation to its environment, as in Rousseau and the Encyclopaedists.)

Weishaupt declared that "accumulated property is an insurmountable obstacle to the happiness of any nation, whose chief laws were framed for its protection and increase."[10] Members of his society were at first called "Perfectibilists"; later the name was changed to "Illuminati", because "the means of attaining our object is Illumination, enlightening the understanding by the sun of reason, which will dispel the clouds of superstition and prejudice."[11] These aims were to be achieved through education in "secret schools of wisdom", or "lights". Like the Freemasons, he modelled his ritual on that of ancient Greek and Egyptian mysteries. Members of the society were divided into three grades: Novice, Minerval, and Illuminatus Minor. The leaders were called Areopagites, and given classical pseudonyms. Weishaupt was known as Spartacus; another leader, Zwack, was Cato; Baron von Knigge, who joined the society later, was Philo. Meetings were held in the utmost secrecy, and the membership was very small. In 1778 there were only twelve members; in 1779 there were seventy – all in Bavaria. Meanwhile Weishaupt had joined the Masonic lodge *Theodor* in Munich, and started to win adherents from among Freemasons.

One of the most active leaders of the Illuminati at this time was Adolf von Knigge, a writer from Hanover, who was a disciple of Rousseau. He had been a member of a Masonic lodge in Frankfurt, but had become dissatisfied with its aims and methods of organisation. In 1779 he joined the Illuminati, and soon rose to prominence in the leadership. In 1781 he travelled all over Germany, recruiting to the movement. At a Convention of Freemasons held at Wilhelmsbad in 1782 the Illuminati succeeded in winning over a number of Freemasons from different sects; in this way they were able to infiltrate and to gain control of Masonic lodges in many places, especially in Austria.

Besides conducting a vigorous recruiting campaign, Knigge reorganised the ritual of the Illuminati, creating new grades which included that of Scottish Knight, or Illuminatus Dirigens. Differences of opinion soon arose between Knigge and Weishaupt over the organisation of the higher grades and ritual, and in 1784 Knigge left the Order. From the content of his writings it seems that his views were more radical than those of Weishaupt.

Meanwhile the rapid growth of this movement and the spread of Illuminist ideas had begun to alarm the clerical authorities. A campaign to discredit the Illuminati was initiated by the Jesuits in Bavaria, with support from members of the rival Rosicrucian Order. The Elector of Bavaria, Karl Theodor, who was under Jesuit influence, published an edict in 1784 forbidding the Illuminati to hold meetings in Bavaria. They appealed against the decree, and continued to meet secretly. The campaign was intensified; spies and informers infiltrated the Order, and in March 1785 a further edict was issued banning the Illuminati. Incriminating documents were discovered, and when four professors, who had been members of the society, turned King's evidence, a witchhunt began. The houses of leading members were searched, including that of Zwack, from whose lodgings a number of documents were seized, and later published; a great many people were arrested. Weishaupt had meanwhile fled to the neighbouring Free City of Regensburg; Knigge had left the Order and was no longer in Bavaria.

Letters were sent by the Bavarian government to the heads of other states, warning them of the dangers of this sect, and asking that measures be taken against the Illuminati. The replies were often lukewarm; a letter from the Viennese authorities to their embassy in Munich stated: "As far as the Illuminati are concerned, the Embassy should do nothing in their favour, since the Elector is so hostile to them, but they should do nothing against them, because these people must be handled with extreme caution, since they have considerable influence in all kinds of business."[12]

After the French Revolution, rulers in many German states became alarmed at the growth and influence of secret societies; there was widespread persecution of Freemasons in general, and of the Illuminati in particular. In Bavaria, the death sentence was imposed on anyone found recruiting to the Illuminati. In Vienna Joseph II tightened control over the lodges, and set up the first secret police in Europe, so as "to discover any discontent arising among the people, all dangerous thoughts, and especially any incipient rebellion, and to nip these in the bud where possible".[13] Throughout the Habsburg dominions there was an atmosphere of fear and suspicion; rumours circulated about the subversive activities of the Illuminati, and it was at this time that the legend of Illuminist responsibility for the French Revolution arose. (We shall return to this subject later.)

The Illuminati have been described as "an association of daring thinkers, who were trying to create a new religion, a new statistic, a new morality, independent of metaphysics, aimed at developing a humanism which was occupied with making life in this world happier, rather than with the possible benefits of a dubious future life".[14] They strongly condemned the Catholic Church for instilling superstition into the minds of the people. But, contrary to general belief, they were not anti-religious nor atheistic, for they believed in a divine Creator of the world.

The Illuminati were never strong numerically, but they were a powerful force in moulding the moral and social ideas of the age. Among their supporters in Germany were Goethe and Herder. In Austria, their leaders included Joseph von Sonnenfels. a Minister of State, and Ignaz von Born, a distinguished mineralogist, founder and Grand Master of the Masonic lodge *True Harmony*. Both these men were friends and patrons of Mozart's, as was Otto von Gemmingen, writer and diplomat, who was also a leading member of the Illuminati. Gemmingen was Grand Master of the lodge *Beneficence*, in which Mozart was initiated in December 1784. This lodge shared a temple with *True Harmony*, and Mozart frequently attended ceremonies in the sister-lodge.

Thus both these lodges were under Illuminist leadership, and a good many of the Brethren were members of the society. Was Mozart himself one of their number? This question is hard to answer. His name does not appear on any of the extant lists, but many records were destroyed during the persecution of Freemasons after the French Revolution, and we know that Constanze disposed of documents relating to her husband's membership of the Freemasons. But we may be certain that he knew something about the ideas and activities of the Illuminati from his friends. It is possible, as Einstein suggests, that he was characteristically making fun of the pseudonyms of the Illuminati when he invented nicknames for himself and his friends, on his journey to Prague in 1787. He wrote to Gottfried von Jacquin: "Now farewell, dearest friend, dearest Hikkiti Horky! That is your name, as you must know. We all invented names for ourselves on the journey. Here they are. I am Punkititi. My wife is Schabla Pumfa. Hofer is Rozka Pumpa. Stadler is Natschibinitschibi. My servant Joseph is Sagadaratà. My dog Gauckerl is Schamanuzky. Madame Quallenberg is Runzifunzi. Mlle Crux is Ramlo Schurimuri. Freistädtler is Gaulimauli. Be so kind as to tell him his name."[15]

This does not mean, of course, that Mozart was necessarily a member of the society, but there is some evidence that he may have attended gatherings of the Illuminati before his initiation as a Freemason. The topographer Lorenz Hübner, writing in 1792, reported that meetings of Illuminati were held by night in a lonely grotto at Aigen, near Salzburg (now known as the "Illuminaten-Höhle", or "Cave of the Illuminati"), attended by Count Gilowsky, one of the Illuminist leaders, "with his friends von Amann, Mozart and Barisani".[16]

If Mozart did indeed attend these gatherings at Aigen – and there seems no reason to doubt the contemporary evidence – he must have retained vivid memories of the grotto, with its rushing waterfall, tall trees and steep, jagged rocks. The atmosphere is mysterious and awe-inspiring, like a setting for the scene of the Men in Armour in *The Magic Flute*, for which the stage directions read: "Two mountains, one containing a rushing waterfall, the other spitting out fire."

After Mozart's death, Constanze told friends that he had drawn up plans for a secret society, to be named "The Grotto". Perhaps he was thinking of those moonlight meetings at Aigen.

Before tracing the steps which led Mozart eventually to become a Freemason, some account must be given of his family background and early life.

(Mozart's parents had become betrothed at Aigen in 1747. The church contains a plaque which erroneously states that Leopold Mozart and Anna Pertl were married there; the error is due to Leopold's jocular reference in a letter of 24 November 1764, stating that he had "joined the order of patched trousers at Aigen seventeen years previously".)[17]

NOTES

1 Deutsch, O. E., *Mozart, A Documentary Biography*, London, 1965, p. 448.
2 Einstein, Alfred, *Mozart*, (1st ed. 1946), London, 1971, p. 93.
3 Schneider, H., *Quest for Mysteries*, New York, 1947, p. 18.
4 Roberts, J. M., *The Mythology of the Secret Societies*, St. Alban's, 1974, p. 38.
5 ibid., p. 38.
6 ibid., p. 52.
7 ibid., p. 49.
8 Massin, J. and B., *W. A. Mozart*, Paris, 1959, p. 1177.
9 Cohen, A., *Lessing's Masonic Dialogues*, London, 1927.
10 Robison, J., *Proofs of a Conspiracy*, Edinburgh, 1797 (repr. Western Islands, U.S., 1967) p. 107.
11 Frost, T., *Secret Societies of the European Revolution*, London, 1876, p. 29.
12 Engel, L., *Geschichte des Illuminaten-Ordens*, Berlin, 1906, p. 197.
13 Wangermann, E., *From Joseph II to the Jacobin Trials*, Oxford, 1969, p. 37.
14 Le Forestier, R., *Les Illuminés de Bavière*, Paris, 1913, p. 110.
15 Einstein, p. 96.
16 Koch, R., *Br. Mozart, Freimaurer und Illuminat*, Bad Reichenhall, 1911, p. 3.
17 Deutsch, p. 5.

2

FAMILY BACKGROUND AND EARLY YEARS

Leopold Mozart was the son of a bookbinder in Augsburg. He was born in 1719, and had originally been destined for the priesthood, but, after studying for two years at the Benedictine University in Salzburg, he was expelled for not attending sufficient lectures. He then took up music, entering the service of Count Thurn und Taxis in Salzburg as "groom of the chamber, with duties as musician". In those days the status of a musician was that of a servant, who frequently had other duties to perform, besides musical ones. An advertisement in a Viennese newspaper, for instance, read: "A servant is required for a mansion in the neighbourhood; he should be a good violinist and able to accompany difficult piano sonatas."[1]

Although Joseph Haydn was fortunate at Esterhazy in having a master who was interested in music and considerate to his dependants, his position was still that of a bond servant; he was obliged to present himself to the prince every morning in the livery of a servant, with white shirt, white stockings and powdered wig. He had to compose whatever his master ordered, and his compositions were the prince's property and could not be passed on to anyone else. Nor could he leave the court without permission, which was not always granted.

Haydn's brother Michael was employed at the court of the Prince-Archbishop of Salzburg, in which Leopold Mozart entered service in 1743.

Salzburg at that time was an independent archi-episcopal state, forming part of the German empire. Most of its population of about 10,000 depended for their livelihood on the Prince-Archbishop. Leopold served under three Archbishops – Firmian, Schrattenbach and Colloredo, of whom the last-named achieved fame through his quarrel with Wolfgang. At first Leopold was employed as fourth violinist in the court orchestra, but in 1757 he was appointed court composer, and by 1763 he had risen to be Vice-Kapellmeister – a position in which he remained to the end of his life, in spite of his efforts to win promotion.

Leopold Mozart was a prolific and competent composer. His compositions include symphonies, concertos, divertimenti and sonatas, as well as a considerable amount of religious music. He supplemented his income by teaching the violin, and in 1756 he published his famous book on violin technique, *Versuch einer gründlichen Violinschule*.

In 1748 he married Anna Pertl, daughter of a petty official from the small town of St Gilgen, of peasant stock. The couple rented three rooms in the house of a wealthy merchant named Hagenauer. (This house is now a Mozart museum.) Of the seven children born to them, only two survived: a girl, Nannerl, born in 1751, and Wolfgang Amadeus, born on 27 January 1756.

By the time that Wolfgang was four his father realised that the child was remarkably talented; he was already playing both the violin and the clavier, and at the age of five he was composing little pieces. Leopold began to plan a series of grand tours for his two gifted children (for Nannerl could play the clavier quite well, too). Between 1762 and 1767 the whole family went on tour, visiting many cities in Europe, including Vienna, Munich, Frankfurt, Brussels, Paris and London. The children were fêted and admired wherever they went, but the financial rewards of these tours were not great, since the aristocracy were more ready to bestow gold watches and snuff-boxes than to part with their money.

These journeys took toll of the children's health; both contracted serious illnesses, including smallpox. But Wolfgang's horizon was widened by seeing many countries and meeting people of different nationalities with differing viewpoints; he was also able to hear a great deal of music. Even in these early years, he came under the influence of Freemasons and supporters of the Enlightenment. At the age of twelve, when he had smallpox at Olomouc, in Moravia, he was tended by Dr. Wolff, a Freemason, for whose daughter he wrote a song.* In Vienna the Mozarts were introduced into Masonic circles by Dr. Mesmer, in whose garden the twelve-year-old Wolfgang's *Singspiel, Bastien and Bastienne*, based on a text by Jean-Jacques Rousseau (*Le Devin du Village*) was first performed.

Between 1769 and 1770 Wolfgang and his father paid three visits to Italy, leaving Anna and Nannerl in Salzburg. Wolfgang received honours from the Pope, and from the Philharmonic Society in Verona; in Bologna he met the celebrated Padre Martini; in Milan he composed three operas and a number of other works, including symphonies and string quartets. These visits to Italy had a considerable influence on the young composer's development. The opera *Lucio Silla* (K.135) and the

---

* It has been suggested that this song was "An die Freude" (K.53), which has a Masonic text. The latest evidence makes this unlikely. (See N.M.A. III, 8, p. 137.)

string quartets written in Milan in 1772 (K.155–160) show a new expressiveness and depth of feeling.

All these journeys were recorded by Leopold in detailed letters to his wife, and to his landlord Hagenauer. They give an interesting picture of society on the continent of Europe and in England at that time, as well as throwing light on the character of the writer. Leopold took a lively interest in politics; he was strongly anti-militarist, making sarcastic comments about the soldiers in Ludwigsburg, who "strut about everywhere dressed to the nines. . . . When you spit, you spit into an officer's pocket or into a soldier's cartridge-box. . . . In the streets you hear nothing but perpetual 'Quick march! Left! right! left, etc.', and you see nothing but arms, drums and war material."[2]

His account of pre-revolutionary Paris is interesting. "And I assure you that it does not require a telescope to see everywhere the evil results of the late war. For the French insist on continuing their external magnificence and therefore only the *fermiers** are rich while the lords are deep in debt. The bulk of the country is divided among about a hundred persons, a few big bankers and tax-farmers, and, finally, most money is spent on Lucretias, who, however, do not stab themselves."[3]

He condemns the nobility for sending their new-born children to be reared in the country. As a result of this custom, he writes: "You will hardly find any other city with so many miserable and mutilated persons. You have only to spend a minute in a church or to walk along a few streets to meet some blind, lame or limping or half-putrefied beggar, or to find someone lying on the street who has had his hand eaten away by the pigs, or someone else who in childhood fell into the fire and had half an arm burnt off while the foster-father and his family were working in the fields."[4]

As a pious Catholic, Leopold was shocked by the lack of religion in England. "I will not bring up my children in such a dangerous place (where the majority of the inhabitants have no religion, and where one has only evil examples before one)."[5]

Leopold's letters show that he was a keen observer of human nature and a shrewd man-of-the-world. He was well-read, and by no means narrow-minded; although a devout Catholic, he had friends among the Freemasons and supporters of the Enlightenment, such as Ignaz von Born and Anton Mesmer in Vienna, Diderot, Grimm and d'Alembert in Paris.

* Tax farmers: financiers who, under the *Ancien Régime*, let out the proceeds of a tax on payment of a fixed sum.

Leopold had the reputation of being a satirical humorist, and in his early days at Salzburg he was censured for writing a lampoon on one of the clergy. He gave his children a good general education, as well as an excellent musical training, though he was inclined to drive them too hard. His attitude to his social superiors was contradictory: he was at the same time haughty and servile. Although he became thoroughly dissatisfied with his treatment at the hands of the aristocracy, he was terrified of offending them. Wolfgang once wrote to him: "You really are too timid. . . . All I insist on and nothing else is that you should show the world that you are not afraid."[6]

Above all, Leopold was ambitious. In exploiting his gifted children he was trying to win for himself, as well as for them, a higher status in society. His determination to achieve this aim became an overriding passion, to which everything must be sacrificed, including his own health, that of his children, of his wife (even her life, as it eventually turned out), and his own dignity and integrity. He would have sacrificed his son's integrity as well, had not Wolfgang rebelled.

The contradictions within the character of Leopold Mozart, as well as those between his character and that of his son, are an interesting reflection of the class conflicts of their time. Both father and son were the products of a decaying social system; both resented the injustices of a society in which wealth and rank counted for everything, natural talent and innate goodness for nothing. But whereas Leopold conformed to the values of that society, and tried to climb the social ladder, Wolfgang, belonging to a later generation, broke right away from the old order. His whole life and his music express a passionate belief in the equality of human beings. "It is the heart which ennobles the man", he wrote to his father after his quarrel with Count Arco, emissary of Archbishop Colloredo, "and, though I am no count, yet I probably have more honour in me than many a count."[7]

The life-story of Mozart illustrates the struggle of a great artist to break the bonds of feudalism and to liberate himself from all feudal ideas, including those expressed in music. In the course of that struggle, Mozart suffered physically and emotionally, and his suffering is revealed in his music. But his story is one of triumph – not over material conditions, for he died in poverty at the age of thirty-five – but a triumph of the spirit, as expressed in the compositions of his last years.

NOTES

1 Stadtlaender, Christina, *Joseph Haydn of Eisenstadt*, London, 1968, p. 21.
2 Anderson, Emily, *The Letters of Mozart and his Family*, New York, 1966, p. 24.
3 ibid., p. 36.
4 ibid., p. 36.
5 ibid., p. 56.
6 ibid., p. 749.
7 ibid., p. 747.

3

THAMOS, KING OF EGYPT

Leopold and Wolfgang returned from their third and last journey to
Italy in March 1773. The results of their travels had been disappointing.
In spite of all Wolfgang's successes, their prospects were no better than
before, and the financial drain on their resources had been heavy. But
their visits to Italy had increased their determination to seek
employment outside the restrictive atmosphere of Salzburg. "<I have
sent Wolfgang's opera [*Lucio Silla*] to the Grand Duke in Florence.
Even if there is no hope of obtaining anything from him I trust he will
recommend us. But if it is all in vain, we shall not go under, for God will
help us. I have already thought out some plans>", wrote Leopold to his
wife, using the code which the family adopted for matters which they
wished to keep secret.[1]*

It was perhaps in furtherance of these plans that father and son set
out on a fresh journey four months later, choosing a time when
Archbishop Colloredo was absent from Salzburg. The exact purpose of
their visit to Vienna is not known. During the three months of their stay
they were frequent guests of Dr. Mesmer, through whom they were
introduced to many Freemasons, including Tobias von Gebler, an
enlightened Councillor and well-known dramatist, for whose play
Thamos, King of Egypt, Mozart composed music.

Gebler was a friend of Lessing and Wieland (who were also
Freemasons), and a supporter of the movement for the reform of the
Viennese theatre. The reformers, led by Joseph von Sonnenfels, aimed
at raising the cultural level of the public through the performance of
serious literary drama in German, such as the plays of Schiller, Goethe
and Lessing. Since the beginning of the eighteenth century improvised
Harlequin, or *Hanswurst* comedies had held the Viennese stage. These
plays, based on folk tradition, and originally introduced into Vienna by
strolling players, had degenerated into what has been described as "a
mixture of elaborate mechanical gimmicks and vulgar buffoonery".[2]
Meanwhile the court and aristocracy patronised only foreign plays,
performed by French and Italian actors and singers, including the

* The use of this code is indicated here by brackets < >.

artificial *opera seria* in Italian, and frivolous French comedies from the court of Versailles. There was thus no serious German drama in Vienna, and it was the aim of men like Sonnenfels and Gebler to establish contemporary plays in German, related to the lives and aspirations of the new bourgeois class, as opposed to the old aristocracy. In this cultural conflict both sides sought to win the support of the monarchy. The theme of the "enlightened ruler" was a popular one in the German literature of the time; it became especially significant in Vienna during the 1770s, since Joseph II, who was co-regent with Maria Theresia, was known to have more enlightened views than his mother.

The establishment of the National Theatre in 1770 was a victory for the reformers. *Hanswurst* comedies were banned; improvisation on the stage was forbidden, and strict censorship imposed. "No dirty or equivocal words shall be allowed, nor shall any of the actors use the same without due punishment."[3] It seems that the comedians continued to defy the censor when the performance was a musical one, for Sonnenfels complained: "But why did the comic sing on the stage, in public, what was not allowed to be printed?"[4]

Meanwhile many French and Italian actors and singers were dismissed, and authors were encouraged to write plays in German. An advertisement appeared in the Gotha Kalendar on 15 February 1778, asking for "Original plays for the German nation, works of true genius, where nature and art are properly allied."[5] For a time German drama flourished in Vienna, and it was during this period that Gebler's play *Thamos, King of Egypt*, was written. The play lacks dramatic interest, and the language is pompous. But it is interesting as an expression of the ideas of the Enlightenment.

On 18 October 1773 Leopold Mozart wrote to his wife: "Wolfgang is composing something most enthusiastically."[6] Evidence suggests that the "something" was in fact the choruses for *Thamos*. Why was Wolfgang enthusiastic about composing music for Gebler's play? No doubt he welcomed the opportunity for collaboration with one of Austria's leading dramatists; perhaps, too, he was glad to accept the challenge of satisfying the author when other composers had failed, for Gebler had already approached J. T. Sattler and Gluck, but had not been pleased with their work. Mozart must certainly have been glad to compose choruses, which he later described as "my favourite type of composition". The fact that these choruses were in German, rather than the Latin of the church masses, must have made the task all the more congenial. Moreover, the high moral purpose of the drama was of a kind likely to appeal to the young composer, whose humanistic ideas were already apparent.

It has been stated that "although Freemasonry may have exerted some influence over Gebler's mind, it can have had none at that time over Mozart".[7] It is true, of course, that Mozart had not yet joined the Order. But, as we have seen, he already had several friends who were Freemasons, and he had composed songs to Masonic texts, including one, "O heiliges Band" (K.148), from a collection of Masonic songs to a text by L. F. Lenz (see p. 44). It is clear that, at the time when Gebler invited him to write music for his play, Mozart was familiar with Masonic ideas, and he may even have known something about the ritual and symbolism of the Order. The music to *Thamos* represents an important stage in Mozart's development, both as a man and as a composer. For the first time, he associated himself openly with the ideas of the Enlightenment. These ideas became increasingly important to him during his short life, finding their noblest expression, in his last year, in *The Magic Flute*.

The subject of *Thamos* is the conflict between the forces of good and evil, of light and darkness, and the triumph of virtue in the person of an enlightened ruler. The Masonic background is indicated by the Egyptian setting, and by the ceremonies of sun-worship. Masonic ideas on Egyptian ritual were based chiefly on Greek sources, like the account given by Diodorus Siculus of the ancient Greek and Egyptian mysteries.[8] One of the immediate sources for *Thamos*, as for *The Magic Flute*, was the novel *Sethos*, written in 1731 by the Abbé Terrasson, purporting to be the work of an Alexandrian Greek of the time of Marcus Aurelius. *Sethos* was translated into German and English; it became popular all over Europe and was much read in Masonic circles. It was one of the books recommended for reading by the higher grades of Illuminati.

The influence of this novel on *Thamos* is evident in several ways. Thamos and Sethos have both been educated by priests in order to become virtuous rulers. In both novel and play strong feelings are expressed against war, as well as the idea of forgiveness and tolerance. For example, in *Sethos* we read that "a king who loves his subjects always looks on war as a misfortune";[9] in *Thamos*: "Do not let citizen rage against citizen, brother disembowel his brother or tear the flesh of his son."[10]

In the introduction to *Sethos*, Terrasson explained that "Since the author has chosen to leave his hero as a pagan, he confines himself wholly to the moral virtues."[11] The idea of the "noble savage", taken over from Rousseau, and that Christianity was not necessarily superior to other religions, ran counter to the teaching of the Catholic Church, as did the idea that love of one's fellow-men was even more important than love of God. Gebler's strong principles on these matters were made clear in 1778, when he upheld the rights of Jews, in opposition to the powerful Cardinal Migazzi, who had complained that "Jewish people, indistinguishable from others by their dress, now frequent inns, ballrooms and theatres and mix with the Christians who are there."[12]

In *Thamos*, the worshippers of Osiris are depicted as possessing the highest virtues. Thamos himself "honours the gods and loves his fellow-men".[13]

Ideas such as these, which are an essential part of Masonic doctrine, are expressed in several of Mozart's operas – in *Zaide*, *Die Entführung*, *La Clemenza di Tito*, and above all in *The Magic Flute*. In that opera Sarastro, High Priest of Osiris, declares that "Within these sacred walls, where man loves his fellow-men, no traitor can be found, for man forgives his enemy."[14]

One of the central themes of *Thamos* is the idea that a ruler is responsible for the welfare of his people, and that he should govern solely in the interests of truth and justice. "The actions of princes are guide-lines for their people. They must be tainted with no injustice."[15] Thamos condemns his father, who had been an unjust ruler, in these words: "Unhappy father! Even if you had held the whole world under your sceptre, you would still have been unhappy. Unless Thamos possesses friends and the love of his people, he cannot rule."[16] Such a statement might be interpreted as a plea to the young Joseph to govern more justly than his mother, whose persecution of Freemasons and others was a living memory.

The democratic belief, that only through an alliance of ruler and people could a just and happy society be attained, was expressed by Gebler through the use of a chorus, in the manner of the ancient Greeks. It is clear that he attached great importance to the musical setting of the choruses, and that he was pleased with Mozart's music. He sent it to Nicolai, commenting: "The first chorus is very fine."[17] Later he sent the music to Wieland, who wrote in reply: "Receive, . . . dearest friend, my most sincere thanks for the beautiful music for *Thamos* which you sent me."[18]

Mozart composed two choruses and four entr'actes for the performances of *Thamos* in Vienna in April 1773. The music was

praised in a review in the *Theaterchronik von Wien*: "The music, by
Herr *Karl Mozzart* [*sic*] is beautifully written."[19] Two years later a
Salzburg critic was less enthusiastic: "The choruses might be entirely
omitted without robbing the piece of anything."[20]

Mozart himself thought highly of the music, which he revised and
added to in 1779 for the travelling company of Johannes Böhm. The
revised version was never performed, and four years later Mozart wrote
to his father from Vienna: "I am sorry that I shall not be able to use the
music of *Thamos*, but this piece, which failed to please here, is now
among the rejected works which are no longer performed. For the sake
of the music alone, it might be given again, but that is not likely.
Certainly it is a pity."[21]*

The revised version consisted of three choruses and five entr'actes,
including a melodrama. In composing the entr'actes, Mozart seems to
have been guided by the principles laid down by J. A. Scheibe, a
Freemason, who was the first German musician to publish a collection
of Masonic songs. "Symphonies between the acts should be connected
both with the act preceding and that which follows, so that the audience
is led insensibly from one frame of mind to another."[22]

The entr'actes in *Thamos* give us a clue towards understanding how
Mozart tried to express thoughts and feelings in instrumental music.
Each entr'acte is prefaced by a description of the situation. "The first
act closes with the resolution of Pheron and Mirza to put Pheron on the
throne."[23] These two characters represent the forces of darkness and
evil. This entr'acte is in the key of C minor, a key often associated with
darkness in Mozart's music, as opposed to C major, the key of light.
Chromatic phrases and diminished sevenths are further indications of
evil, while syncopated rhythms and *tremolandos* illustrate the agitated
state of mind of the two villains. The movement is in sonata form, and
the second subject, in the relative major (E♭), is a tender phrase,
suggesting the character of the heroine, Sais. In the development
section, the two elements are in conflict, and when the second subject is
repeated in the recapitulation in the tonic key (C minor), it is
transformed into a theme of great pathos, expressing the suffering which
has been inflicted on Sais.

The second entr'acte has the following superscription: "Thamos's
good character becomes apparent at the end of the second act; the third
act begins with Thamos and the traitor Pheron."[24] This movement is in
E♭. A flowing melody indicates "Thamos's noble character" (these

* The music was later adapted by Böhm for a play called *Lanassa* (see p. 140).

words are written over the music in the handwriting of Leopold Mozart); while "Pheron's false character" is denoted by strongly-marked syncopated accents, and chords of E♭ minor, with *sforzandos* on the bassoon. In the development, the conflict between the two men is depicted. Both themes are combined in the coda, when Thamos's melody is heard on the oboe, while Pheron's rhythm persists, but now in E♭ major instead of minor, as though subdued by Thamos's "noble" theme. Thus this entr'acte prepares us for the dialogue between Thamos and Pheron which opens Act III.

The entr'acte after Act III contains the melodrama. Mozart had met this musical form in Mannheim in 1778, through the works of Georg Benda, and had been greatly impressed. It consists of words spoken, not sung, to the accompaniment of music. Mozart used melodrama again in *Zaide* (p. 48) but abandoned it later, finding the human voice a more powerful vehicle for expressing emotions. (Beethoven used melodrama with dramatic effect in *Fidelio*.)

In *Thamos* the melodrama accompanies a monologue by Sais, in which she expresses her doubts about the plan proposed to her by the treacherous Pheron, who hopes to marry her and become king instead of Thamos. Sais is torn between her love for Thamos and her loyalty to her country. The changes in the music are closely related to her changes of mood, reflecting agitation, pathos, tenderness, and finally courage and resolution. Eventually she decides to dedicate herself to the service of the Sun-god, rather than to marry Pheron.

The melodrama is in free form, but the repetition of Sais's opening phrase after she has made her vow is comparable in function to the recapitulation in sonata form. (For a full analysis of the melodrama, see *Appendix I*.)

The three choruses in *Thamos* provide a majestic framework to the drama. The first two are antiphonal, with solemn choral sections contrasting with solo passages in lighter style. In the first chorus, the rising of the sun is suggested by rising syncopated chords, which foreshadow the introduction to Sarastro's words in the Finale of *The Magic Flute*: "The sun's golden radiance drives dark night away."[25]

The conflict between light and darkness is illustrated in this chorus by the contrast between major and minor keys, between rising and falling phrases, and between diatonic and chromatic harmonies. In the central section, when the men and women sing antiphonally, thirds and sixths express unity and harmony. The accompaniment of slurred quavers and dancing semiquavers gives a feeling of joy and freedom, as the singers pray for courage and virtue for the young men, grace and beauty for the maidens.*

The second chorus, in D major, is of great power and grandeur. In the 1773 version, it opened with an *Allegro*, but in 1779 Mozart converted the first twelve bars into an *Adagio sostenuto*, preserving the same theme and harmonies, so as to give greater dignity and solemnity to the chorus. After this hymn, there is soft music as the priest ascends to the altar, kneels before the image of the sun, lights the sacrificial fires, and throws incense three times upon them. This music is simple and tender, resembling the *March of the Priests* in *Idomeneo*, and that in *The Magic Flute*.

An address by Sethos, the High Priest, follows, in which the words anticipate those of the Speaker to Tamino in *The Magic Flute*. "Thamos! You have been educated in all the duties of the throne. If these seem too hard, there is still time to discard the burden. Once you have taken it upon your shoulders, it may still be possible for mortals to take it from you. But you yourself are still bound by your promise to the gods."[26]

In *The Magic Flute* Tamino is warned: "Prince! There is still time to turn back. One step further and it will be too late."[27]

In the first stage of the initiation ceremonies it was still possible for the novice to withdraw. There can be little doubt that these ceremonies are alluded to both in *Thamos* and in *The Magic Flute*.

The final chorus is awe-inspiring; it resembles the music of the oracle in *Idomeneo* and of the Commendatore in *Don Giovanni*. In all three scenes trombones are used to suggest the supernatural. The chorus express their fear of the gods' anger in descending semitones, accompanied by fluttering semiquavers on the strings. An *Allegro* section follows, in D major, opening with a phrase which resembles the first phrase of the final chorus in *The Magic Flute* (see p. 167). The people express the hope that Thamos may be guided by truth and justice; these words are set to a dancing, joyous melody.

These choruses are finer than any which Mozart had previously written in his church music. Whatever the weaknesses of Gebler's play, it certainly inspired the young Mozart to compose some of his best music. The additions and alterations of 1779 reflect greater power of expression and depth of feeling. In exploiting the dramatic possibilities of sonata form, he was moving towards the use of symphonic technique

---

* These features were added in the later version.

which he developed in his later operas. Thus, although *Thamos* is a work of Mozart's youth, it points the way towards the supreme masterpieces of his maturity.

NOTES

1 Anderson, p. 226.
2 Wangermann, E., *The Austrian Achievement*, London, 1973, p. 116.
3 Batley, E. M., *A Preface to The Magic Flute*, London, 1969, p. 137.
4 ibid., p. 137.
5 ibid., p. 138.
6 Anderson, p. 246.
7 Jahn, Otto, *Life of Mozart* (1856), London, 1882, II, p. 111.
8 Dent, E. J., *Mozart's Operas* (1913), 2nd ed., London, 1947, p. 228.
9 Brophy, Brigid, *Mozart the Dramatist*, London, 1964, p. 178.
10 *Neue Mozart-Ausgabe* (N.M.A.), Basel, 1957, II/6/1, p. 39.
11 Brophy, p. 137.
12 Wangermann, *The Austrian Achievement*, p. 112.
13 N.M.A., p. 38.
14 *The Magic Flute*, No. 15.
15 N.M.A., p. 74.
16 ibid., p. 75.
17 Deutsch, p. 146.
18 ibid., p. 149.
19 ibid., p. 148.
20 ibid., p. 155.
21 Anderson, p. 840.
22 Jahn, II, p. 104.
23 *King Thamos* (vocal score), London, 1882, p. 18.
24 ibid., p. 22.
25 *The Magic Flute*, No. 21.
26 N.M.A., p. 133.
27 *The Magic Flute*, Act II, scene 2.

4

STRUGGLE FOR EMANCIPATION

Mozart underwent deep and tragic experiences between 1773 and 1779. Apart from a visit to Munich for performances of his *opera buffa*, *La Finta Giardiniera*, he remained in Salzburg until 1777. These were years of increasing frustration and discontent with life in the service of an employer who had no understanding of music and small respect for human beings. Archbishop Colloredo professed to hold enlightened views (he had portraits of Voltaire and Rousseau in his room), but his attitude to his subordinates was far from enlightened. He saw in Wolfgang only an arrogant young servant, whose frequent absences from Salzburg brought little credit to his employer. Colloredo was by no means exceptional in his attitude to his employees. Haydn had recourse to a ruse in the Farewell Symphony to indicate to Prince Esterhazy that the musicians needed a holiday. To the aristocracy of the eighteenth century a musician was an appendage to the court, more or less useful according to the reflected glory which he brought to his master. A letter from Maria Theresia to her son, Archduke Ferdinand, in Naples, throws light on this subject: "You ask me to take into your service the young Salzburger [Mozart]. I know not in what capacity, as I do not believe you have need of a composer, or of useless people. Nevertheless, if that would give you pleasure, I do not wish to prevent you. What I say is, to avoid burdening yourself with useless people and with the expenses people of this sort will cause your service. It demeans the service when these people go about the world like beggars; and besides he has a large family."[1]*

In the summer of 1777 matters came to a head for Mozart, when he was refused permission to travel. He therefore asked for his discharge; the Archbishop's reply is recorded in the following note: "To the Court Chamberlain with my decision that in the name of the Gospel father and son have my permission to seek their fortune elsewhere."[2]

Since Wolfgang had been employed only at a nominal salary, the loss of his earnings created no great hardship for the family. But for Leopold, who had not asked for his discharge, the matter was more serious. In the event, he was not dismissed, and Wolfgang set out alone

* Maria Theresia had clearly been misinformed about Mozart's circumstances.

with his mother in the autumn of 1777, hoping to find employment at one of the courts of southern Germany, and eventually to establish himself in Paris.

The correspondence of the Mozart family during the next fifteen months, consisting of 150 letters between father and son, with occasional letters from Anna and Nannerl, throws light on Wolfgang's artistic and intellectual development. Hitherto Leopold had organised every detail in the life of the family, and Wolfgang had accepted this as part of the established order of things, much as he accepted religion. "Next to God comes Papa",[3] he once said. But with the escape from the drudgery of Salzburg and the tyranny of the Archbishop, Wolfgang began to assert himself and to make his own plans. In Munich his hopes of obtaining a post at the court of the Elector Maximilian failed to materialise. It is likely that politics entered into the matter, since Salzburg was a buffer-state between Austria and Bavaria, and hostilities were soon to break out between these two states in the War of Bavarian Succession.

The Elector questioned Wolfgang closely about his relations with the Archbishop. "So you have left Salzburg for good. Have you had a row with the Archbishop?" "Not at all, Your Highness, I only asked for permission to travel, which he refused. So I was compelled to take this step, though indeed I had long been intending to clear out. For Salzburg is no place for me, I can assure you." "Good Heavens! There's a young man for you!"[4]

Wolfgang proceeded to enumerate his successes in Italy, ending with the words "My sole wish is to serve Your Highness, who himself is such a great——" "Yes, my dear boy, but I have no vacancy. I am sorry. If only there were a vacancy——"[5]

Evidently the Elector was unwilling to risk offending his powerful neighbour by taking into his service this self-confident young man, who had left Salzburg under a cloud.

Wolfgang and his mother then went on to Mannheim, which at that time was an important musical centre, with a famous orchestra. Through the influence of a number of Bohemian composers, such as Joseph Stamic and Georg Benda, some important innovations in orchestral technique, like the so-called "Mannheim crescendo",* had been introduced. Mannheim was also the centre for the German National Theatre, where many plays by Schiller, Lessing and Wieland received their first performance. The Elector, Karl Theodor,

* See Glossary.

encouraged German art and culture, and it was therefore with high hopes that Mozart approached him to ask for employment as court composer. But his application was no more successful than at Munich. After nearly two months of indecision, Karl Theodor finally gave him a negative reply, possibly again for political reasons. It seems that Mozart had an enemy at the court of Mannheim in the Abbé Vogler, a Jesuit, who had considerable influence with the Elector. Although the Jesuit order had been officially banned since 1773, individual Jesuits were still powerful. No doubt Vogler was jealous of Mozart, who had a poor opinion of his pretensions as a composer, describing him as "a dreary musical jester, an exceedingly conceited and rather incompetent fellow."[6]

Meanwhile Leopold's anxiety about his son's prospects increased as time went by and there seemed no hope that he would obtain a post in Mannheim. Even after the Elector's refusal, Wolfgang still lingered, having made many friends in Mannheim, including some of the leading intellectuals – Baron von Gemmingen, the writer, Dalberg, the intendant of the National Theatre, and Wieland the poet. All these men were Freemasons, who later became Illuminati.

Wolfgang's chief reason for wishing to remain in Mannheim, however, was because he had fallen in love with Aloysia Weber, daughter of a musician in the service of the Elector, possessor of a beautiful soprano voice.

Leopold's letters at this time alternate between indignation and self-pity. For the first time in his life he had contracted debts to pay for the expenses of the journey. He painted a pathetic picture of himself and Nannerl, slaving and nearly starving in Salzburg, while his son dallied in Mannheim. When he learned about the Weber family, Leopold's anger knew no bounds. One extract will illustrate the tone of his letters.

"Your desire to help the oppressed you have inherited from your father. But you really must consider first of all the welfare of your parents, or else your soul will go to the devil. . . . Hurt me now, if you can be so cruel! Win fame and *make money* in Paris; then *when you have money to spend*, go off to Italy and get commissions for operas. . . . Then you could put forward Mlle <Weber's> name, which can be the more easily done if you do so personally. . . . Nannerl has wept her full share during these last few days."[7]

In reply, Wolfgang tried to reassure his father by bringing out the well-worn cliché: "I have placed my trust in God, Who will never forsake us."[8]

On 14 March, six months after they had set out from Salzburg, Wolfgang and his mother eventually left Mannheim for Paris. Their hopes of success in the French capital were high. They had several introductions to important people; above all they pinned their faith on Baron Melchior von Grimm, who had assisted the whole family on their previous visit to Paris. Grimm was an important figure in literary circles; he was a friend of Diderot, Voltaire and Rousseau, and secretary to the Duke of Orleans, founder of the first Masonic lodge in Paris. As emissary of the state of Saxe-Gotha, he also had contacts at court and in aristocratic circles. In 1764 he had taken the Mozarts under his wing, and had introduced them into the highest society, both among intellectuals and among the aristocracy.

But in 1778 the situation was not the same. Wolfgang was no longer the charming child prodigy, admired in all the courts of Europe. He was now a self-confident, talented but impecunious young man, in disgrace with his former employer, travelling from place to place virtually begging for a post.

Moreover, in the great controversy then raging in Paris between the supporters of Gluck and those of Piccinni, Grimm sided with Piccinni, and thus had little sympathy for a German musician. However, he gave Wolfgang some introductions, together with advice as to the best way to succeed in Paris. But Wolfgang had his own ideas.

Leopold had painted a rosy picture of the status of an artist in Paris. "There the nobility treat men of genius with the greatest deference, esteem and courtesy; there you will see a refined manner of life, which forms an astonishing contrast to the coarseness of our German courtiers and their ladies."[9] But the reality, as experienced by Wolfgang and his mother in the summer of 1778, was very different. On one occasion, Wolfgang was asked to play at a reception given by the Duchesse de Chabot. After being kept waiting for an hour in an ice-cold room, while the company were occupied with drawing, he was expected to play on a miserable clavier, "while Madame and all her gentlemen never interrupted their drawing for a moment, but went on intently, so that I had to play to the chairs, tables and walls."[10]

Leopold advised his son to "make an effort to get yourself known as a composer . . . , you must look out for opportunities, spur them on relentlessly, wake them up when they seem to be going to sleep."[11]

He adjured him to "write something which is easy, suitable for amateurs, rather popular", and to "be guided by French taste." Wolfgang, however, had no very high opinion of French taste. "If this were a place where people had ears to hear, hearts to feel, and some measure of understanding of and taste for music, these things would only make me laugh heartily; but, as it is (so far as music is concerned), I am surrounded by mere brute beasts."[12]

When he was offered the post of organist at Versailles, his father advised him to take it, since "an appointment of this kind *would be the surest way to win the protection of the Queen* and to make yourself popular".[13] Wolfgang thought otherwise, and turned down the offer.

His failure to follow his father's advice provoked the following comments from Grimm, who was becoming exasperated with his protégé's inability to come to terms with Parisian society: "He is too good-natured, *peu actif, trop aisé à attraper, peu occupé des moyens qui peuvent conduire à la fortune. Ici, pour percer, il faut être retors, entreprenant, audacieux. Je lui voudrais pour sa fortune la moitié moins de talent et le double d'entregent, et je n'en serais pas embarrassé.*"[14] ("Too indolent, too easily taken in, too little concerned with finding means to succeed. To achieve fame here one must be artful, enterprising, daring. For his chances of success, I could wish that he had half as much talent and twice as much worldly wisdom, then I should not worry about him.")

Wolfgang felt ill-at-ease in the society of the aristocracy in Paris. "I can find no *soulagement* here, no recreation, no pleasant and sociable intercourse with anyone." Of the women he wrote: "Most of them are prostitutes, and the few who are not, have no *savoir vivre*."[15]

He had a few friends who appreciated him, however, such as Count von Sickingen, Minister of the Palatinate, to whom he had been introduced by Baron von Gemmingen. Sickingen was a Freemason, and Wolfgang found his company most congenial. "He is very fond of me, and I like being with him", he wrote. "He is such a friendly sensible person, with such excellent judgment and he has a real insight into music."[16]

On one occasion Wolfgang played his newly-finished symphony in D major, the "Paris" (K.297), to Sickingen and the singer, Raaff. "They both liked it very much and I too am quite pleased with it. But I cannot tell whether it will be popular – and, to tell you the truth, I care very little, for who will not like it? I can answer for its pleasing the few intelligent French people who may be there, and, as for the stupid ones, I shall not consider it a great misfortune if they are not pleased. I still hope, however, that even the asses will find something in it to admire –

and, moreover, I have been careful not to neglect *le premier coup d'archet*.[17]*

In spite of his contempt for "French taste", Mozart made efforts to please his audience. When told by Le Gros, the impresario, that the *Andante* for this symphony was too long, and that it contained too many modulations, he wrote a second *Andante*, shorter and simpler.

It is not surprising that Wolfgang suffered from fits of depression, especially after his mother's illness and death, which occurred in July. Anna had endured acute physical and mental deprivation during her stay in Paris. The need to exercise stringent economy meant that, while Wolfgang was frequently invited out to meals, she had to manage on a meagre diet. Even worse, she was often alone all day, and her ignorance of the French language meant that she could communicate with very few people. "I never see him all day long and shall forget altogether how to talk", she wrote.[18] She died on 3 July, after a fortnight's illness.

The letters exchanged between father and son at this time make painful reading. Wolfgang was stunned by his mother's death; perhaps, too, he felt guilty at having allowed her to lead such a dismal life in a foreign country for his sake. Leopold inflamed the wound by writing that his mother had nearly died when he was born, "but she was fated to sacrifice herself for her son in a different way".[19]

Much of Wolfgang's bitterness was turned against the Parisians, and especially against those whom he had expected to help him, like Grimm. Although he disliked Salzburg, he hated Paris even more, and felt himself isolated and friendless in a cold, hard society.

The letters of both father and son express a fatalistic attitude to Anna's death. Leopold's belief in the Catholic faith was deep and lasting, and there is no reason to suppose that Wolfgang had yet begun to question that faith. His desire to please his father, and to exonerate himself from any blame for his mother's death, may have coloured some of his expressions, as when he wrote: "No doctor in the world could have saved her this time – for it was clearly the will of God; her time had come, and God wanted to take her to Himself."[20] His comment on Voltaire's death: "That godless arch-rascal Voltaire has pegged out like a dog, like a beast!"[21] strikes us as exaggeratedly strong; perhaps his attitude to freethinkers at that time may have been influenced by his feelings about Grimm and his circle.

Mozart started on his homeward journey at the end of September. He did not reach Salzburg until the following January, having spent a

* The opening of an orchestral piece by playing in unison.

month in Strasburg and nearly two in Mannheim. In Strasburg he gave two concerts, which were a success artistically, but not financially. He had travelled part of the way with a merchant, whose company he had found congenial.*

Strasburg was then an important centre for Freemasonry, and evidently Mozart felt more at home in this developing centre of commerce among bourgeois circles than he had in Parisian society. He felt even more at home in Mannheim, which he made a détour to visit. "Mannheim loves me as much as I love Mannheim", he wrote.[22]

During his stay there he discussed a project for composing music for a drama by Dalberg, intendant of the theatre; this project did not materialise, but he did compose music for a duodrama by Gemmingen, called *Semiramis*, based on a play by Voltaire on an Egyptian theme. He explained what a duodrama was as follows: "You know, of course, that there is no singing in it, only recitation, to which the music is like a sort of obbligato accompaniment to a recitative. Now and then words are spoken while the music goes on, and this produces the finest effect. . . . Well, imagine my joy at having to compose just the kind of work I have so much desired! Do you know what I think? I think that most operatic recitatives should be treated in this way – and only sung occasionally, when the words *can be perfectly expressed by the music*."[23]

Unfortunately no music for *Semiramis* survives, but we can form some opinion of Mozart's compositions for this genre from the melodramas in *Thamos* and *Zaide*.

Mozart's friends in Mannheim, most of whom were Freemasons, had tried to find a post for him there, but were unsuccessful. Meanwhile the infuriated Leopold was demanding his instant return to Salzburg, where he had secured an appointment for his son as *Konzertmeister*. Wolfgang accordingly set out for Salzburg, via Munich, at the end of December in that fateful year of 1778.

The Weber family had moved to Munich with the court in the previous year. But Wolfgang was to receive another emotional shock when his beloved Aloysia Weber made it clear that she wanted nothing to do with him. A vivid account of their meeting has been recorded: "Some eye-witness account of the scene has rendered it graphic by recollection of the personal appearance of the composer, who was now in mourning for his mother, dressed after the Parisian fashion in a red

* It has been suggested that this merchant may have been F. H. Ziegenhagen (see p. 145), but there is no evidence to support this theory.

coat with black buttons. Perceiving the change which had taken place, he immediately sat down to the clavier and sang aloud: '*Ich lass das Mädel gern, das mich nicht will.*' ('I gladly leave the girl who doesn't want me.')"[24]

Wolfgang eventually arrived in Salzburg in January 1779. The post which his father had obtained for him was on much more favourable terms than his previous appointment, with permission to travel whenever he wished. The Archbishop had virtually apologised for his previous intransigence, excusing himself by saying that "he could not tolerate people going about the world begging".[25]

Wolfgang returned from his travels much wiser and more mature. He had experienced the tragedy of his mother's death, and the bitterness of being rejected by the girl he loved. He had learned to despise the frivolous and corrupt society of the French aristocracy. Alongside his growing social awareness, he was becoming intensely conscious of his nationality, for in Paris he had felt himself to be passionately German. This nascent nationalism was part of the attitude of the German bourgeoisie, which is reflected in the art and literature of the time.

In Mannheim Mozart had made many friends, notably among members of Masonic circles. His artistic experience had been enriched by contact with the orchestra there, and also with the National Theatre, where he had become acquainted with works by contemporary German authors. He had discovered an exciting new form of art, the melodrama; he also had hopes of realising his highly-cherished dream of composing a German opera.

Mozart had learned much from his travels, both in a positive and negative way. It remains to show what effect these experiences had on his music.

NOTES

1 Pusch, G., *Letters of an Empress*, London, 1939, p. 42.
2 Anderson, p. 268 n.
3 ibid., p. 492.
4 ibid., p. 285.
5 ibid., p. 286.
6 ibid., p. 356.
7 ibid., pp. 479 f.
8 ibid., p. 482.

 9 ibid., p. 478.
10 ibid., p. 531.
11 ibid., p. 606.
12 ibid., p. 533.
13 ibid., p. 542.
14 ibid., p. 597.
15 ibid., pp. 570 f.
16 ibid., p. 552.
17 ibid., p. 553.
18 ibid., p. 520.
19 ibid., p. 591.
20 ibid., p. 584.
21 ibid., p. 558.
22 ibid., p. 630.
23 ibid., p. 631.
24 Holmes, E., *Life of Mozart* (1845), 2nd ed., London, 1921, p. 135.
25 Anderson, p. 608.

5

MASONIC IDEAS ABOUT MUSIC

Mozart expressed his ideas about art as early as 1776, in a letter to Padre Martini in Bologna: "We live in this world to learn industriously, and, by interchanging our ideas, to enlighten one another, and thus endeavour to promote the sciences and the fine arts."[1] These words show that he was already familiar with the theories of the Enlightenment on the function of art, which he must have discussed during his stay in Paris, particularly with Sickingen.

Rousseau explained his ideas about music in a letter to d'Alembert: "The art of music consists not in reproducing an exact copy of reality, but in creating for the human spirit a similar condition to the reality."[2] The theorists of the Enlightenment believed that, by studying nature, the composer could learn to depict every shade of emotion.* Rameau stated that harmonies should be chosen specifically so as to awaken certain emotions.† Rousseau, in his article on *Actors* for a Dictionary of Music (1775), laid it down that "the orchestra must not reproduce any emotion which does not flow from the actor's soul; his gait, his glance, his gesture, must all harmonise with the music."[3] Gluck, in his famous Preface to *Alceste*, established "simplicity, truth and naturalness" as the basis for beauty in art.[4]

Music played an important part in Masonic ceremonies, and the ideas of the Freemasons on the purpose of music were similar to those of the Enlightenment, but even more explicit. In his introduction to a collection of Masonic songs, L. F. Lenz set forth certain principles, which are important for an understanding of Masonic music.

According to Lenz, "The purpose of music in the ceremonies is to spread good thoughts and unity among the members", so that they may "unite in the idea of innocence and joy."[5] Music should "inculcate feelings of humanity, wisdom and patience, virtue and honesty, loyalty to friends, and finally an understanding of freedom."[6]

The editor of another collection of Masonic songs, J. A. Scheibe, recommended the antiphonal style in singing as "the best way to spread joy and contentment in society".[7]

* For the meaning of "nature" see p. 14.

† It is not certain whether Rameau was a Freemason, but several of his operas, including *Zoroaster*, are based on Masonic ideas.

A study of early Masonic songs, and of the works of composers who were Freemasons, such as J. G. Naumann, will help us to find out more precisely how these composers tried to achieve their aims.

In the first place, they adopted a simple style, based on German popular song, which had its roots in folk song. Secondly, they used certain rhythmic and melodic figures as musical symbols. Thirdly, they attached significance to particular intervals and harmonic progressions.

Some examples of Masonic musical symbolism may be given. Dotted rhythms, such as

were often used to promote courage and resolution.

The threefold knocking on the door of a lodge by a candidate for initiation was represented in stylised form, as in Naumann's *Beym Eintritt in die Loge* (*On entering the Lodge*).

A different stylisation of the "three knocks" occurs in the *Magic Flute* overture, between the two sections.

In another piece by Naumann, *Die Harmonie* (*Harmony*), the threefold handshake, with which the "chain of brothers" is broken at the end of a meeting, is represented by the figure

at the end of the piece.

Suspensions and slurred notes in pairs are used to indicate the ties of brotherhood. Examples of the former are to be found in Naumann's *Die Harmonie* and *Die Kette* (*The Chain*).

Die Kette also includes a rhythmic figure often used to express fortitude.

   The number three has a special significance in Freemasonry. Most of
the songs are in three-part harmony; they are usually set for male
voices, since the members of the lodges were men. Many songs are in
triple time; threefold repetitions are frequent, and major triads are of
particular importance. Parallel thirds and sixths are used to denote
shared feelings and harmonious relationships. The idea that these
intervals reflect a state of physical harmony and peace was current
throughout the eighteenth century.*

   We find a series of parallel thirds and sixths (6–3 chords) in many of
the songs. This feature may be derived from medieval *faux-bourdon*.[8]
The accompaniment to the songs, for organ or clavier, usually consists
of a melody and figured bass, as in the song "O heiliges Band" ("O
sacred band of friendship's truest brothers") from a Regensburg
Masonic songbook of 1772.

   * For a discussion of the question whether there is a basis for this idea in nature itself,
see D. Cooke, *The Language of Music*.

A familiar example of a series of parallel thirds and sixths is to be found in the *March of the Priests* in *The Magic Flute*.

Chords on the third and sixth degrees of the scale, known as "modal" chords because of their association with the accompaniment of plainsong, are frequently used to evoke a mystical or religious atmosphere. In particular, the progression Dominant–Submediant (V–VI), or interrupted cadence, appears to have some ritual significance.

Mozart was evidently familiar with Masonic music long before he joined the Order. He probably knew the Regensburg songbook, for he set the song "O heiliges Band" (K.148) to music in 1772. The simple, folk-like character of his setting conforms with the principles laid down by Scheibe for music in Masonic ceremonies.

All the features which we have described are to be found in Mozart's Masonic music. He did not invent this musical symbolism, but he developed and transformed it, infusing it with deeper content.

It would, of course, be absurd to suggest that Mozart had Freemasonry in mind whenever he used one of these symbols. Examples of pairs of slurred notes, for instance, occur in many works which can have no connection with Masonry, such as church masses; they are also common in the music of other composers of the time. But a comparison of Mozart's overtly Masonic works, like the *March of the Priests* in *The Magic Flute*, and the *Masonic Funeral Music* (K.477), with other instrumental compositions in which several of these symbols occur together, will help us to identify works which can be said to reflect Masonic ideas, like the E♭ Symphony (K.543).

In Mozart's music certain keys are specifically associated with Freemasonry, notably E♭ major and C major, together with C minor, related to both keys. The choice of E♭ may be connected with the fact that this was an easy key for wind instruments, which played an important part in lodge ceremonies. There may also be significance in the key signature of three flats, in view of the importance of the number three in Masonic symbolism.

In addition to using specific Masonic symbolism, Mozart developed a style which has been described as "humanist". One writer has described some of its characteristics as follows: "Lofty arches of melody; large intervals; serious, song-like melodies reminiscent of the old choral music; quiet, simple rhythms".[9] Several of these features are to be found in the Masonic song-books of the time. Sarastro's aria, "O Isis and Osiris" (*The Magic Flute*, No. 10) is a good example of the humanist style, which may be said to express Masonic ideas about human love and brotherhood. In contrast, the chief characteristics of the *galant* style which was popular in the latter part of the eighteenth century were elegance, brilliance, and a certain superficiality. (Many of the works of J. C. Bach are in this style.)

Much of the music which Mozart composed in Salzburg, both before and after his visit to Paris, is in the *galant* style. But there are indications that he was already searching for a simpler, more expressive style, even in his church music. The Mass in C (K.257), composed in November 1776, has been described as "childlike and songlike", and the piano concerto in E♭ (K.271) contains a deeply-felt *Andantino*. The wonderful *Sinfonia Concertante* for Violin and Viola (K.364), composed in 1779, is the antithesis of *galant*. The second movement, a poignant *Andante* in C minor, seems to reflect Mozart's tragic experiences in Paris. In this work he rose to greater heights of expressiveness than in any of his previous instrumental compositions.

After his return from Paris in 1779 Mozart composed some important works for the stage. He revised and added to the music of *Thamos* for Böhm's travelling company. He also started to compose a German *Singspiel* for the same company. This work, which was later named *Zaide*, was left unfinished, because Mozart received a commission to compose an *opera seria* for Munich. That opera, *Idomeneo*, contains music of great dramatic power and expressiveness. Mozart followed Gluck in giving prominence to the chorus, in the use of trombones for the supernatural scenes, and in the simple serenity of the Priests' March, which foreshadows that in *The Magic Flute*.

The reader must be referred to other books for an account of *Idomeneo*.* But the theme of *Zaide* is directly relevant to our subject, and the *Singspiel* must be examined in some detail. The unfinished score of *Zaide* was discovered after Mozart's death by his widow, Constanze. She wrote to the publisher André: "You will never guess what beautiful things I have found in my treasure-chest! Among them there is a work

* See Dent, *Mozart's Operas*, and Liebner, J., *Mozart on the Stage*.

of which I myself knew nothing . . . it is both an opera and a melodrama. The text itself is fine."[10]

The original text has unfortunately vanished, but the libretto has been reconstructed from a contemporary *Singspiel* on a similar theme, entitled *Das Serail, oder Der Renegat*, by F. J. Sebastiani, with music by Friebert. It is the story of a captive woman enslaved by an oriental despot, who eventually frees her in order to prove that "Not only Europe, but Asia, too, can produce virtuous spirits".[11] (The reconstructed version of Mozart's *Singspiel* was first published in 1866 under the title of *Zaide*.)

The source of the story can be traced back to Montesquieu, who, in his *Lettres Persanes*, set out to show that oriental religions were at least equal to Christianity in moral values. More directly, *Das Serail* is related to Lessing's drama, *Nathan the Wise*, written in 1779. In this play Jews, Christians and Mohammedans are all depicted as possessing virtues such as benevolence, tolerance and courage. In the dénouement several of the characters are discovered to be members of the same family, though of different religions. This, too, resembles the dénouement in *Das Serail*.

We cannot be certain that Mozart and his librettist, Johann Schachtner, knew Lessing's play, which was written in the same year as *Zaide*. But Lessing was an intimate friend of Gebler, and also of Sonnenfels, whom Mozart had met in 1773; moreover Dalberg had produced several of Lessing's plays in Mannheim.

The ideas expressed in *Zaide* are essentially Masonic. Like *Thamos*, *Zaide* is a typical example of the art of bourgeois humanism, with its emphasis on tolerance and human kindness. But whereas *Thamos* is mainly concerned with the theme of an enlightened ruler, *Zaide* is an assertion of the right to freedom for both men and women of all classes, and a denunciation of tyranny and slavery, by which men are reduced to the level of beasts. One of the arias in *Zaide* is a passionate attack on tyranny, and on the idea that the rich have the right to exploit others. This aria foreshadows both the egalitarian theme of *Figaro* and the idea of fraternity which is the main theme of *The Magic Flute*. The words are as follows: "You mighty men, who look down scornfully on your lowly slaves, although you live in luxury, remember your poor brothers. Only the man who has himself experienced the trials of fickle fortune, and been humbled in the dust, can understand pity, mercy and kindness. Only such a man deserves to be raised to the highest rank."[12]

In reading these words we are reminded of a letter written by

Wolfgang to his friend the Abbé Bullinger, on the occasion of his mother's death: "You know well that the best and truest friends are the poor. The wealthy do not know what friendship means, especially those who are born to riches; and even those whom fate enriches often become spoilt by their good fortune. But when a man is placed in favourable circumstances not by blind fate but by reasonable good fortune and merit, that is, a man who during his early and less prosperous days never lost courage, remained faithful to his religion and his God, was an honest man and a good Christian and knew how to value his true friend . . . from such a man no ingratitude need be feared!"[13]

Similar ideas were expressed by Adam Weishaupt in putting forward the aims of the Illuminati: "When we look at this goodly world, and see that every man may be happy, but that the happiness of one depends on the conduct of another; when we see the wicked so powerful and the good so weak, and that it is vain to strive singly and alone against the general current of vice and oppression, the wish naturally arises . . . to form an association of the most worthy persons, who should work together in removing the obstacles to human happiness. . . ."[14]

The aria in *Zaide* is unusual in form as well as in content. It opens with a slow introduction, in which the words "You mighty men, who look down scornfully" are set to a downward leap of an octave, expressing the scorn of the wealthy, while the strings accompany quietly with a figure containing a *gruppetto*.

The section referring to "pity, mercy and kindness", is in F major, in 3–4 time, with a flowing melody which resembles some of Gluck's melodies in its simplicity and serenity. We may note the descending chromatic scale illustrating the words "humbled in the dust", and the modulations which illustrate the "changes of fickle fortune". The word "trials" (*Proben*) is set to strong, detached chords, denoting fortitude.

The words of the opening section are then repeated, and the aria ends with a repetition of the section "But though you live in luxury", which serves as a recapitulation.

In this aria, although Mozart uses only a few of the rhythmic figures and harmonic progressions associated with Freemasonry, the setting of such words as "trials" and "brothers" already indicates how he was to express Masonic ideas musically. The central section of the aria is an early example of his humanist style.

The melodrama in *Zaide* depicts the hero's state of mind. He finds himself in the position of a slave, and expresses his horror at a condition which reduces men to the level of beasts. At the end of the aria he wrestles with his thoughts, while attempting to go to sleep; this vivid representation of insomnia, achieved by startling harmonies and modulations, and disjointed phrases, forms a striking contrast with the beautiful aria, "Ruhe sanft" ("Sleep soft") which follows, sung by the heroine, Zaide.

The ensembles in *Zaide* foreshadow some of the great masterpieces of Mozart's later operas. The quartet, "Freundin, stille deine Tränen" ("Dearest, cease your weeping") is an early example of the use of symphonic technique to depict a dramatic situation, with different themes expressing the tensions and conflicts of the situation, and the different emotions of the four characters. The introduction of such a quartet into a *Singspiel* was certainly daring: we know that one of the singers in *Idomeneo*, an *opera seria*, objected to the insertion of a quartet into the second act of that opera, when he would have preferred an aria.

The quartet was the last number composed by Mozart for *Zaide*. There can be little doubt that the *Singspiel* would have ended happily, like *Das Serail*, in which the final words are in praise of courage and virtue.

The exact reasons for the abandonment of *Zaide* are not known, but Mozart evidently had a high opinion of the work. He wrote to his father from Vienna in 1781, asking him to send him the score, writing that "Stephanie Junior is going to give me a new libretto, a good one, as he says. . . . I could not contradict him; I merely said that, except for the long dialogues, which could easily be altered, the piece was very good, but not suitable for Vienna, where people prefer comic operas."[15]

The new libretto was *Die Entführung aus dem Serail*. But before composing it, Mozart was to take the most decisive step of his life.

NOTES

1 Anderson, p. 266.
2 Knepler, G. *Musikgeschichte des XIX. Jahrhunderts*, Berlin, 1961, p. 31.
3 ibid., p. 32.
4 Einstein, A., *Gluck*, London 1964, p. 99.
5 Ballin, E. A., *Der Dichter von Mozarts Freimaurerlied "O heiliges Band"*, Tutzing, 1960, p. 15.
6 ibid., p. 18.
7 ibid., p. 35.
8 Chailley, J., *The Magic Flute: Masonic Opera* (tr. Weinstock), London, 1973, p. 163.
9 Nettl, P., *Mozart and Masonry*, New York, 1970, p. 59.
10 Bauer, W., and Deutsch, O., *Mozart: Briefe und Aufzeichnungen*, Kassel, 1960, IV, p. 262.
11 *Zaide* (vocal score), Kassel, 1960, p. 185.
12 ibid., No. 14.
13 Anderson, p. 593.
14 Robison, p. 114.
15 Anderson, p. 725.

6

OPEN REBELLION

"The Archbishop had better not begin to play the high and mighty with me as he used to – for it is not at all unlikely that I shall pull a long nose at him!"[1]

So wrote Wolfgang in November 1778, before his return to Salzburg, while he was still hoping to obtain a post in Mannheim or Munich. These hopes had not materialised, and he had been obliged to swallow the bitter pill of returning to the service of the Archbishop. But resentment was still smouldering, and we seem to hear the suppressed anger beneath the polite surface in some of the divertimenti and serenades composed for the court. Sometimes his fury erupts, as in the impassioned aria of Zaide "Tiger! wetze deine Klauen!" ("Tiger! sharpen your claws!")[2]

After the success of *Idomeneo* in Munich in 1781, Mozart had hoped to stay in that city, and to obtain further commissions for operas. When the Archbishop ordered him to go to Vienna along with the rest of his entourage, Wolfgang was at first unwilling to leave Munich. But he hoped that through his friends in Vienna he would find opportunities to make himself known in the capital, and perhaps to stay there altogether.

The Archbishop infuriated him by refusing him permission to perform at concerts. "The Archbishop is so kind as to add to his lustre by his household, robs them of their chance of earning and pays them nothing."[3]

Even for a charity concert in aid of the widows of musicians, permission was only grudgingly given. "Believe me, I am right in saying that he acts as a *screen* to keep me from the notice of others."[4]

The status of a musician in the rigid feudal hierarchy was no higher than that of a valet. "By the way, the two valets sit at the top of the table, but at least I have the honour of being placed above the cooks." . . .[5] "I did not know that I was a valet, and that was the last straw. I ought to have idled away a couple of hours every morning in the antechamber."[6]

Mozart's increasing resentment is illustrated by the epithets he used to describe the Archbishop: "this archbooby of ours", "the inhuman villain", "presumptuous, conceited ecclesiastic". Meantime he was determined to outwit his employer, and, if he were refused permission to play at concerts, to get his own way by cunning. "Oh, indeed, <I shall certainly fool the Archbishop to the top of his bent, and how I shall enjoy doing it!> I shall do it with the utmost politesse."[7]

The famous quarrel took place on 9 May 1781. This date must be regarded as a landmark, not only in the life of Mozart, but in musical history, since it marks the first open rebellion of a musician against feudal society.

The story is vividly told in the letters written by Wolfgang to his father between March and June 1781. These letters should be read in their entirety by all music-lovers. We can only give a brief outline of events, and a few extracts.

The immediate cause of the dispute was Colloredo's peremptory command that he should return to Salzburg with the rest of the prince's household. When Mozart – a servant – dared to question his orders, the Archbishop's fury was aroused, and he hurled invectives at Wolfgang, naming him "the most dissolute fellow he knew", "a scoundrel, a rascal and a vagabond", coupling his abuse with threats of stopping his salary.[8] It is worth quoting part of the dialogue, in which the Archbishop used the contemptuous third person "er" ("he") in addressing him.

"At last my blood began to boil, I could no longer contain myself and I said, 'So Your Grace is not satisfied with me?' 'What, you dare to threaten me – you <scoundrel?> There is the <door!> Look out, for I will have nothing more to do with such <a miserable wretch.>' At last I said: 'Nor I with you!'. 'Well, be off!' When leaving the room, I said, 'This is final. You shall have it tomorrow in writing.'"[9]

Mozart's account concluded with the words: "I want to hear nothing more about Salzburg. I hate the Archbishop to madness."[10]

Leopold's replies to these letters are unfortunately not extant, but there is no doubt that he was terrified, particularly since Wolfgang gradually abandoned the secret code which they habitually used, and even wrote: "Oh, if only he could read this, I should be delighted."[11]

Leopold, fearing that he himself might be dismissed, did everything he could to persuade his son to make up the quarrel; he even wrote to Count Arco, the Court Chamberlain, asking him to mediate. Wolfgang, who was torn between filial piety and anger at the way he had been treated, appealed to his father to "strengthen me in this resolution, instead of trying to dissuade me from it, for if you do you will only make me unproductive".[12] He assured his father that he was able to earn a living in Vienna, and that the Archbishop could hardly punish Leopold for his son's behaviour. However, he agreed to approach Count Arco, with a view to presenting a petition to Colloredo. This attempt at reconciliation ended in the dramatic scene when Count Arco actually kicked Wolfgang out of the antechamber. After that there could be no question of any further attempts at compromise. "Well, that will be the last time. What is it to him [Count Arco] if I wish to get my discharge? And if he was really so well disposed towards me he ought to have reasoned quietly with me – or have let things take their course, rather than throw such words about as 'clown' and 'knave' and hoof a fellow out of the room with a kick on his arse; but I was forgetting that this was probably done by order of our worthy Prince Archbishop."[13]

Although Mozart saw his relations with the Archbishop mainly in personal terms, his attitude was one of deep resentment against a society in which human beings were treated with such indignity by men who were inferior in every respect except their rank and social status. He had the greatest contempt for the servile role played by men like Arco. "I beg you, most beloved father, <not to cringe too much; for the Archbishop cannot do you any harm.>"[14]

Mozart's attitude recalls some of the statements of the Illuminati. "Aim at preventing servile respect of princes. . . . Flattery corrupts men – speak to them as equals, so that they may learn that they are men like other men, masters only by convention."[15]

One is reminded of Beethoven's famous saying: "There are hundreds of princes, and there will be thousands of princes, but there is only one Beethoven."[16]

Nothing illustrates more clearly the difference between Mozart and his father than the difference in their attitude to their social superiors. Leopold was servile; it was second nature to him to cringe and flatter, aiming to succeed by a combination of caution and cunning. He thought his son "far too patient or rather *easy-going*, too *indolent*, perhaps even too *proud* . . . , on the other hand he is too *impatient*, too *hasty*, and will not bide his time."[17]

Wolfgang's attitude was typical of the new class which was to come to power: proud, on the one hand, and confident of itself, and impatient, because it was beginning to know its own strength.

To Leopold, Wolfgang's only hope of establishing himself in Vienna seemed to lie in taking an appointment under some prince. His son believed that he could earn a living as an independent musician on the strength of his talents.

At first his prospects seemed favourable. He had full confidence in continuing to be successful as a virtuoso on the clavier. "It is perfectly true that the Viennese are apt to change their affections, *but only in the theatre*; and my special line is too popular not to be able to support myself. Vienna is certainly the land of the clavier!"[18]

He had little doubt that he could have as many pupils as he wished, and his hopes of establishing himself as a composer were high, since he was becoming well-known in musical circles. He had several influential friends, such as Count Cobenzl, Court and State Chancellor, who was one of the leaders of the Illuminati in Vienna, and Countess Thun (pupil of Haydn, and later a friend of Beethoven), whom he described as "the most charming and lovable lady I have ever met".[19] At one of Countess Thun's musical parties he met Joseph von Sonnenfels, and Baron Gottfried van Swieten, who became his close friend and patron.

Mozart told his father that with four pupils he could earn "twenty-four ducats or 102 gulden, 24 kreuzer. With this sum a man and his wife can manage in Vienna, if they live quietly. . . . I can write, it is true, at least one opera a year, give a concert annually and have some things engraved and published by subscription."[20]

Wolfgang wrote thus in order to prepare his father for the news of his projected marriage to Constanze Weber, a younger sister of Aloysia. Leopold was bitterly opposed to the marriage and did his best to prevent it. But in spite of his father's opposition Wolfgang married Constanze Weber in August 1782.

When he planned to write "at least one opera a year", Mozart was counting on the success of these operas, without reckoning with the fickle taste of the Viennese public. But his first operatic venture in Vienna, *Die Entführung aus dem Serail* (*The Abduction from the Seraglio*), was an outstanding success.

The librettist was Gottlieb Stephanie, actor and stage-manager in the Burg Theater company, author of many plays. He was a member of the circle of Freemasons around Mesmer, whom Mozart had met in 1773. For their new *Singspiel*, Mozart and Stephanie adapted a play called *Belmonte und Constanze*, by C. F. Bretzner, which had been performed in Berlin in 1781. Since there were no laws of copyright at that time, Bretzner could only publish a protest: "A certain individual, *Mozart* by name, in Vienna has had the audacity to misuse my drama *Belmonte and Constanze* for an opera text. I herewith protest most solemnly against this infringement of my rights, and reserve the right to take the matter further."[21]

The theme of the escape of a woman kept in slavery by an oriental despot was a popular one in the eighteenth century, as we saw in reference to *Zaide*. Gluck's *Pilgrims of Mecca*, Jommelli's *La Sciava liberata*, and Grossmann's *Adelheit von Veltheim* (with music by Beethoven's friend Christian Neefe, who was a Freemason), all deal with this subject.

Mozart had long wanted to write a German opera; he was delighted when he received the text, and set to work at once. "I am so delighted at having to compose this opera that I have already finished Cavalieri's first aria, Adamberger's aria* and the trio which closes Act I. The time is short, it is true, for it is to be performed in the middle of September; but the circumstances connected with the date of performance and, in general, all my other prospects stimulate me to such a degree that I rush to my desk with the greatest eagerness and remain seated there with the greatest delight."[22]

Die Entführung is about freedom from tyranny, and about romantic love. In a sense it is autobiographical, for Mozart had just freed himself from the tyranny of an autocratic employer, and he had married for love, carrying off Constanze from her overbearing mother and marrying in haste and secrecy, against his own father's wishes. (His friends teased him about his "Abduction from the 'Eye of God'" – that being the name of the house where Constanze lived.)

His views on love and marriage were linked with the idea of freedom: they are clearly stated in a letter written in 1778 about a friend who had married a rich wife.

"His, I daresay, is one of those money matches and nothing else. I should not like to marry in this way. . . . People of noble birth must never marry from inclination or love, but only from interest and all kinds of secondary considerations. . . . But we poor humble people can not only choose a wife whom we love and who loves us, but we may, can, and do, take such a one, because we are neither noble nor highly born, nor aristocratic, nor rich, but, on the contrary, lowly born, humble and poor; so we do not need a wealthy wife, for our riches, being in our brains, die with us – and these no man can take from us unless he chops off our heads, in which case – we need nothing more."[23]

In *Die Entführung* two pairs of lovers, Belmonte and Constanze, and their servants, Pedrillo and Blonde, face dangers and difficulties for the sake of their love. When Constanze is threatened by the Sultan, Pasha Selim, with torture and death if she does not submit to his wishes, she defies him in a magnificent coloratura aria, "Marter aller Arten":

* Adamberger, the tenor, was a Freemason. Mozart wrote many parts for him.

> "Torture me and flay me,
> Martyr me and slay me,
> All you threaten
> Is but idle talk to me."[24]

Blonde replies to the advances of the Sultan's rascally steward, Osmin, in spirited fashion. "Your slave? I your slave? . . . girls are not commodities to be given away! I am an Englishwoman, born to freedom, and I shall defy anyone who tries to force me."[25]

Osmin is both a symbol of tyranny and a figure of fun – a bully and a fool. In this caricature of a despot, Mozart was perhaps taking his revenge on the Archbishop ("that stupid booby") and his obsequious servant, Count Arco. In spite of his furious blustering Osmin is ineffectual and in the end he is outwitted and defeated. The Sultan, though a tyrant, proves that he can be magnanimous. As in *Zaide*, the dénouement shows that a pagan can have noble feelings as well as a Christian. In Bretzner's play the Sultan turns out to be Belmonte's father, which provides a plausible reason for his sudden change of heart. But in *Die Entführung* Belmonte is revealed as the son of Pasha Selim's former enemy, who had done him great harm. His action in forgiving the lovers is one of sheer humanity. "Take your freedom, take Constanze, sail back to your country, and tell your father that you were in my power, that I set you free so that you could tell him that it would be a greater pleasure to repay injustices with kindness than to requite injury with injury."[26]

These sentiments are Masonic: the words are not set to music, since Pasha Selim is a non-singing part, but their meaning is brought out in the *Andante sostenuto* section of the *Finale*. "Nothing is so hateful as revenge; to be humane and kind, to pardon without selfishness – that is the action of the loftiest spirits."[27] These words, which remind us of Sarastro's famous aria, "Within this sacred dwelling", are sung *sotto voce*, like other passages in which a moral sentiment is uttered. We may note certain features which we shall find in Mozart's Masonic works: the appoggiaturas on the words "humane" and "kind"; the diminished seventh with a *sforzando* accent on the word "hateful"; the rising scale, ending on a dominant seventh, illustrating the words "loftiest spirits".

The theme of lovers' constancy and courage in the face of death is one which recurs in several of Mozart's operas – in *Zaide, Idomeneo,* and *The Magic Flute*. Belmonte and Constanze display their fortitude in the beautiful duet in Act III of *Die Entführung* (No. 20). As in *The*

Magic Flute, it is the woman who takes the lead, showing that true love can overcome even the fear of death. The recitative to this duet opens in D minor (a key often associated with tragedy). In the first bar, syncopated chords and a falling seventh express Belmonte's anxious sorrow. An interrupted cadence, leading to E♭ major, introduces Constanze's calmer phrases. "What is death? A path that leads to peace", she declares,[28] in words which suggest the Masonic view of death as a friend. Belmonte is calmed by her words (chord of E♭), but the strings (in C minor) continue to utter the despairing falling sevenths. An *Andante* section follows, in which Belmonte appears to have been strengthened by Constanze's example. The syncopations continue, but we hear no more diminished sevenths; then he thinks of her death: his thoughts are expressed by throbbing semiquavers, discords and minor chords, in a passage which anticipates Pamina's threatened suicide in the *Finale* of *The Magic Flute*. In the final *Allegro* section, the lovers declare that they will face death gladly together; their unity and harmony are indicated by parallel tenths.

Mozart himself described how he had expressed Belmonte's love for Constanze in his A major aria (Act I, No. 4). "Would you like to know how I have expressed it – and even indicated his throbbing heart? By the two violins playing octaves. . . . You feel the trembling – the faltering – you see how his throbbing breast begins to swell; this I have expressed by a crescendo. You hear the whispering and the sighing – which I have indicated by the first violins with mutes and a flute playing in unison."[29]

Several of the letters written at this time illustrate Mozart's ideas on composition. As usual he insisted on alterations in the text to suit the music. "In an opera the poetry must be altogether the obedient servant of the music."[30]

In one instance he even composed the music first. "I have explained to Stephanie the words I require for this aria – indeed I had finished composing most of the music for it before Stephanie knew anything whatever about it."[31] The aria in question is sung by Osmin (Act I No. 3). "As Osmin's rage gradually increases, there comes (just as the aria seems to be at an end) the *allegro assai*, which is in a totally different tempo and in a different key; this is bound to be very effective. For just as a man in such a towering rage oversteps all the bounds of order, moderation and propriety and completely forgets himself, so must the music too forget itself. But since passions, whether violent or not, must never be expressed to the point of exciting disgust, and as the music, even in the most terrible situations, must never offend the ear, but must please the listener, or in other words must never cease to be *music*, so I have chosen a key remote from F (in which the aria is written) but one related to it – not the nearest, D minor, but the more remote A minor."[32]

Mozart is here applying to music the principle of order and moderation in all things which was part of the Pythagorean doctrine of the mean – an idea which was adopted by the Freemasons. In composing this aria, Mozart was surely remembering the occasion when the Archbishop's rage "overstepped all bounds of order, moderation and propriety".

A year later, referring to an ode which he had been asked to set to music, he wrote: "The ode is beautiful, sublime, anything you like, but too exaggerated and pompous for my fastidious ears. But what is to be done? The golden mean of truth in all things is no longer known or appreciated. In order to win applause, one must write stuff which is so inane that a *fiacre* [fool] could sing it, or so unintelligible that it pleases precisely because no sensible man can understand it. . . . I should like to write a book, a short introduction to music, illustrated by examples, but, I need hardly add, not under my own name."[33]

It is a pity that this book was never written, for Mozart was profoundly concerned with the precise expression of his musical ideas. But a comparison between examples of his vocal music with similar passages in his instrumental music should help us to obtain a clearer understanding of his meaning. We shall return to this subject later.

In spite of the success of *Die Entführung* with the general public, Mozart's opera encountered opposition. Cabals were organised against it by supporters of the Italian opera. On 20 July he wrote to his father: "I hope you received safely my last letter informing you of the good reception of my opera. It was given yesterday for the second time. Can you really believe it, but yesterday there was an even stronger cabal against it than on the first evening! The whole first act was accompanied by hissing. But indeed they could not prevent the loud shouts of 'bravo' during the arias."[34]

Certain journals criticised the *Singspiel* as being too difficult, and for containing too many syncopations, modulations and discords. The Emperor himself had commented: "Too fine for our ears, and an immense number of notes, my dear Mozart," to which Mozart had replied: "Just as many notes, Your Majesty, as are necessary."[35]

The rivalry between the Italian and German opera companies was a reflection of that between the aristocracy and the bourgeoisie, in which the latter were in favour of opera in the vernacular. Mozart was a supporter of German opera; as he once wrote: "I prefer German opera, even though it means more trouble for me."[36]

Although the Emperor Joseph had established the National Theatre in 1776 for the performance of German drama, Italian influence was strong at court, and Italian opera was in the ascendant. The German company was finally dissolved in March 1783, thus putting an end to Mozart's hopes of obtaining a commission for another German opera.

NOTES

1 Anderson, p. 632.
2 *Zaide*, No. 13.
3 Anderson, p. 714.
4 ibid., p. 716.
5 ibid., pp. 713–14.
6 ibid., p. 730.
7 ibid., p. 721.
8 ibid., p. 728.
9 ibid., p. 728.
10 ibid., p. 729.
11 ibid., p. 726.
12 ibid., p. 733.
13 ibid., p. 741.
14 ibid., p. 741.
15 Le Forestier, R., p. 323.
16 Turner, W. J., *Beethoven*, London, 1927, p. 57.
17 Anderson, p. 816.
18 ibid., p. 739.
19 ibid., p. 717.
20 ibid., p. 795.
21 Deutsch, p. 211.
22 Anderson, p. 755.
23 ibid., p. 467.
24 *The Abduction from the Seraglio*, tr. Dent, London, 1952, p. 16.
25 *Die Entführung* (vocal score), Act II, scene 1.
26 *The Abduction from the Seraglio*, p. 33.
27 *Die Entführung*, No. 21.
28 ibid., No. 20.
29 Anderson, p. 769.
30 ibid., p. 773.

31 ibid., pp. 768–9.
32 ibid., p. 769.
33 ibid., p. 833.
34 ibid., p. 807.
35 Jahn, II, p. 212.
36 Anderson, p. 839.

7

MASONIC INFLUENCES

Among the leaders of the movement for promoting German art and culture were several Viennese Freemasons, some of whom, like Sonnenfels and Gemmingen, held important positions in Joseph's government.

During the first four years of his reign, Joseph introduced a number of reforms, which, though primarily aimed at strengthening his own position in relation to the aristocracy, were beneficial to supporters of the Enlightenment. These reforms included the Edict of Toleration of 1781, which gave some freedom of worship to others besides Catholics, the partial lifting of the censorship, and reforms of the legal system and of the universities.

Freemasonry flourished during this period. Joseph was considered to be friendly towards the Order; some even called him "a Freemason without an apron". It became quite fashionable at this time to join one of the many different groups of Masons which had sprung into existence. Caroline Pichler, daughter of a Privy Councillor named Greiner, who was a Freemason, wrote in her Memoirs: "Many members joined the Order out of curiosity, and enjoyed the pleasures of the table at least. Others joined with less pure intentions, for it was useful to belong to this Order, the members of which were everywhere, and had valuable acquaintances in every circle."[1]

In spite of this report, there is no doubt that most of the leading men in the Order, especially those connected with the Illuminati, were men of great integrity. Many of them were friends of Mozart, and it will be useful at this point to give a short biographical account of some of them.

Otto van Gemmingen, diplomat and writer, whom Mozart first met in Mannheim, came to Vienna in 1782 as ambassador to the state of Baden. He was a strong partisan of the supporters of German drama. "I am a German, and I want to remain German", he once declared.[2] In Mannheim he had worked in close collaboration with Dalberg at the National Theatre, promoting performances of plays by Schiller, Lessing and other German authors. In Vienna he edited several journals whose purpose was to spread the ideas of the Enlightenment. He was a member of the Illuminati, and at a later date he assisted Adam Weishaupt to escape from the Bavarian authorities.

Mozart's relations with Gemmingen were evidently close and cordial. He had composed the music for *Semiramis* free of charge. "To please Herr von Gemmingen and myself I am now composing the first act of the declaimed opera (which I was commissioned to write) and I am also doing this *for nothing*", he wrote on 3 December 1778.[3]

It was probably Gemmingen who persuaded Mozart to take the step, in December 1784, of joining the lodge *Beneficence*, of which he was Grand Master. Gemmingen introduced Mozart to Gottfried van Swieten, who became one of his closest friends and patrons.

Van Swieten was the son of Maria Theresia's doctor. Like Gemmingen, he was a diplomat and a writer. He had travelled widely, having lived in Paris, Brussels, Warsaw and Berlin, where he was Ambassador to the King of Prussia. In 1777, during the War of Bavarian Succession, he was dismissed from Prussia; he then returned to Vienna, and in 1781 he became Chairman of the Commission on Books. He was in charge of the reforms of the censorship introduced by Joseph; he has been described as "the bastion of Enlightened influence within Joseph's government".[4] Upon hearing the news in 1774 that general primary education was to be provided in the Habsburg dominions, he had exclaimed: "At last the time has come when the truth is emerging in new splendour from the dark clouds which have enveloped it, and is entering upon its rights."[5]

After 1783 Joseph's reforms were attacked by Cardinal Migazzi and conservative ministers; Van Swieten fought to retain the reforms, but Joseph's enlightened policies were modified in the later years of his reign, and, after his death in 1790, the Commission on Books was dissolved by Leopold II. Van Swieten was dismissed from his post on 5 December 1791 – the very day on which Mozart died.

Van Swieten was a great lover of music. In Prussia he had become interested in the music of Bach, Handel and other baroque composers; he was a friend of C. P. E. Bach. In Vienna he held regular Sunday morning concerts for the performance of baroque music, and it was there that Mozart was introduced to the music of the polyphonic school, which had a profound influence on his own music.

Van Swieten was also a friend of Haydn's; he wrote the text of the *Creation* (in which Masonic ideas are prominent) and of the *Seasons*. He too was a member of the Illuminati.

Another friend was Count Johann Philipp Cobenzl, Court Vice-

Chancellor and Chancellor of State. He and his brother were leading members of the Illuminati in Vienna, under the pseudonyms of Memerades and Arrian. The latter was criticised by Weishaupt for "acting as though Vienna and Austria were his personal property, and as though the whole Austrian monarchy was under his thumb".[6]

Mozart was on intimate terms with the Cobenzl family. He visited the Count frequently in Vienna, and spent several days at the family's country residence at Reisenberg in the Wienerwald (now named Cobenzl). Mozart described the surroundings in a letter to his father in July 1781:

"The little house is nothing much, but the country – the forest – in which my host has built a grotto which looks just as if Nature herself had fashioned it! Indeed the surroundings are magnificent and very delightful."[7]

Joseph von Sonnenfels was one of the leaders of the Illuminati in Austria, with the pseudonym of Fabius. He was an important figure in eighteenth century Vienna; in 1763 he had been appointed to the Chair of Administration and Commerce, and later he became Minister in charge of the police, in which capacity he was responsible for important legal reforms. He conducted a campaign for the abolition of torture and of the death penalty, which eventually proved successful in 1776; he also advocated improvements in the condition of the peasants. Sonnenfels was of Jewish origin; for this reason, as well as for his advanced views, he had many enemies, among whom was Cardinal Migazzi. His opponents called him "the insolent Sonnenfels".

Like so many other public men of that time, he was also a writer and a journalist. He fought for reforms in art and literature, and founded a "German Society", with the aim of popularising the works of writers such as Gellert and Klopstock. He sponsored a journal, *Letters on the Viennese Theatre*, to which he contributed a number of articles and reviews. Among these was an enthusiastic review of Gluck's *Alceste*, in which he wrote: "The music is by a man who not only manipulates chords and harmonies, but who has discovered the accents of emotion, or if I might be allowed the phrase, the accents of the soul."[8]

Sonnenfels was one of Mozart's subscribers; he must have met him on many occasions, since he was a member of the lodge *True Harmony*, whose meetings Mozart frequently attended. Four volumes of his collected works were among Mozart's books.

The name of Sonnenfels is well known to musicians, because Beethoven dedicated to him his piano sonata in D major, Op. 28.

But of all Mozart's Masonic friends the man who probably exerted the greatest influence on the composer was Ignaz von Born, scientist and satirist. Educated at a Jesuit seminary, Born, like Adam Weishaupt, soon learned to detest the fanaticism and superstition encouraged by the Jesuits. In Prague, where he had a distinguished career as adviser to the Department of Mint and Mines, he had founded a Masonic Lodge, and when he came to Vienna to take charge of the Imperial Natural History Collection, he founded the lodge *True Harmony*, which became the leading centre for intellectual and cultural life among the Freemasons of the city. Born was a member of the Illuminati, and his lodge was run on Illuminist lines. One of its declared aims was: "To combat superstition and fanaticism in the persons of the monkish orders, the main supports of both these evils."[9]

Born's writings, many of which were published in the magazine edited by Gemmingen, included a number of scientific works, several satires on the clergy, and a book on the Egyptian mysteries.

Born was highly esteemed by all who knew him. One of his contemporaries said of him: "I know of no one whom people would rather meet, or hear with greater interest. He has not written much, but everything he says should be published, for it is always witty, relevant, and his satire is without insult. . . . He has read and investigated everything from Church Fathers to fairy tales."[10]

In 1785 Born made a stand against the persecution of the Illuminati in Bavaria, withdrawing his name from the Bavarian Academy of Sciences as a protest. (We shall return to this subject in a later chapter.)

Born's acquaintance with the Mozart family was of long standing. As early as 1777 Nannerl recorded in her diary that he had "taken coffee" with them. In June 1787, when travelling through Salzburg with the poet Blumauer, he again called on Leopold Mozart and spent an evening with him.

He subscribed to Mozart's concerts, and wrote an inscription in his album (see p. 117). He was the Grand Master of the lodge *True Harmony*.

Although Born's name is not mentioned in Mozart's extant letters, there is enough evidence to show that the two men were on intimate terms. Mozart is known to have visited him at his residence in the Dorotheergasse during the summer of 1790, one year before the composition of *The Magic Flute*. There is a tradition that he was the prototype of Sarastro, and it has also been suggested that he had some hand in planning the libretto. Certainly his article on the Egyptian mysteries is one of the sources for the ritual scenes.

Mozart had many other acquaintances among Freemasons. He regularly attended musical gatherings at the house of Countess Wilhelmine Thun, where he met a number of distinguished foreign guests. Among these was Georg Forster, the writer, who became one of the leaders of the Mainz Republic in 1792. Forster described Countess Thun as "the most virtuous and enlightened woman in Vienna"; he mentions Born, Gemmingen, Cobenzl and Kaunitz among those who attended her receptions "to enjoy brilliant conversation or music".[11]

From Caroline Pichler we learn that gatherings at her father's house were attended by the poets Leon, Haschka, Alxinger and Blumauer (all well-known Freemasons), and that "the celebrated traveller Georg Forster" had been entertained there by musicians, including "our native artists Mozart, Haydn and Salieri".[12]

Mozart does not seem to have renewed his intimacy with the Mesmer family, although he had been a frequent guest at their house on previous visits to Vienna. The Mesmers were Freemasons, but their interests were in the occult and mystical aspects of the Craft, whereas Mozart's friends were mostly Illuminati, with rationalist ideas.

NOTES

1 Jahn, II, p. 402.
2 *Neue deutsche Biographie*, Berlin, 1963, VI, p. 179.
3 Anderson, p. 638.
4 Wangermann, *The Austrian Achievement*, p. 142.
5 ibid., p. 149.
6 Engel, p. 195.
7 Anderson, p. 751 f.
8 Wangermann, p. 120 f.
9 Jahn, II, p. 401.
10 Nettl, p. 13.
11 Jahn, II, p. 354.
12 ibid., pp. 354 f.

MUSIC OF 1782-4

It is sometimes stated that Mozart can have had no knowledge of Masonic ritual before his own initiation. Yet he had depicted Masonic ceremonies in his music for *Thamos* several years before he joined the Order. Two works composed in 1782 and 1783 also provide evidence of his association with the Brotherhood before he became an initiate.

The first of these is an *Adagio* for two clarinets and three basset horns (K.411), of which Jahn writes: "The combination of instruments so nearly related, with their full, soft, and, in their deeper notes, sepulchral tones, produces an impression of solemnity, which is in accordance with the general character of peace after conflict expressed by the *Adagio*."[1]

Nothing is known of the circumstances in which this piece was composed; Jahn suggests that it was written for some Masonic occasion, while Dr. William Ober writes that it was "probably intended for a solemn entrance procession by members of the lodge, as the Masonic knocking theme is softly indicated".[2]

Woodwind instruments, especially clarinets, were frequently used in lodge ceremonies; they were known as "columns of harmony".[3] Basset horns play an important part in Mozart's Masonic works, such as the *Masonic Funeral Music* (K.477). The *Adagio* contains certain Masonic symbols, such as pairs of slurred notes, and a series of 6–3 chords. The opening theme, with the rhythm

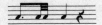

on a rising major chord, occurs in several of Mozart's Masonic works, as in the opening of the cantata K.623. It has been suggested that the rests which punctuate the phrases denote pauses for the insertion of some act of ritual.

The unfinished cantata *Dir, Seele des Weltalls* (*To Thee, Soul of Creation*) (K.429), is undoubtedly Masonic. The words are by Haschka, a member of the lodge *True Harmony*; the sentiments expressed in the opening chorus, which is a Hymn to the Sun, resemble those of the first chorus in *Thamos*.

The occasion for which this cantata was written is not known. Ober suggests that it was composed for some Masonic celebration to which non-members were invited.[4] Massin thinks that it may have been intended for a meeting of Illuminati, and that Gemmingen may have enrolled Mozart among them before 1783.[5] Unfortunately there is not enough evidence to support this theory, and we do not know whether the Illuminati made use of music on the scale required for a performance of this work. Other critics, such as Saint-Foix, have suggested that the cantata dates from the last year of Mozart's life, on account of its affinity with the style of his later compositions. But the resemblance of the chorus to those in *Thamos*, as well as in *The Magic Flute*, shows that we cannot dismiss the earlier date on stylistic grounds. Rather we may see in this work an early example of a style associated with Masonic ideas, whose chief characteristic is its noble simplicity. Constanze described the cantata in the following words:

"The first chorus, in E♭ major, is quite complete. It begins with a magnificent unison, and there prevails throughout it a noble, simple, pleasant melody. In the words 'From thee cometh fruitfulness, warmth, light', the word 'light' is particularly prominent, through a surprising *forte* on the chord of the seventh, and would doubtless make a strong impression on listeners if set to the prescribed instruments — flutes, oboe, clarinets, bassoons and so on. After this comes a tenor aria in B♭, full of the tenderest melody, with a wonderful melody for contrabass. . . . Lastly follows a second tenor aria in F, of which only seventeen bars remain."[6]

The so-called "aria" is in fact a duet for two tenors, opening with the words "The lights, which to thousands . . ." Perhaps this is a reference to the "secret schools of wisdom" of the Illuminati, which were known as "lights".

The cantata contains various Masonic symbols, such as the rhythmic figure

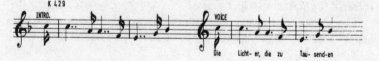

with an interrupted cadence, pairs of slurred notes, descending 6–3 chords, and dotted rhythm in the unfinished duet. The opening of this duet is identical with that of the song "Lied der Freiheit" ("Song of Freedom") (K.506), composed in 1786, to words by Alois Blumauer, a leading member of the Illuminati. The poem expresses contempt for the slaves of love, ambition or fortune.

LIED DER FREIHEIT K 506

Wer un- ter ei- nes Mäd-chens Hand

The opening phrase of the chorus, with its wide leaps on the tonic chord, foreshadows Sarastro's recitative in the *Finale* of Act II of *The Magic Flute*, alluding to the sunrise. (The resemblance of this phrase to the opening of Beethoven's "Creation's Hymn" suggests some connection with the idea of Nature.)

There is thus evidence that Mozart was already using Masonic symbolism in his music in 1783.

In considering Mozart's Masonic music, attention may be drawn to the use of counterpoint, which plays an important part in the *Masonic Funeral Music*, and in parts of *The Magic Flute*. It may help us to understand the significance of counterpoint for Freemasons if we refer to a speech made on the occasion of Haydn's initiation. J. Holzmeister, Grand Master of the lodge, praised Haydn "for inventing a new order of things in the orchestra. . . . If every instrument does not considerably diminish its own volume, in order not to do damage to the utterances of its companions, the end, which is beauty, would not be attained. Instead of melting, moving music, an intolerable hodge-podge of ill-united sounds would be produced."[7] This is clearly a statement of Masonic ideas on democracy in music, expressed through polyphony, as opposed to the typical *galant* style of a leading melody, to which the other parts are subservient.

Mozart had been introduced to the music of Bach and Handel by Baron van Swieten during the year 1782; he had composed a number of fugues, modelled on Bach, and had arranged five fugues from the *Well-tempered Clavier* for string orchestra (K.405). We shall see later how he applied these studies in counterpoint to his Masonic compositions.

The instrumental works of 1782 and 1783 may be divided into two categories, the first consisting of music intended for public performances, like the Haffner and Linz symphonies (K.385 and 425) and the three piano concertos (K.413–5), and the second of more intimate works, such as the string quartets dedicated to Haydn. The first three of this series (K.387, 421 and 428) were composed in 1782 and 1783.

The Masonic significance of the last three quartets will be discussed later. But certain Masonic features can also be seen in the earlier quartets. In the E♭ quartet (K.428), for example, we may note the suspensions in the opening of the *Andante con moto*, and the pairs of slurred notes in the Minuet. The seven bars of detached notes, played *piano*, in the second part of the Minuet, are in the style of *sotto voce* moralising passages, like the famous duet between Pamina and Papageno in *The Magic Flute*.

Meanwhile Mozart was endeavouring to reach a wider audience. In the summer of 1782 he associated himself with a certain Philip Martin, who was organising a series of concerts for amateurs in the Augarten. This part of the Imperial gardens had recently been thrown open to the public by Joseph, with an inscription over the entrance: "Public place of recreation dedicated to all men, by one who esteems them."

Mozart described the scheme to his father enthusiastically. "You know that there are a great many amateurs in Vienna, and some very good ones too, both men and women. . . . Well, this Martin has now got permission from the Emperor under Charter (with the promise too of his gracious patronage) to give twelve concerts in the Augarten and four grand serenades in the finest open places of the city. The subscription for the whole summer is only two ducats. So you can imagine we shall have plenty of subscribers, the more so since I am taking an interest in it and am associated with it. . . . The Baron van Swieten and Countess Thun are very much interested in it. The orchestra consists entirely of amateurs, with the exception of the bassoon-players, the trumpeters and drummers."[8]

Similar concerts for amateurs had been given in Paris and in Mannheim, where they were organised by Freemasons. It is most likely that in Vienna, too, much of the support came from Masonic circles.

Mozart composed three piano concertos (K.413–5) for these concerts in the Augarten. These works represent a compromise between the need to please the public and the desire to express his own deepest feelings. He wrote to his father: "These concertos are a happy medium between what is too easy and too difficult; they are very brilliant, pleasing to the ear, and natural, without being vapid. There are passages here and there from which the connoisseurs alone can derive satisfaction; but these passages are written in such a way that the less learned cannot fail to be pleased, though without knowing why."[9]

Girdlestone writes of these concertos that "they represent the collective soul of his hearers, rather than his own".[10] The first (K.413), in F major, is in typical *galant* style, with an old-fashioned minuet for its last movement – "a product of the Ancien Régime".[11] The second

(K.414), in A major (not to be confused with the better-known A major concerto, K.488), is more personal in character. Its mood is predominantly tender and joyous, reminding us of *Die Entführung*, to which some of its themes bear resemblance. The third theme in the opening *ritornello* of the first movement, for example, is almost identical with a theme from the quartet in that opera, in which the two pairs of lovers are reconciled after a quarrel.

(Dearest Blondchen, ah, forgive me, I am sure that you are constant.)

In the second movement, an *Andante* in D major, triple time, we find a new element – that of mystery. The slow, solemn strains of the opening bars and the use of the "modal" chord on the Mediant (III), evoke an atmosphere described by Girdlestone as "almost religious".[12] We may note the pairs of slurred notes,

and the transitions from major to minor, which, as Girdlestone points out, always have special significance in Mozart. Such transitions often indicate a change from darkness to light, as in the last chorus of *Thamos*.

The atmosphere of this *Andante* is similar to that of the Priests' choruses in *The Magic Flute*. Mozart knew something about the mysteries of initiation from his Masonic friends, even if he had not yet taken part in the ceremonies. Although this concerto avoids "not only what might shock, but even what might merely astonish the public",[13] it appears to contain a message of profound significance for those who can understand it. Perhaps that is what Mozart meant when he referred to passages "from which the connoisseurs alone can derive satisfaction".

The third concerto in this series (K.415), in C major, is chiefly notable for its *Finale* – a light-hearted rondo in 6–8 whose gaiety is suddenly shattered by a change to C minor, with a poignant melody in 2–4 time.

Mozart wrote no more piano concertos until the beginning of 1784 – a gap of fifteen months. On 9 February he started to keep a catalogue of his works, opening with a piano concerto in E♭ (K.449). This was the first of six concertos written in that year, which was one of the most productive in his life. The preponderance of piano concertos during this period was the result of his success as a virtuoso performer of his own works. On 10 February he wrote to his father: "I have works to compose which *at the moment* are bringing in money, but will not do so later. The opera will always bring in some, and besides, the more time I take the better it will be."[14]

He begged his father not to allow his concertos to be copied. In those days composers had no protection against unscrupulous copyists and engravers. "How can I protect myself from being cheated by the engraver? For he can surely print off as many copies as he likes and therefore swindle me."[15]

In December 1783 the Mozarts moved to lodgings at the house of Johann von Trattner, a bookseller, who owned a large room where concerts were given. It was there that Mozart gave a series of subscription concerts at which his new piano concertos were played. He sent his father a list of over a hundred subscribers, of whom many were Freemasons. (His landlord, Trattner, was also a member of the Order.) He played frequently at musical receptions given by members of the nobility, among whom were Count Esterhazy (another Mason) and Prince Galitzin, Russian Ambassador to the Viennese Court.

Each of the six concertos composed in 1784 is a masterpiece, and each has its distinctive personality. The first, in E♭(K.449) marks a new stage in Mozart's development, and is therefore worthy of detailed study.

The difference between this concerto and all the preceding ones (with the possible exception of the earlier E♭ concerto, K.271) is summed up by Girdlestone as displaying "elaboration of form and deepening of thought."[16] It seems as though Mozart is no longer afraid of startling his audience; no longer does he compromise with the *galant*. The opening *Allegro vivace* is in triple time; this in itself is unusual for this period.

The first *Tutti* is full of modulations, and the prevailing mood of this movement is one of restlessness and uncertainty, created by tonal instability and agitated rhythms. Within a few bars of the opening we reach the key of C minor (of which there is already a hint in the second bar); the section which follows, with its agitated *tremolando* accompaniment and fluttering semiquavers on minor and diminished chords, reminds us of the portrayal of Tamino's flight from the serpent in the opening scene of *The Magic Flute*. There is also some resemblance to the first entr'acte in *Thamos*, which depicts the clash between the forces of good and evil. All these passages are in C minor.

Just before the recapitulation, four bars of chromatic harmonies, played by the soloist, remind us of a passage at the same point in the first movement of the E♭ Symphony (K.543) – a work generally recognised as Masonic.

The *Andantino* of K.449 is simple and serene, conforming to Masonic ideals. It contains pairs of slurred notes in thirds, played first on the piano, then taken up by the strings and oboes. This theme expresses tenderness and unity.

The climax of this concerto is its *Finale*. In this movement the restlessness of the opening *Allegro* is transformed into an unceasing flow of purposeful motion. The theme itself, with its bold sequences of fourths, is related to the E♭ fugue in Book II of the *Well-tempered Clavier* – one of those which Mozart had transcribed for string quartet, and of which he was particularly fond. In this *Finale* homophonic and polyphonic elements are combined, in a manner which foreshadows the *Finale* of the "Jupiter" Symphony. It also combines diversity of form with continuity, by combining rondo and variation form. Thus this movement is an example of a unity of opposites.

We must call attention to a phrase, heard first on the piano, which occurs in several other of Mozart's compositions, notably in the Clarinet quintet (K.581) and in the Trio sung by Pamina, Tamino and Sarastro in *The Magic Flute* (No. 19).

K449

K 581

Magic Flute

Der Göt- ter Wil— le mag ge— scheh- en

Massin suggests that this phrase may have Masonic significance. The idea expressed in the Trio is acceptance of Fate – a recognition of necessity which is identifiable with freedom. In Masonic ideology freedom and joy were closely related; the acceptance of Fate may be joyous. Tamino sings "The will of the Gods must be accepted"; he gladly undertakes the trials which lie before him, knowing that he will conquer through the power of love, aided by Pamina and under Sarastro's wise guidance. Knowledge and wisdom have given him strength to overcome his ordeals; he no longer fears the serpent.

The mood of the *Finale* of K.449 is one of joyous acceptance, as it presses towards its goal. The first movement of this concerto is full of anxiety and conflict, which is assuaged in the tender *Andantino*, and finally overcome in the triumphant progress of the *Finale*.

The same mood of confidence is evident in the next two concertos, in B♭ (K.450) and D major (K.451), entered in Mozart's catalogue on 15th and 22nd of March. He wrote to his father: "I really cannot choose between the two of them, but I regard them both as concertos which are bound to make the performer perspire."[17]

In these two concertos the orchestra is larger than in K.449; in K.450 woodwind is especially prominent. The *Andante* of this work, in E♭ and in triple time, is calm and tender, and may be described as humanist in style.

The D major (K.451) is on a grander scale, with drums and trumpets. The first movement, though outwardly conventional, contains some surprises, like the syncopated chromatic phrases heard towards the end of the opening *ritornello* (bars 43–52), and the series of descending 6–3 chords, starting unexpectedly on the Mediant chord (III), which evoke an atmosphere of mystery.

During the spring of 1784 Mozart wrote several other works of great beauty and significance, including the Quintet for piano and woodwind (K.452), which he considered "the best work I have ever composed,"[18] and the G major piano concerto (K.453), sometimes known as the "Starling" concerto because he taught his pet starling to whistle the theme of the *Finale*. This air reminds us of Papageno, the bird-catcher in *The Magic Flute*.

The sonata for Violin and Piano in B♭ (K.454), written for the Italian violinist Regina Strinasacchi, and performed in the presence of the Emperor on 29 April, is one of Mozart's finest in that genre, although it was composed in such haste that he had no time to write down the piano part. This sonata was published by Torricella, a Freemason, with Masonic emblems on the title-page. (These were omitted in a later edition, published by Artaria in 1787.)[19] Masonic influence may perhaps be traced in the serene *Andante* in E♭, and in the opening phrase of the last movement, which consists of a joyous upward leap of an octave, followed by a series of descending pairs of slurred notes.

After this period of intense creativity Mozart wrote little until the end of September 1784. His prospects at that time seemed good; his fame as a composer had spread all over Germany, with performances of *Die Entführung* as far afield as Dresden and Hanau. It was well-received everywhere, even in Salzburg, where Leopold reported that "the whole town is delighted with it. Even the Archbishop was gracious enough to say, 'Really it wasn't bad at all'."[20]

Years later Goethe described the impact which Mozart's music had made on him. "All our endeavour . . . to confine ourselves to what is simple and limited was lost when Mozart appeared. *Die Entführung aus dem Serail* conquered all."[21]

The Mozarts must have felt comparatively secure financially at this time, for in June they moved to larger, more expensive apartments, probably on account of the birth of their son, Karl Thomas. During that summer Mozart made friends with Paisiello, for whom he formed a strong attachment. Paisiello was a man of enlightened views, who later became a supporter of the French Revolution.

At the end of August Wolfgang fell seriously ill, and was attended by his old friend Dr. Barisani. His first composition after five months of silence was another piano concerto, in B♭ (K.456), written for the blind pianist, Maria Theresia Paradis. The poignant *Andante* of this concerto, in G minor, might suggest the pathos of the blind girl for whom it was composed. The last movement contains sudden and startling changes of key and tempo, with astonishing modulations. The suppressed passion in this part of the *rondo* is related to the mood of the piano sonata in C minor, composed at about the same time (K.457).

This sonata, together with the *Fantasia* in the same key written in the following summer (K.475), is dedicated to his former landlord's wife, Therese von Trattner, who was his pupil. Mozart is known to have described how the sonata ought to be played, in letters which are unfortunately not extant. Therese von Trattner is said to have refused Constanze's request for them after Mozart's death. There has been some speculation as to whether Mozart was in love with Therese; however that may be, this sonata certainly appears to reflect some crisis in his life. The tragedy which it expresses seems like that of an individual struggling against his fate. The first movement, with its *sforzando* accents and short, rhythmic motifs, has an explosive character usually associated with the music of Beethoven. (It is said to have been Beethoven's favourite among Mozart's sonatas.)

The *Adagio* in E♭ conveys an atmosphere of resignation, combined with pathos, resembling the Countess's first aria in *Figaro*. It is worth noting that the *Adagio* of Beethoven's Pathetic Sonata echoes one of the phrases in this movement.

The agitated *Allegro assai*, with its fragmentary themes, syncopations and diminished sevenths, offers no solution to the tragedy of the first movement. The *Fantasia* which Mozart wrote in the following year (K.475) to precede this sonata is even more sombre. It bears some resemblance to the *Masonic Funeral Music* (K.477) written shortly afterwards. But, whereas the latter ends on a chord of C major, expressing the change from dark to light, both the Fantasia and the Sonata end in unrelieved gloom.

A few weeks before he composed this sonata Mozart had been at death's door. C minor was the key associated with darkness and death. For whatever reasons, whether personal or more general, his mood was one of despair when he wrote it. A few months later he joined the

Brotherhood, and found his hopes renewed through companionship and community of ideals. The two remaining compositions of 1784 express his revived hopes and renewed confidence.

NOTES

1   Jahn, III, p. 28.
2   Ober, Dr. W., on sleeve of *Music for Masonic Occasions*, Vol. I.
3   Chailley, p. 210 n.
4   Ober, op. cit.
5   Massin, p. 1131.
6   Farmer, H. G., *New Mozartiana*, Glasgow, 1935. p. 58.
7   Jacob, H. E. *Joseph Haydn, his Life and Times*, London, 1950, p. 155.
8   Anderson, pp. 804 f.
9   ibid., p. 833.
10 Girdlestone, C. M., *Mozart's Piano Concertos*, London, 1948, p. 130.
11 ibid., p. 130.
12 ibid., p. 140.
13 ibid., p. 137.
14 Anderson, p. 866.
15 ibid., p. 868.
16 Girdlestone, p. 175.
17 Anderson, p. 877.
18 ibid., p. 873.
19 Deutsch, p. 226.
20 Anderson, p. 884.
21 Deutsch, p. 305.

MOZART AND THE BROTHERHOOD

Mozart's lodge *Beneficence* was a small one, whose founder and Grand Master was Otto von Gemmingen. Shortly before Mozart's admission, the secretary, Leopold Aloys Hoffmann, left Vienna to become professor of German at Pest University. On 5 December 1784 the lodge issued the following communication: "Proposed: Kapellmeister Mozart. Our departed secretary, Bro. Hoffmann, forgot to circulate this nominee among the most honourable sister lodges; his name was already submitted 4 weeks ago to the highly honoured District Lodge, and we should therefore wish to proceed to his admittance next week, if the most honourable sister lodges have no objection to him."[1]

Hoffmann had seemed to be a zealous member of the Order, but he subsequently published an attack on Freemasonry, and eventually became one of its most violent opponents. In view of his later treachery, of which we shall give an account in due course, we may wonder whether his failure to notify the sister lodges of Mozart's application was due to forgetfulness, or whether it was deliberate.

The Viennese lodges at that time were grouped in district lodges. *Beneficence* was in the same group as *True Harmony*, with which it shared a temple, and whose meetings Mozart frequently attended. On 7 January 1785 he was admitted to the second grade of Masonry there. His promotion was unusually rapid.

The lodge *True Harmony*, whose founder and Grand Master was Ignaz von Born, was the largest and most important in Vienna. Many writers, scientists and artists were members, and meetings and concerts were frequently held there, as well as the traditional Masonic feasts. The lodge had a library and a museum, and it published a quarterly journal, *Journal für Freymaurer*, edited by the poet Blumauer, with a circulation of between five and six hundred. This journal published articles on a wide range of subjects, both scientific and cultural. Many members of *True Harmony* were Illuminati, including the poets Blumauer, Leon and Alxinger. The last-named was well known for his criticism of the church; one of his poems had been censored on the grounds of atheism. Alxinger maintained that the Edict of Toleration, aimed at giving freedom of worship, did not go far enough. He also criticised the Emperor for his parsimony towards the arts.

The doctrines of the Illuminati had made a strong impression in the Viennese lodges, chiefly under the influence of Born. The lodge *True Harmony* had been in correspondence with Weishaupt's lodge *Theodor* in Munich, and among the papers seized from the house of Zwack during house-searchings in 1786 were a number of copies of the *Journal für Freymaurer*. Born aimed at reforming Freemasonry in the spirit of the Illuminati. The latter were not anti-religious, since they believed in a Divine Creator, and thought that many of Christ's teachings were similar to their own. But they attacked the Catholic hierarchy, declaring that "the oppression of priests and princes is the result of their conceit, ambition, greed, envy and thirst for power".[2] In the ritual for the Regent grade of the Illuminati the candidate was asked certain questions, among them the following: "Who has brought you to this miserable condition of slavery?" Answer: "Society, the State, the Scholars, false religion."[3]

In his pamphlet against the monastic orders, Born attacked "the wealth and power, superfluity of goods, superstition and spiritual corruption of the clergy",[4] declaring that the church "condemns freedom of thought and enlightenment, and nourishes superstition",[5] and that "every man should be free to choose his way of life, for the man who is a slave can never be a really useful member of society."[6]

It should be stated that discontent with orthodox religion was not confined to the Freemasons: we learn of student contempt for religion, and growing scepticism among artisans. A Piarist* preacher named Wieser was suspended by Cardinal Migazzi for stressing the moral elements in Christianity; he received such strong support from his congregation, led by the cobbler Felberer, that he was reinstated. The occasion was celebrated at a festive dinner, among the guests being "the master tailor Engel, a florist called Bichler, the auditor Kramer with his two sons, Wieser's two brothers, a [female] cook from the General Hospital who had also written a pamphlet against Fast [see below], the upholsterer Storch from Neubach and many others – all in all some fifty people."[7]

The spread of anti-clerical ideas caused the church authorities increasing anxiety, and the conflict with supporters of the Enlightenment grew sharper as a result of events in Bavaria. During

---

* A Catholic teaching order with special responsibility for youth.

the persecution of the Illuminati in 1785, Born sent in his resignation to the Bavarian Academy of Sciences, and wrote an open letter to the press protesting at the actions of the Bavarian government: "I declare myself to be an open enemy of ignorant monks . . . , who ought never to be entrusted with the education of youth: I declare that the words Jesuitry and Fanaticism can be equated with roguery and ignorance, superstition and stupidity; in short, my opinion is completely opposed to what seems to be the official opinion in Bavaria."[8]

The immediate occasion for Born's protest was the trial and conviction of a young officer called Meggenhofen, accused of having had contact with the Illuminati after the Order had been banned (Appendix II). Born's letter elicited the following reply from Father Fast, Jesuit curate and choirmaster of St. Stephen's Cathedral, a zealous writer of pamphlets against the Enlightenment: "The Church of God is now in continual conflict with the Enlightenment in Vienna, and has now fallen almost completely under the yoke of rationalism. But a small group of Catholic believers join with me in rejoicing at the wise and enlightened verdict against the impertinent philosopher Meggenhofen, who has been compelled to atone for his crimes by incarceration, because he was not ashamed openly to place upon his bookshelves the works of heathen writers such as Cicero, Sallust and Livy, and, worse still, to read them."[9]

Father Fast proceeded to offer to supply copies of his *Catholic Instruction* for use in the army, where they might "perhaps be useful in converting men from this bestial and damnable freethinking"; he concluded with a fulsome eulogy of Meggenhofen's judge as "one who is worthy to be made Grand Inquisitor in Madrid or Lisbon".

Attacks on the Illuminati in Vienna, as in Bavaria, came from two sources: the Jesuits and the Rosicrucians. In 1786 an anonymous brochure accused the Brothers of *True Harmony* of "not being true Masons". Sonnenfels, it was said, had "made the Masonic oath look ridiculous", while Born "had gone too far in belittling the importance of magic".[10]

Among Mozart's friends, Born was not the only one who supported the Illuminati against their enemies. Gemmingen was Austrian ambassador at Regensburg when Adam Weishaupt took refuge there. The Bavarian authorities demanded his extradition as "a criminal scoundrel who does not deserve protection".[11] Gemmingen refused to be intimidated, and he assisted Weishaupt to obtain asylum at the court of Saxe-Gotha, where the Duke was friendly to the Illuminati.

It is hard to believe that Mozart was completely indifferent to the political struggle which was taking place, in which several of his friends were actively engaged, even though he was fully preoccupied with musical events during the spring and summer of 1785. We can form a picture of his busy life from descriptions sent by Leopold to his daughter when he visited Wolfgang during the Lent season. "We never get to bed before one o'clock and I never get up before nine. We lunch at two or half-past. The weather is horrible. Every day there are concerts; and the whole time is given up to teaching, music, composing and so forth. I feel rather out of it all. If only the concerts were over! It is impossible for me to describe the rush and bustle."[12]

All the same, Wolfgang found time to attend lodge meetings, and to persuade his father to join the Order. Leopold was initiated in the lodge *Beneficence* on 1 April, and promoted to the second grade in *True Harmony* ten days later. Before his departure from Vienna, he was promoted to the third grade at a ceremony over which Born presided, in the lodge *True Harmony*.

On 16 February Joseph Haydn had been initiated in the same lodge. The ceremony should have taken place on 28 January, but Haydn was prevented from attending, and Mozart, who had been present on the first date, was unable to attend on the second occasion. In applying to join the Order, Haydn had written: "The highly advantageous impression which Freemasonry has made on me has long awakened in my breast the sincerest wish to become a member of the Order, with its humanitarian principles."[13]

To his friend Count Apponyi he wrote: "Oh if only it were Friday – so that I could have the inexpressible Joy of being among a circle of such worthy men. . . ."[14]

Haydn's zeal for the Order has been questioned, since he attended no more meetings after his initiation, but the distance from Esterhazy, and the difficulty of obtaining leave from his employer might well account for this.

On the day after his initiation, Haydn visited Mozart and heard the last three of the quartets dedicated to him. Leopold described the occasion. "On Saturday evening Herr Joseph Haydn and the two Barons Tinti* came to see us and the new quartets were performed, or rather, the three new ones which Wolfgang has added to the other three which we have already. The new ones are somewhat easier, but at the same time excellent compositions. Haydn said to me: 'Before God and

* Members of *True Harmony*.

as an honest man I tell you that your son is the greatest composer known to me either in person or by name. He has taste, and, what is more, the most profound knowledge of composition.'"[15]

Mozart's first composition for a Masonic occasion after he joined the Brotherhood was the song, "Gesellenreise" (K.468), composed for Leopold's promotion to the second grade. The words are by J. F. Ratschky, a member of *True Harmony*. "You who are now approaching a new grade, be firm as you wander on your path; know that it is the path of wisdom. Only a man who is tireless can approach the source of light."

The song is for solo voice, with organ accompaniment. It has a gentle, flowing melody; the undulating shape of the opening phrase resembles phrases found in Mozart's later Masonic works, often connected with the idea of wandering. The song contains some of the Masonic symbols, such as dotted-quaver rhythms, 6–3 chords and suspensions.

On 4 April 1785 Mozart's cantata *Die Maurerfreude (Mason's Joy)* (K.471) was performed at the lodge *Crowned Hope*, in honour of Ignaz von Born, whose discovery of a new method of amalgamating metals had been praised by the Emperor as "one of the most important discoveries of the century".[16] A contemporary writer, Franz Graeffer, gave a vivid account of a supposed conversation between Born and the Emperor, ending with Joseph's handing Born a letter of congratulation from the distinguished American scientist and Freemason, Benjamin Franklin.

The preface to the cantata reads as follows: "Touched by the kindness which the wisest and most just of Monarchs, Joseph II, has bestowed on one of its Brothers, and full of sympathy with the impending happiness of this noble man, this profound scholar, this meritorious Mason, the assembly of Brothers known as *The Crowned Hope* of Vienna, resolved to express its sentiments in fraternal concord at a friendly and joyous repast, and to give vent to them in conviviality through the arts of poetry and music. The present cantata is a distinguished item of the songs of joy sung at the feast. The Brothers of the said lodge believe that they fitly interpret the views of their Monarch, the opinions of their honoured guest and the feelings of their own hearts by making this cantata generally known and by dedicating its proceeds to the benefit of their needy fellow-men."[17]

On the title-page is an engraving depicting Born as a bearded figure being crowned by the goddess of Wisdom, while the goddess of Hope is seated at her side, with crown and anchor. The background is a

Masonic temple, with books, musical instruments and statuary in front
of it, and a landscape of trees, mountains and waterfall alongside. The
inscription reads: "Mason's Joy, a Cantata, sung on 24 April 1785 in
honour of our Worthy Brother Born, by the Brothers of Crowned Hope
Lodge in Orient in Vienna. The words are by Br[other] P[etra]n, the
music by Br[other] W. A. Mozart."[18]

The cantata expresses the joy of Freemasons at the honour shown to
one of their Brothers by Joseph. The praise of Joseph seems to us
fulsome; but it must be remembered that at that time the Emperor was
thought to be friendly to the Order, and even that he might intend to join
it. The opening words: "See how Nature step by step reveals her face to
the steadfast seeker, how she fills his mind with wisdom and his heart
with virtue", may be compared with part of the Speech to the Illuminati
Dirigentes, edited by Knigge: "As diligent and exact observers of
Nature, we pursue her majestic course with admiration, rejoicing in our
race and in our good fortune, as human beings and the children of
God."[19]

The cantata, which is in E♭ major, is for solo tenor (specially
composed for Adamberger), three-part male-voice chorus, and
orchestra of strings, two oboes, one clarinet and two horns. It contains a
number of Masonic symbols – dotted rhythms, slurred notes and
suspensions. The *gruppetto* in the opening bar may represent Masonic
joy, while the wide leaps on the tonic chord suggest a connection with
Nature. (See first ex., p. 92.) In the short choral section rising scales
illustrate songs of triumph rising to the skies; the general tone of the
cantata is one of dignified joy. There is a passage of haunting beauty in a
short recitative which links the two sections, accompanied by oboes in
thirds, with pizzicato basses. The words are as follows: "Take, beloved,
this crown; from noble Joseph's hands receive this honour."

DIE MAURERFREUDE

This cantata became one of Mozart's most popular Masonic works; it was performed on a number of occasions, including twice in Prague in the composer's presence, in 1787 and 1791.

In July 1785 Mozart composed the *Masonic Funeral Music* (K.477). The work was performed at a meeting held in November to commemorate the death of two Masons, Count Esterhazy and Count Mecklenburg. It may have been written for some ritual ceremony of death and resurrection; it cannot have been composed for the funeral of the two Masons (as is sometimes stated), since their death occurred in November, while the work was written in July.

The music is remarkably beautiful, and full of significance, foreshadowing the scene of the Men in Armour in *The Magic Flute*. The key is C minor (symbolic of death and darkness); the sombre tones of the lower woodwind, including basset horns; the throbbing quavers of the basses; the chromaticism and harsh discords – all these features combine to express the depths of human sorrow. The *Cantus Firmus*, based on a Protestant psalm-tune, which is itself derived from an ancient Jewish melody, seems to affirm an inexorable fate, against which the strings struggle in dotted-quaver rhythm

Three bars from the end an interrupted cadence suggests a glimmer of hope; the effect of the final C major chord is like a sudden transition from darkness to light, such as that expressed by Haydn in the *Creation*, in his setting of the words "And there was light". Man's triumph over death, by acceptance of his fate, was in accordance with Masonic ideas. This is expressed by the C major chord at the end of the *Masonic Funeral Music*.

Einstein writes: "If one wished, one could find all the symbols of Masonry in the 69 measures: the parallel thirds and sixths, the slurs, the knocking-rhythm."[20]

The work is Masonic, not only through the use of specific symbols, but through its tonality, rhythms and harmonies, through the use of counterpoint, and especially through the introduction of a *Cantus Firmus*, whose Protestant and Jewish connotations express the unity of all religions. This was one of the fundamental beliefs of Freemasons. Thus this short piece is of supreme importance in helping us to understand how Mozart expressed his Masonic ideas in instrumental music.

Two songs composed at the end of 1785 record an event of considerable importance to Viennese Freemasons. On 11 December Joseph issued a decree ordering that the eight lodges in Vienna be amalgamated into three, and that records of meetings and membership be regularly submitted to the police. This measure was a severe blow to those lodges which were predominantly Illuminist, since members of the Rosicrucian lodges were now combined with the Illuminati.

The changes were not accepted without controversy. On 20 December at 5 p.m. delegates from all the lodges met to discuss the new measures. All Masonic documents were handed in to be locked up and sealed. It was proposed that membership of the three new lodges should be decided by ballot, but this proposal was considered unbrotherly by some of the delegates. Among those who opposed the ballot were Sonnenfels and Gemmingen, while Born was in favour of a compromise, which was eventually reached. As a result, the total membership was reduced from 600 to 360, divided between two lodges, called *Truth* and *Newly-crowned Hope*. Sonnenfels and Gemmingen ceased to be Grand Masters, and a number of members left the Order. Mozart joined the lodge *Newly-crowned Hope*, whose Grand Master was his old friend, Tobias von Gebler. It was for the first meeting of the new lodge that he composed the two songs "For the Opening of the Lodge" (K.483) and "For the Closing of the Lodge" (K.484). Both songs are for solo voice and three-part male-voice chorus, in simple style. The first song praises Joseph's wise action in giving protection to the Order. Since Joseph's purpose was to control rather than to protect the Freemasons, the words seem to us somewhat ironic, but no doubt the Brethren hoped to retain the Emperor's favour. The song contains references to Mozart's former lodge *Beneficence*, as well as to the new lodge in the phrase "the crowning of our hopes". Dotted-quaver rhythm is used in the accompaniment to illustrate the word "striving".

The second song is an appeal to the lodge's new leaders to "guide the Brothers in the path of wisdom, rejoicing in the chains of brotherhood which bind them together, helping them to be better men". The opening bar contains the dotted-quaver rhythm so often associated with Masonic music, and the words "chain of brothers" are set to pairs of slurred semiquavers. The refrain, with its simple, tender melody and three-part close harmony, reminds us of the music of the Three Boys in *The Magic Flute*. It is worth noting that the words "bind us to better men" are set to a phrase almost identical with one in Schubert's "An die Musik" ("To Music"), which describes the power of music to make men better. Is this a mere coincidence? Some have thought that Schubert, too, had an interest in Freemasonry.[21]

Early in 1786 Mozart composed two more songs for the Order, "Zur Eröffnung der Meisterloge" ("For the Opening of the Grand Lodge") and "Zum Schluss der Meisterarbeit" ("For the Conclusion of the Work"). These songs are unfortunately lost, and apart from them Mozart wrote no more specifically Masonic music until 1791. It is therefore all the more important to look closely at some of the other compositions written in the intervening years, and to compare them with the works which we have described.

NOTES

1 Deutsch, p. 230.
2 Le Forestier, p. 322.
3 ibid., p. 290.
4 Born, Ignaz von, *Der Klostergeist geschildert in der Untersuchung des Kirchenwesens überhaupt, insbesonders des Ordenstandes*, Vienna, 1781, p. 2.
5 ibid., p. 120.

6 ibid., p. 128.
7 Wangermann, *From Joseph II to the Jacobin Trials*, p. 8.
8 Engel, p. 310.
9 ibid., pp. 320 f.
10 Lewis, L., *Geschichte der Freimaurerei in Oesterreich und Ungarn*, Vienna, 1861, p. 28.
11 Engel, p. 310.
12 Anderson, p. 888.
13 Robbins Landon, H. C., *The Collected Correspondence of Joseph Haydn*, London, 1929, p. 48.
14 ibid., p. 49.
15 Anderson, p. 886.
16 Nettl, p. 51.
17 Deutsch, O. E., *Mozart und die Wiener Logen*, Vienna, 1932, p. 10.
18 ibid., p. 7.
19 Engel, p. 158.
20 Einstein, p. 366.
21 Chailley, p. 71.

10

STRING QUARTET AND PIANO CONCERTO

"Vienna, 1 September, 1785.
"To my dear friend Haydn.

"A father who had decided to send his sons into the great world thought it his duty to entrust them to the protection and guidance of a man who was very celebrated at the time and who, moreover, happened to be his best friend.

"In like manner I send my six sons to you, most celebrated and very dear friend. They are, indeed, the fruit of a long and laborious study; but the hope which many friends have given me that this toil will be in some degree rewarded encourages me and flatters me with the thought that these children may one day prove a source of consolation to me."[1]

With these words, in Italian, Mozart dedicated his six quartets to Haydn (K.387, 421, 428, 458, 464, 465). This dedication throws light on the relationship between the two composers, and also on Mozart's method of work, which was not as care-free as is sometimes supposed. He clearly attached great importance to these quartets.

It is significant that the A major quartet (K.464) was his first composition after joining the Order of Freemasons. Massin has suggested that the key signature of A, with its three sharps, is itself symbolic, and that the "question and answer" formula of the opening *Allegro* depicts the questioning of the candidate for initiation. The *Finale* contains a chorale-like theme, which foreshadows the *Cantus Firmus* in the *Masonic Funeral Music*.[2]

The C major quartet (K.465) was composed a few days later; thus the two works form a pair. In an interesting article[3] Jacques Chailley has pointed out the Masonic significance of the C major quartet, often called the "Dissonance" quartet on account of the strange discords in the opening introduction. Mozart's contemporaries thought that these discords were due to copyists' errors. Chailley shows that similar harmonies were used in other eighteenth-century works to represent chaos. He quotes the French composer J. F. Rebel, who in 1737 composed a work entitled *Le Cahos*, which contains harmonies very like those in the C major quartet. Rebel describes chaos as "the confusion which reigned between the elements before the moment when, obeying immutable laws, they took their prescribed place in Nature's order ... I have dared to add the confusion of harmony to that of the elements. ... I thought that chaos could be still better depicted in harmony if I could, without shocking the ear, render the final tonality vague, until it returns definitely at the moment of clarification."[3]

Chailley quotes examples from Handel's *Israel in Egypt* and from the introduction to Haydn's *Creation* to illustrate similar representations of chaos. He suggests that the idea of darkness may be associated with the darkness and confusion of ignorance surrounding the profane man before the moment of illumination when he is initiated.

As we listen to the *Allegro* which follows the introduction to the first movement of the C major quartet, we may well feel that we are emerging from darkness into light. The *Andante cantabile*, in F major, triple time, with a tender, serene melody, is an example of Mozart's humanist style. The poignant central section is full of discords, recalling the introduction; when the first theme returns, we feel as though we were emerging once more from the realms of darkness into the light. The *Finale*, with its uncompromising C major tonality, expresses joy and perfect harmony, and is thus the antithesis of the introduction.

These two quartets were composed just after Mozart's initiation, and it is not surprising to find in them an expression of Masonic ideas. But the earlier B♭ quartet (K.458) (the "Hunt") also has Masonic connotations. The *Adagio*, in E♭, is in Mozart's humanist style.

This movement contains several features which occur frequently in his Masonic compositions, such as the rhythm of the opening bar, the harmonic progression in the second bar, the sudden changes from *forte* to *piano*, and the interrupted cadence when the first phrase recurs just before the end.

Four days before his admission to the lodge *Beneficence* Mozart completed a piano concerto in F major (K.459). This is one of the most joyful of his piano concertos. The theme of the opening *Allegro*, with its militant, march-like rhythm and rising fifths, at once proclaims a mood

of self-confidence. The rhythm is all-pervasive, asserting itself even in
the brief minor section. Question and answer formulas and threefold
repetitions suggest connections with the ceremonies of initiation. The
second movement is an *Allegretto* in C major, in 6–8 time, with echoes
of Susanna's aria in the pinewoods. In the minor section we hear a series
of descending 6–3 chords, with *sforzando* accents sounding a note of
warning. A few bars before the end an enchanting dialogue between
piano and woodwind is interrupted by three soft chords on the strings,
including the "modal" chord on VI, like a reminder of a solemn
occasion.

The mood of confidence and joy is asserted once more in the *Finale*,
which foreshadows the *Finale* of the "Jupiter" Symphony in its
combination of harmony and counterpoint, and fusion of learned and
popular elements. Like the opening *Allegro*, this movement has a
pervasive rhythm.

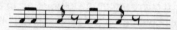

It is similar to that of Naumann's *Eintritt in die Loge* which indicates
the "triple knocking" (see p. 42).

"Never more in his work shall we hear so whole-hearted a joy so
ingenuously expressed"[4] was Girdlestone's comment on this concerto.
In deciding to join the Brotherhood, Mozart affirmed his belief in the
future happiness of mankind. It is significant that he chose to play this
work when he went to Frankfurt in 1790 for the coronation of Leopold
II, at a time when his personal hopes of happiness were at their lowest
ebb. On that occasion the F major concerto must have seemed a
proclamation of courage in the face of adversity.

The concertos in D minor (K.466) and C major (K.467) form a pair,
since they were composed within a few weeks of each other for a series
of subscription concerts during the Lent season of 1785. Leopold
referred to the D minor concerto in a letter to his daughter, written soon
after his arrival in Vienna. "Then we had a new and very fine concerto
by Wolfgang which the copyist was still copying when we arrived, and
the rondo of which your brother did not even have time to play through,
as he had to supervise the copying."[5]

D minor has been called Mozart's "demonic" key; most of his
important works in that key have sinister undertones, like Don
Giovanni's descent into hell, and the Queen of Night's rage against
Sarastro. The opening theme of the Queen's second aria bears a striking

resemblance to the opening of the first movement of the D minor concerto.

In *The Magic Flute* the Queen of Night represents the forces of darkness and superstition, as opposed to the enlightened wisdom of Sarastro. The similarity between her second aria and the D minor concerto suggests that in this work Mozart was expressing the conflict between superstition and Enlightenment. In joining the Order of Freemasons he had ranged himself firmly and openly on the side of Enlightenment. His confidence in the ultimate victory of Masonic ideals is indicated in the coda of the *Rondo*, with the sudden change to D major and the stirring call of horns and trumpets. The triumphant ending of this concerto leads inevitably to the militant march of the first movement of K.467, aptly described by Girdlestone as the "luminous" C major.

If the D minor concerto reflects the struggle against darkness and superstition, the C major may be said to express the victory of Enlightenment. It is perhaps significant that one of the themes in the first movement resembles the melody played by Tamino on his magic flute while undergoing his trial by Fire and Water.

The *Andante* of this concerto is a movement of such loveliness that it defies description. But certain features relevant to our subject may be pointed out. The repeated triplets, the rising pizzicato bass, the poignant harmonies, the conflict of duple and triple time, the stressed minor sixth – all these elements combine to produce an atmosphere which is both deeply human and hauntingly mysterious. The effect is similar to that of the passage in *Die Maurerfreude*, quoted on p. 81. We are reminded of the music of Sarastro, a character who is both mysterious and humane. The resemblance is significant, since *Die Maurerfreude* was dedicated to Born, who was thought to be the prototype of Sarastro. The melody contains the wide leaps and pairs of slurred notes characteristic of Mozart's humanist style.

(a)   K 467

Thus it seems clear that this movement is related to Mozart's Masonic beliefs, embracing a sense of mystery as well as deep human feelings.

The mood of the final *Rondo* is joyous and carefree, although conflict is expressed in the central section.

Mozart did not write another piano concerto until December, when he composed the concerto in E♭ (K.482). The tonality of the three concertos of 1785 is significant. D minor is the key associated with forces of evil and superstition; C major is the key of light; E♭ is the tonality most frequently used in Mozart's Masonic compositions.

On 28 December Wolfgang wrote to tell his father that he had given "without much preparation, three subscription concerts to 120 subscribers, that he composed for this purpose a new piano concerto in E♭, in which (a rather unusual occurrence!) he had to repeat the *Andante*".[6]

This concerto was completed on 16 December. On the previous evening he had played at a concert at the lodge *Crowned Hope*, arranged at the request of two visiting Freemasons from Prague, named David and Springer, virtuosi on the basset horn. Mozart had already played at a benefit concert for these two Brothers, who, according to an invitation issued by the united lodges *The Three Eagles* and *The Palm-tree*, "some time ago came to Vienna with the intention of finding shelter here, but have meanwhile fallen into difficult circumstances". A postscript to the invitation stated that "Brother Mozart will entertain the Brothers with his much-loved extemporisations".[7]

The programme on 15 December included "the Cantata in honour of the very hon. Brother Born with music by the hon. Bro. Mozart sung by the hon. Brother Adamberger, . . a concerto on the piano played by the hon. Brother Mozard, . . . Fantasias by the hon. Brother Mozard".[8]

It is highly probable that the concerto performed on that occasion was the one in E♭ which he had just completed. This concerto contains a number of features associated with Freemasonry; it must therefore be examined in some detail.

The key of E♭ and the use of clarinets instead of oboes are characteristic of Mozart's Masonic works. The opening theme of the first movement is in the "question and answer" form which, though typical of the *galant* style, may also have Masonic implications (see p. 86).

This theme consists of two phrases, the first of which is frequently found in Mozart's music (as in the "Padlock" quintet in *The Magic Flute*), while the responsive phrase is composed of a series of suspensions, denoting the "chains of brotherhood" in Masonic symbolism. Thus the opening theme of the first movement may be considered Masonic.

A second theme, heard a few bars later, resembles a phrase in *Die Maurerfreude*.

This theme is stated first by the flute, and then by the clarinets in thirds; it is then repeated by the bassoons in sixths. In *Die Maurerfreude*, the words which this phrase accompanies refer to the study of Nature as a means of obtaining wisdom (see p. 81). The threefold repetition of this theme in the concerto illustrates the Masonic triad referred to in the cantata: Nature, Wisdom, Virtue.

In the opening aria of *Die Maurerfreude* the orchestral introduction contains *gruppetti*, which in this context signify Masonic joy. The wide leaps on common chords suggest a connection with Nature (see p. 81). In the first movement of K.482, the first solo section contains both *gruppetti* and wide leaps.

In the concluding aria and chorus of the cantata, the words "Let our jubilant singing reach the clouds" are set to a rising scale, illustrating the joyful sounds rising to the skies. In the first movement of the concerto, the second subject, played by the soloist alone, consists of a rising scale, which expresses similar joy.

To Freemasons, the ideas of joy and of freedom were closely linked. *The Marriage of Figaro* is an expression of joy at liberation from feudal tyranny. In December 1785 Mozart was occupied in composing *Figaro*, and it is therefore not surprising to find echoes of the overture to that joyous opera in this concerto.

If the first movement of K.482 expresses joy, the *Andante* is certainly its antithesis. It is in C minor (the key of darkness); the opening theme has been described as "a long lament, irregular and tortuous" . . . like "a blind man groping towards the light".[9] The analogy is justified by a comparison with a theme in the cantata *Davidde penitente* (K.469), set to the words "Among the dark shadows" (see below). Should we not go further, and associate this music with the darkness in which the candidate for initiation is surrounded before admission to the temple? "Leaving the Temple with his eyes blindfolded, the profane man is . . . led to a dark place, the Cabinet of Reflection, where his guide removes the blindfold and leaves him alone for a long time."[10]

Two features of this theme – the descending minor scale and the drop of a seventh – remind us of Pamina's anguish in her G minor aria ("Hours of joy for ever vanished").

The structure of this *Andante* is a combination of variation and rondo form. (A B A C A Coda) In the first episode (bar 64) the woodwind introduce a theme in E♭ major, tender and consoling, as though trying to assuage the anguish. The first three notes of this theme (E♭ D C) are the same as the last three notes of the opening theme. But their character has been transformed. Instead of representing the last

three notes of the scale of C minor they have become the first three
notes of the descending scale of E♭ major. This change is of considerable significance. Girdlestone comments on this movement: "In
spite of its partly episodic structure, the flow of its emotion is unbroken.
It progresses towards increasingly clearer definition. Confused and
uncertain at first, it begins already to know itself in the first variation;
the E♭ episode defines it by its contrary, by showing what it is not. The
second variation with its greater vigour is the result, and a heightened
consciousness of what it is. A further manifestation of its opposite, the
C major episode, is followed by an outburst of wrath; then in the
'tragic' song of the coda, it possesses itself and is fully revealed."[11]

The first episode is in E♭; the second, in C major (bar 124), opens
with a dialogue for flute and bassoon which resembles Tamino's
charming of the wild animals with his magic flute. The contradictory
elements in this movement, as represented by the "dark" C minor
tonality, and the opposing, yet related, Masonic keys of E♭ major and C
major, may be said to represent the struggle between the forces of
darkness and superstition and those of the Enlightenment. The
throbbing semiquavers which open the coda recall the *Masonic Funeral
Music*. Clarinet and bassoon in unison state a theme derived from the
descending minor scale; the solo takes up this theme against a
background of sighs from the strings. Then there is a magical
transformation of the theme from the E♭ episode. For a moment the
music moves into the major, with E natural, but the solo, with its minor
version of the clarinet theme, leaves us in no doubt about the tragic
ending. There is no major chord, as in the *Masonic Funeral Music*, to
bring us hope; the movement ends with a chromatic scale, and three soft
chords of C minor.

The last movement, a *Rondo* in 6–8, is sparkling with gaiety. But still
Mozart's consciousness of the Order is present. The opening theme
contains a *gruppetto*; there is a series of 6–3 chords in the refrain, and
the clarinets in thirds, in the second subject, express unity and harmony.
The second episode is an *Andante cantabile* in A♭, 3–4 time, in which
the clarinets in thirds again suggest unity and harmony. This theme
resembles, not only the canon in the *Finale* of *Così fan tutte*, in which
the lovers pledge their troth, but also, as Massin points out, the Masonic
Adagio for clarinets and basset horns (K.411) (see p. 65). The
solemnity of this episode is enhanced by the use of pizzicato strings,
held woodwind chords and soft, syncopated arpeggios on the piano.
Modulations to minor keys and diminished seventh chords convey an

atmosphere of mystery, reminding us again of the Masonic character of this concerto.

There is a further touch of mystery at the end, when Mozart, combining seriousness with humour, plays one of his practical jokes. The movement seems to be at an end, with conventional tonic and dominant chords, followed by the tonic chord repeated six times in anapaestic rhythm, suggesting the Masonic "three knocks". We then hear three soft chords on the tonic, followed by three chords on the submediant (VI) – a "modal" chord associated with the mysteries – while the solo wistfully echoes the opening theme. It is as though Mozart is reminding us of the solemn side of life. Can it be taken as a reminder to the Brethren, in the midst of their revelry?

Some critics have seen in this concerto a return to the *galant* style, after the turbulence of the D minor concerto. But, though the E♭ concerto may be *galant* in form, Mozart imbued it with profound significance. If this was indeed the concerto which he played to the members of the lodge *Crowned Hope* on 15 December, they must surely have understood its meaning.

NOTES

1 Anderson, p. 891.
2 Massin, pp. 985 ff.
3 Chailley, J., *Sur la signification cachée du quatuor de Mozart K.465 dit "les Dissonances", et du 7e quatuor en fa majeur de Beethoven* (in *Natalicia musicologica Knud Jeppesen*), Copenhagen, 1962, pp. 283–7.
4 Girdlestone, p. 280.
5 Anderson, p. 886.
6 ibid., p. 895.
7 Deutsch, p. 254.
8 ibid., p. 257.
9 Girdlestone, pp. 357 ff.
10 Chailley, *The Magic Flute*, p. 134.
11 Girdlestone, p. 361.

THE MARRIAGE OF FIGARO

On 11 November 1785 Leopold Mozart wrote to his daughter: "At last I have received a letter of twelve lines from your brother, dated November 2nd. He begs to be forgiven, as he is up to his eyes in work at his opera, *The Marriage of Figaro*. . . . I know the piece; it is a very tiresome play and the translation from the French will certainly have to be altered very freely, if it is to be effective as an opera. God grant that the text may be a success. I have no doubt about the music. But there will be a lot of running about and discussions before he gets the libretto so adjusted as to suit his purpose exactly."[1]

The author of the libretto, Lorenzo da Ponte, was an Italian Jew, who had been brought up in a Jesuit convent and trained for the priesthood. After leading a rather disreputable life in Venice, he had finally been expelled from Italy for political reasons. He arrived in Vienna in 1781, not long after Mozart, whom he first met in 1783.

Mozart wrote: "Our poet here is now a certain Abbate da Ponte. He has an enormous amount to do in revising pieces for the theatre, and he has to write *per obbligo* an entirely new libretto for Salieri, which will take him two months. He has promised after that to write a new libretto for me. But who knows whether he will be able to keep his word – or will want to? For, as you are aware, these Italian gentlemen are very civil to your face. Enough, we know them!"[2]

Soon afterwards da Ponte brought Mozart a libretto for an *opera buffa*, *Lo sposo deluso* (K.430), which was never finished. It was not until 1785 that Mozart approached da Ponte with the suggestion that they should turn *The Marriage of Figaro* into an opera.

Beaumarchais's play had been written in 1776, but it was not produced until 1784 owing to difficulties with the censorship. The play aroused controversy all over Europe on account of its bitter social and political satire. His previous play, *The Barber of Sevile*, had caused trouble enough, but compared to *Figaro* that had been a storm in a teacup. As the author himself wrote in his preface to *The Marriage of Figaro*: "In *The Barber of Sevile* I merely cause the authorities to quake a little, but in this new venture, even more infamous and seditious, I overthrew the whole structure of society, from top to bottom. If such a work were permitted, there would be an end to everything sacred."[3]

Da Ponte describes in his *Memoirs* how the opera came to be written. In the course of a conversation about librettos, Mozart asked him if he could easily adapt Beaumarchais's play. "The proposal pleased me very well, and I promised to do as he wished. But there was a great difficulty to be overcome. Only a few days before, the Emperor had forbidden the company at the German theatre to act this same comedy, as it was, he said, too outspoken for a polite audience. How could one now suggest it as an opera?"[4] Da Ponte then explained that he had "left out and shortened whatever might offend the refinement and decorum of an entertainment at which Your Majesty presides . . . 'Very well,' he answered, 'if that is so I'll trust your taste as to the music and your discretion as to the morals.'"[5]

We can imagine some of the difficulties encountered by Mozart and da Ponte when we read Beaumarchais's account of passages in the play to which objections were made. He mentions, for example, the following remark of Figaro's: "Why should they [soldiers] kill and be killed for other people?",[6] and the definition of a courtier in three words as one who knows how to "ask, take and get".[7]

Beaumarchais's attitude to women met with disapproval; Marcellina's attack on the injustice of laws which punished a woman for an offence considered trivial in a man was omitted in all stage performances. The play was criticised on general grounds of immorality. In defending himself, Beaumarchais stated that the true moral of the play was that a nobleman who is vicious enough to wish to prostitute to his caprices everything that comes under his rule, and who attempts to seduce all the young girls in his dominion, must end by becoming the laughing-stock of all his vassals. Further, he pointed out that the numerous intrigues in the play are caused by the struggle between the Count – "young, profligate, flirtatious, a bit of a rake, very like other young noblemen of the day" – who sets aside all moral principles in order to assert his power as supreme master, and Figaro, the servant, who is driven to use all possible ingenuity and skill to frustrate the Count's designs. During the course of the play the Count is continually foiled, and eventually obliged to ask his wife's pardon, for the third time in a single day, in front of all his servants.

Beaumarchais goes on to say that he has depicted the Countess as a model of virtue – generous, forgiving, sensitive. Even her affection for Cherubino is intended to show her noble character, since she struggles to overcome her feelings and all her tricks are designed to win back her husband. As for Cherubino, whom the critics attacked so strongly, Beaumarchais says that we must remember that he is only a child, intended as a foil to the Count, who is made to look ridiculous by his fear of being discovered by Cherubino, like a lion frightened of a mouse.

It is often maintained that although Beaumarchais's play is a social and political satire, Mozart's opera is nothing of the kind. Yet it is remarkable how closely da Ponte and Mozart have followed the play. The plot of the opera is in all essentials the same. And it is in the plot itself that the play is most subversive. Beaumarchais made this clear in describing his characters: "In this work which I am defending I am not attacking states; it is only people with guilty consciences who can find it harmful. . . . I evoke my characters and put them in a certain situation: take care, Figaro, your master will find you out; run away, Cherubino, you are provoking the Count; Ah! Countess, how imprudent, when your husband is so violent. I don't care what they *say*; I am only interested in what they *do*."[8]

The most notable omissions in the opera are as follows:

(1) The scene in which Figaro makes some extremely insolent remarks, such as "If I'm no worse than my reputation, how many *gentlemen* are there who can say the same?"[9]

(2) Marcellina's attack on the injustices of the laws against women.[10]

(3) Figaro's long, satirical speech in Act IV, in which Beaumarchais gives an account of his own life.[11]

(4) The couplets at the end of the play, when Figaro says: "By chance of birth one man is born a king, another a shepherd. Fortune keeps them apart; only skill can change things. Death puts an end to twenty kings, but Voltaire is immortal."[12]

It is obvious that such passages would never have passed the censor. It is also clear that Mozart and da Ponte had read the Preface, since the characterisation in the opera follows Beaumarchais's analysis very closely.

Although the play was not allowed on the stage in Vienna, a German translation was circulating in 1785. Mozart had probably also read the French original, since he occasionally inserts into the score directions which are not in the libretto. We know that Mozart was interested in the literature of the French Revolution. When Vincent and Mary Novello visited his widow in Salzburg in 1829, they asked her which were Mozart's favourite authors. She replied that "one of his favourite authors is at present in her possession, and which she most frequently peruses. It is in nine volumes, but being a forbidden fruit in the Austrian states, she did not name it. I suspect some of the French revolutionary authors."[13]

The difficulties faced by Mozart and da Ponte in obtaining permission to stage *Figaro* were eventually overcome and the first performance was given on 1 May 1786. But there were innumerable intrigues against the opera, as Leopold Mozart had foreseen when he wrote to his daughter: "*Le Nozze di Figaro* is being performed on April 28th for the first time. It will be surprising if it is a success, for I know that very powerful cabals have ranged themselves against your brother."[14]

The *Wiener Zeitung* for 11 July gave an account of the first performance: "The public . . . did not really know on the first day where it stood. It heard many a *bravo* from unbiased connoisseurs, but obstreperous louts in the uppermost storey exerted their hired lungs with all their might to deafen singers and audience alike with their *St!* and *Pst!*; and consequently opinions were divided at the end."[15]

Among those in the audience was a certain Count Zinzendorf, who recorded in his diary: "At seven o'clock to the opera *Le Nozze di Figaro*, the poetry by da Ponte, the music by Mozhardt [*sic*], Louise in our box, the opera bored me . . ."[16] At a later performance, this aristocratic member of the audience made the further comment, "Mozart's music singular, hands without head".[17]

In spite of the cabals against it, the opera was so popular that Joseph issued a special decree forbidding encores for any piece written for more than a single voice.[18] In view of the unusually large proportion of ensembles in *Figaro*, this decree was clearly aimed at that opera.

Only nine performances were given that summer in Vienna, but the opera was received with enormous enthusiasm in Prague in the autumn. Mozart visited the city in December, and wrote to his friend Gottfried von Jacquin: "Here they talk about nothing but 'Figaro'. Nothing is played, sung or whistled but 'Figaro'. No opera is drawing like 'Figaro'. Nothing, nothing but 'Figaro'."[19]

There were several reasons for the popularity of *Figaro* in Prague, one being the high level of culture in that city. There is no doubt that the political satire must have been appreciated there. Bohemia was a centre for anti-feudal ideas. A secret agent, sent to investigate the unrest in that province, some years later, reported that he had found among the Bohemians "a universal hatred of their lords, and a determination to rid themselves of their excessive burdens".[20]

Many of Mozart's friends in Prague were Freemasons, including Count Thun, with whom he stayed, and Count Canal, a distinguished botanist and enthusiastic musician, Grand Master of the lodge *Truth and Harmony*. On several occasions Mozart attended meetings at this lodge, which was the chief centre for the activities of the Illuminati in Prague. But he had his enemies in the city, too. When he returned in 1787 for *Don Giovanni*, he wrote to Jacquin that "a few of the leading ladies here, and in particular one very high and mighty one", found it "very ridiculous, unsuitable, and Heaven knows what that the Princess should be entertained with a performance of *Figaro*". . . . "In short by her persuasive tongue the ringleader brought things to such a pitch that the government forbade the impresario to produce the opera on that night. So she was triumphant! '*Ho vinto*' ['I have conquered'], she called out one evening from her box. No doubt she never suspected that the *ho* might be changed into a *sono* ['I am']. But the following day *Le Noble* appeared, bearing a command from His Majesty to the effect that if the new opera could not be given, 'Figaro' was to be performed! My friend, if only you had seen the handsome, magnificent nose of this lady! Oh, it would have amused you as much as it did me!"[21]

In view of all the evidence, there can be little doubt that Mozart was fully aware of the political implications of Beaumarchais's play, and that he went as far as he dared in bringing out its meaning. All the feelings of hatred, contempt and rebelliousness which he had expressed against the Archbishop are to be found in *Figaro*. But whereas in 1781 his anger was chiefly directed against one man, by 1786 he had a deeper insight into the social conflicts of his time. Figaro's denunciation of the Count is an attack on the whole feudal aristocracy.

In plot, characterisation, and often in dialogue, the opera is close to the play. In some places the music underlines the satire and even brings out the irony. We may take Figaro's first aria as an example.

Figaro has just learned from Susanna that the Count intends to exercise on her his feudal privilege of the "right of the first night" with any bride in his dominions, although he has declared that he will abolish that privilege. The Count is planning to go to London, taking Figaro with him, and accompanied by Susanna. In the recitative preceding the aria, Figaro expresses his anger, ending with the words "No you shan't, no you shan't. Figaro says so." These words are taken from the opening of Figaro's political monologue in Act IV of the play, which Napoleon described as "the revolution in action".

The aria is in the form of a court dance, a minuet, in the old-fashioned Da Capo form (A1 and 2, B, A 1, Coda). Figaro says that he too will play the courtier, outwitting his master in cunning. "You may go dancing, but I'll play the tune on my guitar, my little Mr. Count." Thus a feudal form, the minuet, is used to express anti-feudal feelings. The pizzicato string accompaniment illustrates Figaro's guitar, while the horns hint at the Count's intention of cuckolding Figaro. The sudden interjection of the word "Yes" after the formal cadence is like a rude gesture. (We remember Mozart's own phrase about "pulling a long nose at the Archbishop".) His anger increases; the strings rush upwards, then drop a seventh – an interval associated with fear, as with Leporello in the graveyard scene in *Don Giovanni*, or anxiety, like that of Belmonte in the duet in *Die Entführung*. In *Figaro* the fear and anxiety are to be experienced by the Count at the hands of his servant.

The second section of the aria is in the rhythm of a fashionable English dance-tune of the day, a *Presto* in 2–4. Figaro makes the Count dance faster, to a tune of a different character. When the courtly dance is repeated, the implied irony is enhanced by the contrast. The Coda echoes the first eight bars of the *Presto*, played as Figaro goes out. He intends to have the last word; his wit and native cunning will prove him superior to the nobleman.

This aria may be taken as Figaro's signature-tune. When he comes to tell the Countess of his plan to foil the Count, in Act II, he enters singing the Coda to "La"; he leaves singing the words "You may go dancing, but I'll play the tune."

The central theme of the opera, as of the play, is that of equality. Mozart held strong views on this subject, as we know from his letters. On Sunday, 19 February 1786, he went to a masked ball, disguised as an Indian philosopher, and distributed printed sheets with eight riddles and fourteen "Selections from Zoroaster's Fragments", invented by himself. Many of these "Fragments" display an irony and barbed satire which remind us of *Figaro*. "If you are a poor dunce, become a K——r [?Kleriker . . . cleric]. If you are a rich dunce, become a tenant. If you are a noble, but poor dunce, become what you like, only – pray – not a man of sense." "If you are poor, but clever, arm yourself with patience and work. If you do not grow rich, you will at least remain a clever man. . . . If you are an ass, but wealthy, take advantage of your good fortune and be lazy. If you do not become poor, you will at least remain an ass."[22] (We are reminded of Basilio's aria about the asses' skin.)*

* The broadsheet was published in the Salzburg journal *Oberdeutscher Staatszeitung* on 23 March 1786. It was sent to the editor, Lorenz Hübner, by Leopold Mozart.

The connection between Zoroaster and Sarastro need hardly be pointed out. The philosophy of Zoroaster was connected with an allegory used by the Illuminati in the higher grades of their ritual. Further, the egalitarianism underlying the sentiments expressed in the "Fragments of Zoroaster" is similar to that expressed in some of the writings of the Illuminati. We may quote first part of the Speech to the Illuminati Dirigentes (see p. 81): "Fortune's favourites, kings and princes, are supposed to possess by right of birth qualities which they do not have to prove, and they retain a power which neither virtue nor intelligence can make up for among those condemned to slavery."[23]

Secondly, we may quote the vow made by the Illuminatus Minor: "I, A . . . B . . . , acknowledge my natural weakness and inability, and that I, with all my possessions, rank, honours and titles which I hold in society, am only a man; I can enjoy these things only through my fellow-men, and through them I may also lose them."[24] Thirdly, the vow made in the initiation ceremony for the degree of Scottish Knight was as follows: "To be a fighter for wisdom and virtue, the equal of kings by thy cleverness, and a friend of beggars and princes equally, if they are virtuous."[25]

The Illuminati stated as one of their principles: "The Order is one great Society in which consideration given to wealth and rank in the old world would only be given to worth and talent." Enemies of the Order accused them of aiming "at checking the tyranny of princes, nobles and priests and establishing universal equality of condition and religion".[26]

Since Mozart was a member of a Viennese lodge which was under the influence of the Illuminati, and since some of his closest friends were leading members of that Order, it is clear that he must have been familiar with their ideas on equality, which are similar to the basic theme of *The Marriage of Figaro*.

There is another aspect of Freemasonry which is expressed in the opera – the idea of reconciliation. The concept of forgiveness is, of course, typically Christian, but its Masonic form – the idea that man is reconciled to man on a basis of equality – is Protestant rather than Catholic. Sarastro's aria in *The Magic Flute*, "Within this sacred dwelling", is a typical example of Masonic thought on forgiveness. Mozart himself expressed similar ideas in a letter to his wife, written a few months before his death. "For I maintain that kindness cures everything, that magnanimous and forbearing conduct has often reconciled the bitterest enemies."[27]

Reconciliation is one of the main themes of several of Mozart's operas: *Zaide*, *Die Entführung*, and *La Clemenza di Tito*, for example. In *Figaro*, resolution of the various conflicts is attained in the final scene, when the Count kneels to beg his wife's pardon, and is forgiven.

Let us examine this scene in detail. The Count has discovered Figaro making love to a woman whom he supposes, by her dress, to be the Countess, although it is really Susanna disguised as her mistress. The Count, in a fury, summons all his household: "Ho! my servants! To arms! To arms!" (His exaggerated language is illustrated musically in typical *opera buffa* style, with repeated tonic and dominant chords in G major, 4–4 time.) He goes to the left-hand arbour, where he supposes his wife to be hidden, and drags out in turn Cherubino, Barbarina and Marcellina, who have all been hiding there. Finally he pulls out Susanna, in the Countess's clothes, and denounces her. All the other characters, even the cynical Basilio, beg him to pardon her, but the Count refuses, with angrily-repeated "No's". Then the real Countess emerges from the right-hand arbour, and asks for forgiveness, in a phrase which echoes the Count's angry refusal, but which has been transformed into one of dignity and tenderness. The last cadence ends unexpectedly in G minor, and there follow nineteen bars whose effect is truly magical, expressing the utter astonishment of the men whom the Count has called to witness his wife's humiliation.

> "O Heavens! what do I see? Am I deluded?
> Can I believe my eyes?"

The five men (all the male characters except Figaro, who, of course, is in the plot) sing in three-part harmony, with the Count singing the middle part alone. The violins rush up and down in staccato quavers; the music modulates through D minor, E♭, C minor and back to G minor, with suspensions in the vocal parts. At last the Count realises that he has been exposed and humiliated; he kneels at his wife's feet. "My lady, forgive me." We are back in G major now; a calm *Andante* follows the *Allegro assai*. The Count's voice rises a major sixth – an interval which has been defined by Deryck Cooke as producing "a pleasurable longing, or longing for pleasure"[28] – then a seventh; he repeats "forgive me" twice more. The third time he leans heavily on a discordant A♯ (see p. 167), then there is a long pause. (One may ask whether the chromaticism and discordant harmony indicate remorse or hypocrisy.) After a crotchet's rest and another pause, the Countess replies: "I am kinder than you, and I say 'Yes'." She sings these words to a phrase which begins with a rising fifth, with simple, diatonic harmonies and an interrupted cadence. There can be no question about *her* sincerity. All the characters then join in singing "We shall all be happy now ("*Ah! tutti contenti saremo così*") expressing unity of thought and purpose in perfect harmony of voices and instruments. But one may wonder whether the Count can really be happy with a solution of the conflict achieved at his expense. Will he accept that "things will be *thus*"?

Throughout the opera, as in the play, the action revolves around the struggle between two opposing classes, the privileged and the under-privileged, as represented by the Count and Figaro respectively. (In this conflict the Countess, though aristocratic, is on the side of the under-privileged on account of her sex.) In the *Finale* of Act II, Marcellina, Bartolo and Basilio are all on the side of the Count, against Figaro, Susanna and the Countess. In that ensemble the Count's group express their joy at the apparent defeat of Figaro, singing in harmony, while the other three show their agitation and distress in breathless and syncopated phrases. In the sextet in Act III (which is said to have been Mozart's own favourite number in the opera) the boot is on the other foot. Marcellina and Bartolo have joined Figaro's camp; they sing of their "*dolce contento*" ("sweet happiness") in melodious phrases, while the Count and Don Curzio mutter furious threats of revenge. The Count's fury at being thwarted by his servant – a "vile thing ("*vile oggetto*"), as he calls Figaro – is magnificently expressed in his aria in Act III.

> "Must he, my servant, laugh at me,
> While I am mortified?"

But in the end this proud autocrat becomes, in Beaumarchais's words, "the laughing-stock of all his vassals". Three times, during the course of that "folle journée" (crazy day), he has been humiliated; finally he has been forced to kneel at his wife's feet, begging her to forgive him, in front of all his servants. Thus in *Figaro* the reconciliation represents a victory over the autocrat.

We may recall Mozart's own words, quoted earlier (p. 22). "It is the heart that ennobles the man, and, though I am no count, I probably have more honour in me than many a count."

The themes of three of Mozart's greatest operas have been aptly compared to the slogans of the French Revolution.[29] The subject of *Die Entführung* is Liberty, while that of *Figaro* is Equality. In his last opera, *The Magic Flute*, Mozart was to complete the triad with a message of Fraternity.

NOTES

1 Anderson, p. 893.
2 ibid., p. 848.
3 Beaumarchais, P. A. de, *Le Mariage de Figaro* (ed. Arnould), Oxford, 1952, p. 6.
4 da Ponte, L., *Memoirs* (tr. L. A. Sheppard), London, 1920, p. 129.
5 ibid., p. 129.
6 Beaumarchais, p. 16.
7 ibid., p. 18.
8 ibid., p. 9.
9 ibid., p. 161.
10 ibid., p. 126.
11 ibid., p. 128.
12 ibid., p. 151.
13 Novello, V. and M., *A Mozart Pilgrimage* (ed. Medici and Hughes), London, 1955, p. 95.
14 Anderson, p. 897.
15 Deutsch, p. 278.
16 ibid., p. 274.
17 ibid., p. 278.
18 ibid., p. 275.
19 Anderson, p. 903.
20 Wangermann, *From Joseph II to the Jacobin Trials*, p. 118.
21 Anderson, p. 911.
22 Deutsch, p. 268.
23 Le Forestier, pp. 322 f.
24 Frost, p. 34.
25 Engel, p. 365.
26 Robison, p. 131.
27 Anderson, p. 964.
28 Cooke, D., *The Language of Music*, London, 1959, p. 69.
29 Massin, p. 520.

12

MUSIC IN THE YEAR OF FIGARO

At the beginning of 1786 Mozart's prospects seemed good, although he was more popular in Vienna as a virtuoso than as a composer. A Salzburg journal gave the following account of him: "He is uncommonly liked, and his expression has to be marvelled at. He is also so agreeable as to give frequent public performances. His harvest is not confined to Lent, for he also appears during Advent, or, if the public so desires, in the summer. His opera, too much filled up with accompaniments . . . did not receive the approbation that is usually vouchsafed to his art when he is heard on the fortepiano."[1]

The opera referred to was the one-act German *Singspiel, Der Schauspieldirektor (The Impresario)*, commissioned for an elaborate entertainment in the Orangerie at Schönbrunn in February 1786. The occasion was described in contemporary records:

"At the end of the banquet, and during the time that His Majesty with all his guests repaired to one of the theatres set up at the end of the Orangerie, the entire table was removed from the building; and at once the whole length of the Parterre was brilliantly illuminated. Whereupon His Majesty with his guests repaired to the theatre erected at the other end of the Orangerie, where a German play with arias intermingled was performed.

"When this was finished the entire company repaired to the theatre at the other end, where an Italian *Singspiel* was at once performed.

"After which, at about 9 o'clock, the company rode back to the city in the order in which they came, in barouches and carriages, each preceded by two outriders with lanterns."[2]

Mozart received fifty ducats for his music to the "German play", while Salieri was paid a hundred ducats for his "Italian *Singspiel*". Singers and actors were given the same fee as Mozart. We do not know how much money was spent on the banquet, coaches or illuminations. Count Zinzendorf commented in his diary: "The whole was very mediocre."[3]

No doubt Mozart welcomed the opportunity to compose music for a play in German, especially since the words were by his old friend Stephanie, author of *Die Entführung*. But *Der Schauspieldirektor* did not lead to any further commissions for German opera, and Mozart wrote no more operas in the vernacular until *The Magic Flute*, in 1791.

Meanwhile he was hard at work on *The Marriage of Figaro*, with high hopes of establishing himself as a composer of Italian opera. But although *Figaro* was a popular success, his enemies at court ensured that the opera was not retained long in the repertoire. Mozart was bitterly disappointed. In the summer he began to make plans for a visit to England, encouraged by his friends Stephen and Nancy Storace and Michael Kelly, who had taken part in the performances of *Figaro*. Leopold wrote to tell his daughter that Wolfgang had asked him to look after his two children "because he was proposing to undertake a journey through Germany to England in the middle of the next carnival". Leopold rejected the proposal indignantly. "Not at all a bad arrangement! They could go off and travel – they might even die – or remain in England – and I should have to run after them with the children."[4]

Relations between father and son had been strained ever since Wolfgang's marriage; moreover the aging Leopold was looking after Nannerl's son at the time, and no doubt he would have found three grandchildren too much for him.

The visit to England never materialised; but meanwhile Mozart was trying to find a market for his works outside Vienna. He wrote to his childhood friend Sebastian Winter, formerly the family valet and friseur, who was in service at the court of Donaueschingen, asking him to try to obtain a commission from the Prince to compose "every year a certain number of symphonies, quartets, concertos for different instruments, or any other compositions which he fancies".[5] The Prince ordered some symphonies and concertos, but Mozart did not obtain a regular commission, which might have provided him with a small but steady income.

The financial difficulties which overwhelmed him during his last years were not yet acute, but he had already been obliged to borrow from friends, such as the publisher Hoffmeister, to whom he had written in November 1785; "Dearest Hoffmeister! I turn to you in my distress and beg you to help me out with some money, which I need very badly at the moment. . . . Forgive me for constantly worrying you, but as you know me and are aware how anxious I am that your business should succeed, I am convinced that you will not misconstrue my importunity. . . ."[6]

In July 1785 Mozart had composed a piano quartet in G minor

(K.478), which was intended to be the first of a series. In June 1786 he composed a second, in E♭ (K.493). But Hoffmeister thought both works too difficult. "Write more popularly", he is reported to have said, "or else I can neither print nor pay for anything more of yours!" To which Mozart is said to have replied: "Then I will write nothing more, and go hungry, or may the devil take me!"[7]

It was perhaps as a means of repaying his debts to Hoffmeister that Mozart composed the quartet in D major (K.499), often called the "Hoffmeister" quartet, because it is believed that it was written for the publisher. In an illuminating article on this quartet, Georg Knepler has revealed close thematic connections between the first movement and certain passages in *Figaro*. He draws attention to the relationship between the closing cadence of the opening theme and the two-bar recitative after the sextet in Act III, in which Figaro, Susanna, Bartolo and Marcellina express their delight at having foiled the Count.

> "And if my Lord is furious,
> So much the better!"

Knepler compares these two bars to a short, satirical march of triumph, which expresses both the dramatic situation of the four characters and the historical situation in the epoch of revolution. He shows convincingly that in this piece of instrumental music Mozart was expressing some of the fundamental beliefs of the Enlightenment.[8]

The music composed in 1786 includes a good deal of chamber music, probably intended for the many amateur groups in Vienna. The Trio in E♭ (K.498) for piano, clarinet and viola, was written for the sister of Mozart's friend Gottfried von Jacquin. Massin has suggested that this work has Masonic significance, as shown by the key of E♭, the use of the clarinet, and the *gruppetto* in the opening theme of the first movement. (We may note also the pairs of slurred notes, suspensions and descending parallel thirds and sixths in the last movement.)

By the autumn of 1786 Mozart's popularity as a virtuoso had begun to decline. The concert at the Burg Theater on 7 April, at which he played the C minor concerto (K.491), was the last which he gave there; he played only one more concerto that autumn, and after that wrote only two more piano concertos.

The three piano concertos of 1786 represent the summit of his achievement in that genre. The concertos in A major (K.488) and C minor (K.491) were composed on 2 and 24 March respectively. The contrast between the two works is striking.

The A major, like several other works in that key, is tender, lyrical and warm, with a poignant *Andante* and a sparkling *Finale*. The first movement of the C minor is full of harsh discords and chromaticism; its second movement is serene and solemn, but not tragic. The *Finale*, a march with eight variations, is grim and tense, ending on a note of despair, in spite of some calmer episodes. In the A major concerto clarinets take the place of oboes, imparting a warm tone; the C minor has both oboes and clarinets, as well as drums and trumpets. (This concerto has the largest orchestra in the whole series.) In structure, too, these two concertos are different. The A major belongs to what has been designated as the "melodic" concertos: these are full of lovely melodies, and depend for their unity on a melodic thread which runs right through them. This thread was called "il filo" (the thread) by Mozart and his father.[9]

The C minor concerto, on the other hand, is symphonic in structure. In the first movement, the whole development depends on the interplay and clash of various elements in the opening theme, which is remarkable for its strong, terse rhythms and wide, awkward intervals. Both the theme and the working-out remind us of Beethoven, who in fact greatly admired this concerto.

The A major concerto has some affinity with two later works for clarinet, also in A major: the quintet (K.581) and the concerto (K.622). There is also some kinship between this concerto and *Figaro*. Girdlestone has described the *Finale* as typically *opera buffa* in style, with its "cascade of tunes". He compares the first and second couplets to a point in the *Finale* of Act II of *Figaro*, when, after one of the most serious and poetic moments in the score, Antonio, the drunken gardener, rushes in to complain about his broken flower-pots, and the music jumps into F major and becomes as frivolous and clownish in its bustle as it was meditative and grave a moment earlier. Such changes, Girdlestone points out, would be readily acceptable to an audience accustomed to *opera buffa*, although a modern audience no longer responds "to the allusions to dramatic music that we hear in the instrumental works of the eighteenth century".[10]

This comment, like Knepler's analysis of the D major quartet (see p. 108) gives an important clue to the understanding of Mozart's instrumental music. We may remember that Beethoven, when asked why, since he had given words to the *Finale* of his Ninth Symphony, he had not explained the "poetic ideas" of his earlier works, replied that the earlier age was "more poetic", and that in the former period words would have been "superfluous".[11]

Nothing could be further from *opera buffa* style than the last movement of the C minor concerto, which Einstein described as "an uncanny, revolutionary quick-march".[12] The fourth variation brings some relief from the tension, with clarinets in thirds and pairs of slurred notes suggesting unity and brotherhood. The sixth variation, in C major, contains a beautiful dialogue for woodwind, in which the flute plays an important part, reminding us of Tamino taming the wild beasts. The "heavenly peace" of this variation is succeeded by a desperate struggle between solo and tutti, in which the former becomes increasingly agitated, while the orchestra remains inexorable. The last variation, in 6–8, suggests a dance of death, with its creeping chromatic harmonies. A series of 6–3 chords, rising chromatically, seems like a mockery of the Masonic progression, as though the harmonies intended to promote unity and peace had been turned into their opposite. In this concerto there is no happy solution to the conflict – no major ending, as in the D minor concerto.

It has been suggested that the concertos in E♭ (K.482), A major (K.488) and C minor (K.491) form a trilogy, since they were all composed for the Lent season of 1786. The tonality of all three works is associated with Freemasonry; Massin sees in them a portrayal of the three stages of initiation. But the C major concerto (K.503), though composed after an interval of nine months, must also be considered in relation to its predecessors, and indeed to the whole series composed in Vienna, since it was the last until 1788. The C minor concerto was full of unresolved conflicts, but the C major expresses triumph almost as confidently as the "Jupiter" Symphony, which it resembles in several ways besides its tonality.

This concerto was completed on 4 December, two days before the "Prague" Symphony (K.504). Both works received their first performance in Prague in January 1787. Many years later an elderly viola-player in Vienna recalled that he had played in a performance of the concerto in Prague, when Mozart himself had played the solo part. Recollecting that occasion, the old man was moved to tears, saying that no one had played like Mozart.[13]

It is not certain whether this concerto was composed specifically for this visit to Prague. But its triumphant optimism is certainly in tune with his mood in that city. After the indifference with which his latest works had been received in Vienna, the enthusiastic welcome of the people of Prague cheered him greatly, "As the Bohemians understand me so well, I must write an opera on purpose for them", he is reported to have said.[14] (Later that year he composed *Don Giovanni* for Prague.)

A member of the lodge *Truth and Harmony*, Gottlieb Meissner, reported that on one occasion when Mozart visited the lodge, the Brethren welcomed him by forming a guard of honour and singing *Die Maurerfreude*. In thanking them, Mozart said that he hoped soon to pay tribute to Freemasonry in a better way, thus indicating that he already had it in mind to compose a Masonic opera.[15] It is not surprising, therefore, to find that both the "Prague" Symphony and the concerto in C major contain features which we can recognise as Masonic. The theme of the *Allegro* in the first movement of the symphony closely resembles the *fugato* theme in the overture to *The Magic Flute*, which is said to represent Masons "working on the rough stone".[16] (The fact that the theme was borrowed from a sonata by Clementi is irrelevant.) The *Andante*, in Massin's words, expresses "universal harmony and fraternity",[17] while in the *Presto* suspensions and parallel thirds and sixths play a prominent part. The absence of a Minuet in this symphony has been attributed by some critics to the aristocratic associations of this dance-form, which would be less likely to find favour with an audience in Prague than in Vienna.

The C major concerto (K.503) is marked by a number of Masonic characteristics. In the first movement the conflict between C major and C minor, which may symbolise the struggle between forces of light and darkness, is of supreme importance. The opening fanfare consists of a C major triad, in dotted-quaver rhythm, closely resembling the opening of a Masonic cantata composed in 1791 (K.619) (see p. 149).

A few bars later (bar 15) a figure heard first in C major, then in C minor, is played by the oboes in thirds. At bar 49 the rhythm

is proclaimed in unison, on the dominant (G). This leads to a march-like tune (described by Girdlestone as a "mock second subject") played first in C minor, then C major. In its major form, this theme has been compared to Papageno's second aria in *The Magic Flute*, and also to the *Marseillaise*. (Since the latter was not composed until 1792, the resemblance is, of course, fortuitous.)

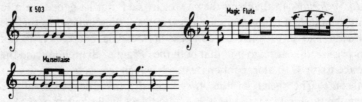

The recurrent rhythmic figure

assumes great importance in the development section. It resembles the rhythm of a phrase in the Trio between Pamina, Tamino, and Sarastro in *The Magic Flute* (No. 19). Tamino is about to undergo his final ordeals; he is bidding farewell to Pamina. Sarastro sings the words: "The hour is come." (The theme in the concerto has been called the "Fate" motif, because of its resemblance to the opening of Beethoven's Fifth Symphony.)

We may note also the ascending tonic triad in dotted rhythm played by the horns in the opening *ritornello* (bar 74), which may be compared with the setting of the words sung by the Three Boys in the *Finale* of Act I of *The Magic Flute* (No. 8) ("Go, be a man, and thou shalt conquer"). Other significant features are the three chords, repeated three times by the strings, before the entry of the soloist, and the descending 6–3 chords, with suspensions, in the eighth bar of the solo part.

The second movement is an *Andante* in F major, in triple time. In key, tempo and general character it resembles the *Andante* of the C major quartet (K.465), and that of the "Jupiter" Symphony, and also the *Andante* section of the Masonic cantata, K.619 (see p. 149). All these works are examples of Mozart's humanist style, foreshadowing the music of Sarastro.

The *Andante* of K.503 contains a passage of haunting beauty, which suggests the mysteries of initiation (bars 47 ff.). Four chromatic chords on the woodwind, causing us to lose all sense of tonality, seem to indicate the darkness with which the candidate is surrounded. They are followed by a simple harmonic progression, including a "modal" chord (Supertonic, II). Thus a religious atmosphere is evoked, reminding us of Sarastro's aria with chorus of priests (*The Magic Flute*, No. 10).

The *Finale* is in sonata rondo form, with a refrain based on a gavotte in *Idomeneo*. It contains what is perhaps the most significant passage in the whole concerto. After the second *Tutti* there is a short solo section in A minor. Then the orchestra modulates to F major, in three chords. The soloist then introduces a new melody, of great simplicity and tenderness, which is taken up by the oboe and flute, and developed in eight-part counterpoint. Girdlestone describes this passage as revealing the perfect union in Mozart between form and thought.[18] It may help us to understand the meaning of this section if we refer once again to *The Magic Flute*.

When Tamino and Pamina meet for the first time face to face (*Finale* of Act I) they greet each other ecstatically, in a phrase echoed later in their Trio with Sarastro (No. 19). Is there not a certain kinship between this phrase and the theme of this section of the *Finale* of K.503?

The development of this theme takes us through various keys, including the "dark" minor keys. The theme undergoes chromatic transformation, while the triplet arpeggios in the solo part enhance the sense of struggle. Eventually a long dominant pedal leads us back to C major (the key of light), with a joyous cascade of descending sixths, in triplets, on the piano. This passage may perhaps be associated with the trials of Tamino and Pamina, and their ultimate victory over the forces of darkness, through the power of love, aided by music. At the end of the movement an echo of the same theme is heard again on the piano; this time it resembles the outburst of joy at the end of the Masonic cantata, K.619, where it depicts man's joy at the thought of his eventual triumph over evil and suffering (see p. 151).

Mozart's Masonic beliefs found their fullest expression in the works of his last year – the Masonic cantatas K.619 and 623, and in *The Magic Flute*. But in 1786 the ideas were already present in his mind, and it is therefore relevant to link this concerto with the optimistic beliefs of the Illuminati.

The three great concertos of 1786 may perhaps be taken as a trilogy expressing different aspects of human life. The A major depicts warm, human feelings of tenderness and love, together with deep sympathy for human suffering. The C minor is full of struggle, and almost prophetic of the Revolution of 1789. The C major is a triumphant assertion that right and justice will conquer in the end.

NOTES

1 Deutsch, p. 270.
2 ibid., p. 261.
3 ibid., p. 262.
4 Anderson, pp. 901 f.
5 ibid., p. 898.
6 ibid., p. 894.
7 Jahn, II, pp. 295 f.
8 Knepler, G., *Geschichte als Weg zum Musikverständnis*, Leipzig, 1977.
9 Forman, D., *Mozart's Concerto Form*, Borough Green, 1971, pp. 70 ff.
10 Girdlestone, p. 386.
11 Finkelstein, S., *Composer and Nation*, London, 1960, pp. 83 f.
12 Einstein, p. 325.
13 Köchel, L. von, *Chronologisch-thematisches Verzeichnis sämtlicher Tonwerke Wolfgang Amadeus Mozarts* (2nd ed.), Leipzig, 1905, p. 476.
14 Holmes, p. 226.
15 Nettl, pp. 20 f.
16 ibid., p. 91.
17 Massin, p. 135.
18 Girdlestone, p. 440.

13

FRIENDSHIP, LOVE AND DEATH

When Mozart returned from Prague in the middle of February 1787, he brought with him, besides happy memories of his enthusiastic reception in that city, a commission for a new opera, which was to be *Don Giovanni*. But his fortunes in Vienna were at a low ebb. During the Lent season he gave no concerts, and composed no concertos or symphonies, turning instead to chamber music. The two string quintets in C major and G minor (K.515 and 516) were completed in April and May; apart from these and *Don Giovanni*, which was finished in October, the compositions of 1787 consist of less important works, such as songs, sonatas for piano duet, and a quantity of dance-music, composed to earn money to pay some of his debts. It seems as though the Viennese public had no use for Mozart as a serious composer at that time. What, one may ask, had become of the support which he had previously had from Masonic circles?

In order to answer this question, it is necessary to give some account of political developments relating to Freemasonry in the mid-1780s. By 1786 the strength and influence of the movement had declined considerably. Joseph's decree of December 1785 had struck the first blow at the Brotherhood by imposing official control of Masonic activities. The amalgamation of the lodges had caused internal schisms, and led to resignations, including that of Born. In 1787 a publication inspired by the enemies of the Illuminati in Bavaria, appeared under the title *Original Documents of the Illuminati*. This work was supposedly based on papers seized from the house of Zwack and other leaders of the Illuminati. One of the members of the lodge *True Harmony*, the poet Leon, described the impact of this book in Vienna. "Have you seen the 'Original Documents' – a fairly large book which has just been published by the Elector of Bavaria? It has made a great sensation here. From its contents I cannot imagine that the transactions of this society in Bavaria can have been honourable – unless (as may well be the case) material has been intentionally introduced into Zwack's papers which will present to the world the most odious and horrible aspect."[1]

Persecution of the Illuminati was intensified in Bavaria during the next few years. In August 1787 all lodges were closed, and any gathering behind closed doors "or in suspicious circumstances" was treated as subversive. The death penalty was imposed on anyone found trying to make recruits to the Order. There were repercussions from these events in Vienna, too. In 1786 an anonymous brochure appeared, attacking the Viennese lodges in general, and Born's lodge (*True Harmony*) in particular. The author of this pamphlet was Leopold Aloys Hoffman, the renegade Freemason who had resigned from the secretaryship of the lodge *Beneficence* shortly before Mozart's initiation there. A flood of pamphlets, mostly hostile to the Freemasons, appeared during the next few years. Informers and *agents provocateurs* were rife, and in such circumstances it was natural that Freemasons were wary of publicising their activities.

We have comparatively few records of events in Masonic circles after 1787. In that year the poet Leon declared: "There has been no question of the Illuminati here for a long time. The Order has simply ceased to exist – it only lasted for a year and a few months."[2]

One may wonder whether the Illuminati had in fact gone underground: the bans imposed later on "reading-societies, coffee-clubs and the like" might lead one to such a conclusion. But it is certain that their ideas, which had been widespread in the Viennese lodges, survived. A book published in 1786, intended to expose the dangerous doctrines of the Illuminati, stated that their aims were "to emancipate all of mankind from religious and political slavery".[3] On the eve of the French Revolution, many citizens of Vienna must have sympathised with these aims, even though they were too frightened to express their support openly.

The attacks on the Illuminati reached a climax in 1789, and will be discussed in a later chapter. Meanwhile, since the Masonic documents give little information after 1786, and since we know that Constanze Mozart destroyed letters containing references to Freemasonry after her husband's death, we must turn to other sources for evidence of what Mozart and the members of his circle were thinking at this time.

The fashion of keeping an album in which one's friends inscribed their thoughts was current in the latter part of the eighteenth century. Mozart kept such an album in 1787, and he also contributed to the albums of his friends, many of whom were Freemasons. Some of the entries in Mozart's book pay tribute to his musical talents; others refer to the close ties of friendship.

Among the contributions was one by Ignaz von Born, in Latin, dated

27 April 1787: "O gentle Apollo! who gavest thine arts and thy gifts to our Mozart, so that at his request the string yields whatever sounds his hand and mind desire; be they shrill, solemn, fast, slow, tuneful, plaintive, great or small, sounding together without offence; decree that the number of his happy days may accord with the agreeable music of his lyre and that such may be the harmony of his fate."[4]

This inscription is interesting, since it shows that Born's friendship with Mozart continued after he had left the Order; moreover it throws light on Masonic attitudes to music, which is presented as the art of reconciling opposites by means of harmony.

Mozart clearly attached great importance to friendship: this may have been one reason for his adherence to the Brotherhood. He wrote in the album of Gottfried von Jacquin the following words in English (which he was studying at the time for a projected visit to England): "Don't never [sic] forget your true and faithfull friend, Wolfgang Amadé Mozart."[5] Jacquin's inscription in Mozart's album was as follows: "True genius without heart is a thing of naught – for not great understanding alone, not imagination alone, nor both together, make genius – Love! Love! Love! that is the soul of genius. – Your friend Emilian Gottfried Edler von Jacquin. Vienna, 11 April 1787."[6]

For another friend and fellow-Mason, a teacher named Kronauer, Mozart wrote – again in English: "Patience and tranquillity of mind contribute more to cure our distempers, as the whole art of medecine. Vienna, March 30 1787. Your true, sincere friend and Brother, Wolfgang Amadé Mozart, member of the very hon. Lodge of the *New-crowned Hope* in the Orient of Vienna."[7]

Mozart was certainly in need of tranquillity at the time when he wrote these words. Thoughts of death were in the forefront of his mind, for he had just lost a dear friend, Count von Hatzfeld. On 4 April he wrote to his father, who had been seriously ill, expressing his ideas on the subject of death. This is one of the few surviving letters which allude to Masonry.

"As death, when we come to consider it closely, is the true goal of our existence, I have formed during the last few years such close relations with this best and truest friend of mankind, that his image is not only no longer terrifying to me, but is indeed very soothing and consoling! And I thank my God for graciously granting me the opportunity (you know what I mean) of learning that death is the *key* which unlocks the door to our true happiness. I never lie down at night without reflecting that – young as I am – I may not live to see another day. Yet no one of all

my acquaintances could say that in company I am morose or dis-
gruntled. . . . I expressed my views to you on this point, in connexion
with the sad death of my dearest and most beloved friend, the Count
von Hatzfeld. He was just thirty-one – my own age. I do not feel sorry
for him, but I pity most sincerely both myself and all who knew him as
well as I did. I hope and trust that while I am writing this, you are feeling
better. But if, contrary to all expectation, you are not recovering, I
implore you by . . .* not to hide it from me, but to tell me the whole truth
or get someone to write it to me, so that as quickly as is humanly
possible I may come to your arms. I entreat you by all that is sacred – to
both of us."[8]

Leopold did not recover; on 29 May Wolfgang wrote to Jacquin: "I
inform you that on returning home today I received the sad news of my
most beloved father's death. You can imagine the state I am in."[9]

Later that year he was to lose another friend, Sigmund Barisani, the
doctor who had twice treated him during severe illnesses, and with
whom, according to report, he had attended meetings of the Illuminati
at Aigen in Salzburg days (p. 17). Barisani had inscribed verses in
Mozart's album, which concluded as follows:

> Do not forget thy friend, whose happiness
> And pride it is to know he served thee twice
> To save thee for the world's delight. This boast
> Is yet surpassed by joy and pride to know
> Thou art his friend, as he is ever thine.
> > > Thy friend Sigmund Barisani.[10]

Underneath this inscription Mozart wrote: "Today, 3 Sept of this same
year, I was so unfortunate as quite unexpectedly to lose by death this
noble man, dearest, best of friends and preserver of my life. – He is at
rest! – but I, we, all that knew him well – we shall *never* be at rest again –
until we have the felicity of seeing him again – in a better world – and
nevermore to part. – Mozart."[11]

To Catholics, thoughts of death brought fear of hell and retribution.
Freemasons, on the other hand, taught men to overcome their fear by
accepting death as something inevitable, to be faced with courage and
calmness. Both attitudes are reflected in Mozart's music. The idea of
hell and punishment is expressed in the *Dies Irae* of the *Requiem* and in
Don Giovanni. Belmonte and Constanze, Ilia and Idamante, Tamino
and Pamina, all face death courageously, strengthened by human love.

* Omission marks as in original.

In that same summer of 1787 Mozart composed the beautiful song "Abendempfindung" ("Evening thoughts"), which reflects the Masonic view of death, combining calm acceptance of its inevitability with grief at parting from a friend or loved one. The poem (once attributed to J. H. Campe) is by J. F. Schink, a Freemason; it was published later in a Masonic song-book with the title "Abendempfindung an Laura"; Mozart extended the scope of the poem by omitting the dedication and by substituting the words "O friends" for "Beloved one". The general mood of the song is one of serenity, but sadness is reflected in the sudden changes to the minor, and the tranquil flow of quavers is broken at the words "Then, O friends, will I appear to you "by the introduction of the rhythm

The Rondo in A minor (K.511) for piano, is an isolated work (composed after a gap of three months), which seems to reflect Mozart's mood of sadness, caused by the death of his friend Count Hatzfeld and by his father's illness. It is full of chromaticism, discords and unusual modulations.

Although it would, of course, be wrong to suggest that Mozart's works in general can be related to particular events in his life, the G minor quintet (K.516), completed ten days before his father's death, in May 1787, must surely be seen as an expression of his thoughts on human suffering and death. Georg Knepler, in a masterly analysis of the work, describes it as an expression of the conquest of sorrow and suffering.

The first movement is full of fear and longing for consolation; the slow movement "opens with a five-part instrumental song, like a solemn, festive gathering, recalling Mozart's Masonic compositions. But in the third bar the first violin detaches itself from this choral theme, and announces a sobbing motif, which plays an important part in the other movements too. This detachment of the first violin has a significant meaning: the sorrow of the individual breaks through the group; the individual sufferer can find no comfort in the society of men. Thus this movement is an expression of a surrender to sorrow, loneliness and tears."[12]

There is a similarity between the central section of this movement and the scene in *The Magic Flute* (*Finale* of Act II) when Pamina tries to commit suicide. Knepler has also noted a resemblance between the slow introduction to the last movement of the quintet and part of the same

Finale in *The Magic Flute*, when Tamino and Pamina show their determination to face their trials. Thus this introduction may be seen as an attempt to overcome sorrow, and to see the terrible experiences of the first three movements in a new light.

The introduction leads into a *rondo* in G major, 6–8 time. This *rondo* has sometimes been described as trivial and unworthy of the rest of the quintet. But in choosing such a theme for his refrain – a folk-like waltz, which in key, tempo and mood resembles the music of Papageno – Mozart was demonstrating his close ties with ordinary people. His melodies are not always recognised as folk-like, because, as Vaughan Williams pointed out, "If we look at a collection of German Volkslieder we are apt to be disappointed, because the tunes look exactly like the simpler Mozart, Beethoven and Schubert. The truth is, of course, the other way about. The tunes of Mozart, Beethoven and Schubert are so very much like Volkslieder."[13]

Knepler has shown that the second subject of the *Finale* is related to the second subject of the first movement of this quintet, with the important difference that it contains a major third instead of a minor third. Mozart is thus clearly asserting the message of the whole work: that even the deepest sorrow can be overcome in a community of men.

During the summer of 1787 Mozart worked on *Don Giovanni*. Da Ponte describes how he suggested the theme of the opera to Mozart: "a subject which pleased him exceedingly". He goes on to relate how he worked simultaneously on three librettos, one for Salieri, one for Martini, and one for Mozart, "with a little bottle of Tokay on my right hand, the inkstand in the middle, and a box of Seville tobacco on my left", and how the landlady's beautiful sixteen-year-old daughter inspired him, so that "between the Tokay, the Seville tobacco, the coffee and my young Muse", he wrote the first two scenes of *Don Giovanni* in a day, and completed most of all three operas in sixty-three days.[14]

Mozart and his wife went to Prague on 1 October for the production of *Don Giovanni*. The story that he wrote the overture on the eve of the first performance while Constanze kept him awake by telling him fairy-stories and plying him with punch, may not be true; but it is quite possible that the overture was not written down until the last minute.

The opera, if not quite as popular as *Figaro*, was a success in Prague. But when it was performed in Vienna in the following year it "failed to please". The Emperor Joseph wrote to Count Rosenberg, the impresario of the National Theatre, that "Mozart's music is certainly too difficult for the singers".[15] A similar opinion was expressed by

Count Zinzendorf, who recorded that "Madame de la Lippe finds the music learned, little suited to the voice".[16] The opera was given only fifteen times in Vienna, and although, like *Figaro*, it was later played in many parts of Germany, these performances brought Mozart no profit. In Munich it was at first forbidden by the censor, and only performed at the command of the Elector.

It is not hard to guess one of the reasons why *Don Giovanni* did not succeed in Vienna, and why it was banned in Munich. It is a satire on the morals of the aristocracy, and the people of Prague, for whom it was written, would certainly have appreciated the significance of the title "Il dissoluto punito" ("The libertine punished"). Current unrest and the recent peasant insurrections are reflected in the scenes between Don Giovanni and the peasant Masetto, whose first aria is a violent attack on the aristocracy. (By a strange coincidence one phrase foreshadows the French revolutionary song, "Ça ira".) Don Giovanni's F major aria in Act II expresses his brutal contempt towards the peasantry, and class distinctions are emphasised in the ballroom scene in Act I by the use of three orchestras, playing three different dance tunes simultaneously – a courtly minuet, a contredanse and a peasant waltz.

All the same it is an over-simplification to regard the opera merely as an attack on the profligate aristocracy. Mozart's characters are not types, but complex human beings, many-sided and true to life. We may admire the class-consciousness of Masetto, but he is jealous and cruel to Zerlina, the peasant girl, who is herself a mixture of naïvety and coquettishness. Don Giovanni is both hero and villain, fascinating and repellent. We admire him for his audacious defiance of society, and we despise the conventional and self-righteous Ottavio, who is an intolerable prig.

We may feel that there is an underlying irony in the moralising sentiments uttered by the six characters who represent the views of respectable society in the *Finale*, after Don Giovanni has been carried off to hell. And we cannot think that Mozart, friend and admirer of Ignaz von Born, really believed in hell-fire and eternal damnation. But there is no doubt that he condemned the Don Giovannis of this world. His hero must be punished, because he is completely selfish. He is ranged against the whole of humanity, riding rough-shod over every other human being in pursuit of his pleasures. He breaks all bounds of moderation and ignores the rule of the "Golden Mean" which was an essential part of Masonic teaching. There can be no forgiveness for him, because he rejects the idea of reconciliation. For Mozart, to whom friendship and brotherhood were all-important, such isolation would indeed have seemed like hell.

One of the most discerning of our Mozartean scholars, E. J. Dent, suggested that a generally frivolous standpoint must be adopted towards the whole opera. Da Ponte, however, tells us that Mozart insisted on treating the subject seriously; moreover, the solemn D minor opening of the overture, which must have startled contemporary audiences, warns us at the outset that this is no ordinary *opera buffa*.

Brigid Brophy has put forward the view that "only in *Don Giovanni* is Mozart on the side of Christianity against the Enlightenment", and that the Don is "an Enlightenment individual asserting the Ego's right to pleasure against God, honour and society".[17] This interpretation is hardly acceptable. Supporters of the Enlightenment did not believe in the freedom of the individual to trample on the rights of others; they based their teaching on love of humanity and brotherhood.

Some examples may be given from the writing of the Illuminati, such as Weishaupt's "Instructions on Initiation": "Whoever does not close his ears to the lamentations of the miserable, nor his heart to gentle pity; whoever is a friend and brother of the unfortunate; whoever has a heart capable of love and friendship . . . whoever does not mock and despise the weak . . . whoever, when truth and virtue are in question, is sufficiently courageous to follow the dictates of his own heart, despising the approbation of the multitude – such a one is a proper candidate."[18]

Goethe, who was himself one of the Illuminati, stated in an address to members of the lodge *Amalia* in Frankfurt: "Not only do all advantages of rank, position, age, wealth and talents disappear in our union and lose themselves in fraternal unity, but individuality also must recede."[19]

On another occasion he said that Mozart, whose music he greatly admired, was the only person who could have set *Faust* to music. Don Giovanni, like Faust, illustrates the downfall of an individual who sets himself up against humanity, asserting his right to complete freedom, regardless of others. In both cases the interpretation of freedom as self-gratification is condemned.

NOTES

1 Le Forestier, p. 501.
2 ibid., p. 541.
3 Roberts, p. 148.

4　Deutsch, p. 291.
5　ibid., p. 290.
6　ibid., p. 289.
7　ibid., p. 287.
8　Anderson, pp. 907 f.
9　ibid., p. 908.
10　Deutsch, p. 289.
11　ibid., p. 296.
12　Knepler, G., *Musikgeschichte des XIX. Jahrhunderts*, Berlin, 1961, pp. 105 ff.
13　Vaughan Williams, R., *National Music*, London, 1934, p. 85.
14　Da Ponte, L., *Memoirs*, pp. 152 f.
15　Deutsch, p. 315.
16　ibid., p. 314.
17　Brophy, B., *Mozart the Dramatist*, London, 1964, p. 83.
18　Frost, p. 32.
19　Banner, H. S., *These Men were Masons*, London, 1934, p. 159.

14

STRUGGLE AGAINST BLACK THOUGHTS

When Haydn was asked to compose an opera for Prague, in December 1787, he refused, saying: "I should be risking a good deal, for scarcely any man can brook comparison with the great Mozart. . . . It enrages me to think that this incomparable Mozart is not yet engaged by some imperial or royal court! Forgive me if I stray from my path. I love the man too much."[1]

In the same month Mozart was in fact given a court appointment as Chamber Musician to Joseph II. His duties consisted solely in composing dance music for the masked balls in the Redoutensäle; his salary of 800 gulden was less than half of what Gluck had been paid for the same position. "Too much for what I do, too little for what I could do", was Mozart's comment.[2] Although he often signed himself as "*Kapellmeister*", his official position was that of "*Kammermusikus*" (Chamber Musician).

His financial prospects during 1788 were bad. He gave no subscription concerts for the Lent season, and a series planned for the autumn, for which the three symphonies in E♭ (K.543), G minor (550) and C major (551) were probably intended, failed to materialise. His Italian operas had "failed to please" in Vienna, and, since the German company had been disbanded, there was no hope of another commission for a *Singspiel*. By that summer Mozart was in desperate straits. The begging letters which he wrote to his friend and fellow-Mason, Michael Puchberg, make tragic reading. Puchberg was a wealthy merchant, and a lover of music. He usually responded to Mozart's requests for loans, though not as generously as his circumstances might have permitted.

Mozart appealed to him on the grounds of their common membership of the Order of Freemasons. "I have now opened my *whole* heart to you in a matter which is of the utmost importance to me; that is, I have acted as a *true brother*. But it is only with a *true brother* that one can be *perfectly* frank. . . . I do not know, but I take you *to be a man* who, provided he can do so, will, *like myself*, certainly assist a friend, if he be a *true* friend, or his brother, if he be *indeed a brother*."[3]

After moving to cheaper lodgings in the suburbs of Vienna he wrote to Puchberg: "Do come and see me. I am always at home. During the ten days since I came to live here I have done more work than in two months in my former quarters, and if black thoughts did not come to me so often, thoughts which I banish by a tremendous effort, things would be even better."[4]

Mozart was never able to repay his debts to Puchberg. But he composed several works for him, including the beautiful Piano Trio in E major (K.542). This key is an unusual one for Mozart, and in general it has no particular association with his Masonic music, although Sarastro's famous aria, "Within this sacred dwelling" (*The Magic Flute*, No. 15) is in that key. The Trio contains some Masonic symbolism, such as the slurred quavers in the second subject of the first movement, which recur in the last movement. When the phrase is heard in the coda, played in parallel tenths by the violin and cello, it expresses a mood of joy which is far removed from the "black thoughts" of which he had written a few days earlier.

The *Adagio* for piano in B minor (K.540), composed in March, expresses deep sorrow and anguish, with its chromaticism, diminished sevenths and poignant dissonances. The element of struggle is denoted by the rhythm

The movement is an isolated one, perhaps intended for a sonata. Like the *Masonic Funeral Music*, it ends on a major chord, conveying the idea that there may, after all, be some hope.

In the summer of 1788 Mozart wrote his three great symphonies in E♭ (K.543), G minor (K.550) and C major (K.551). They were composed within six weeks, and should be taken as a trilogy. The tonality of the three works is significant: the first is in the Masonic key of E♭; the second in G minor, a key reserved for his most poignant and pathetic music; the third in C major, the key associated with light.

Einstein describes the E♭ symphony as a mysterious work, containing some secret Masonic meaning. He compares the slow introduction with the overture to *The Magic Flute*. "And just as in the overture the adept knocks at the gate and waits anxiously in the dark, so does he here again, until the six-four chord brings the light."[5] The introduction opens with the rhythm:

Darkness is portrayed by discords, syncopations and chromatic phrases, while the radiant *Allegro* opens with a theme consisting of a rising chord of E♭ and a major sixth, expressing hope and joy. In the second subject pairs of slurred quavers denote the ties of brotherhood.

The opening theme of the A♭ *Andante* is clearly Masonic; we may compare it to one of the themes in the first movement of the "Jupiter" Symphony (see p. 127).

Einstein suggests that this movement may be interpreted in the light of Mozart's famous letter on death, quoted in the previous chapter. It is quite true that the first episode, in F minor, resembles the Masonic Funeral Music, with throbbing semiquavers in the bass, syncopated inner string parts, and dotted-quaver rhythms on the violins. This is followed by a transitional passage in E♭ for woodwind (including clarinets), whose calm and peaceful atmosphere may well be related to those "thoughts which are indeed very soothing and consoling".

The "ties of brotherhood" are indicated again in the pairs of slurred notes in the Minuet; woodwind is prominent in the Trio, with a playful dialogue between clarinet and flute.

The theme of the *Finale* is like that of one of the Contredanses which Mozart was composing for the court dances at the Redoutensäle. It resembles one of Haydn's finales in its irrepressible gaiety and good humour, as well as in its monothematic structure. Just before the recapitulation the clarinets and bassoons bring a calming influence, with gentle, staccato crotchets, seeming to restrain the turbulent gaiety of the whirling violins.

Like many other of Mozart's works in E♭, this symphony expresses

Masonic ideas in terms which must have been understood by members
of the Order. But these symphonies were never performed in Mozart's
lifetime, and the message of hope and confidence in the future which
might have given courage to the Brethren in difficult times, remained
unheard.

The symphony in G minor is related to other works in that key, such
as Constanze's aria "Traurigkeit" ("Endless grief"), Pamina's aria
"Ach! ich fühl's ("Ah! 'tis gone"), and the G minor quintet.

Deryck Cooke has described the interval of a minor sixth as
signifying "an expression of anguish in a context of flux".[6] This might
well be a description of the emotional impact of this symphony. In a
detailed analysis of the work, Rudolph Reti shows how the theme,
based on the rise of a minor sixth, undergoes various transformations
throughout the symphony, until finally "the work's prime thought is
heard at the end of the symphony – no longer with the dramatic effect
and emphasis of the first movement, but in a transformation conveying
ease and liberation".[7]

During the summer of 1788 Mozart endured great personal suffering.
The G minor Symphony may best be understood as his "struggle
against black thoughts". He finished the E♭ Symphony on 26 June, the
G minor a month later, and he completed the trilogy with the C major,
the so-called "Jupiter", on 10 August. To appreciate fully the message
of confidence and triumph of this symphony, it is necessary to hear all
three symphonies in succession. In the words of Massin, the "Jupiter" is
"at the same time Wolfgang's victory over loneliness and misery, and
the future towards which mankind is progressing".[8]

It will be useful to point out some of the Masonic ideas which are
implicit in the "Jupiter" Symphony.

The first movement opens with a triple affirmation of the key of C
major; the threefold repetition may be associated with the apprentice's
threefold knocking at the door of the lodge. The dotted rhythm in the
third and fourth bars resembles the opening of the *Finale* of Act I of *The
Magic Flute*, when the Three Boys lead Tamino to the Temple of
Wisdom ("The goal appointed here behold"). This figure is
accompanied by three chords on the lower strings: the number three is
Masonic.

In the closing section of the exposition we hear a light-hearted theme in G major, which forms part of the second subject group, providing a striking contrast with the solemnity of the opening theme. The melody, derived from an *arietta* composed a few weeks previously for an *opera buffa*, recalls Papageno's chattering; it is also reminiscent of the first duet of Susanna and Figaro. The key of G major is associated with the "profane" elements in *The Magic Flute*, especially with Papageno. Perhaps this melody in the "Jupiter" Symphony may be taken to represent the songs and laughter of the common people? In the development section it undergoes transformation by means of modulations and interplay with other themes. In the recapitulation it is further transformed by the addition of woodwind and brass, which impart greater solemnity. The theme is restated at a higher level. We remember that Papageno, too, undergoes trials and is transformed, though he never attains to a state of enlightenment.

The second movement of the "Jupiter" Symphony is an *Andante* in F major, in triple time, resembling the *Andante* of the C major quartet (K.465) and of the C major piano concerto (K.503). All three movements are related to the music of Sarastro.

In this theme we note the rising major sixth, expressing hope, the dotted rhythm and the strong, detached chord denoting courage and resolution. The bridge passage, in C minor, is full of discords and syncopations, painting a picture of darkness and evil, like the portrayal of chaos in the "Dissonance" quartet. The second subject, with parallel thirds in C major, brings a return to order and light, and the final cadence resembles the last phrase in Sarastro's E major aria. (Jacques Chailley suggests that the choice of a seven-note formula for the cadence in that aria may be connected with the fact that seven was the number of Wisdom in Masonic symbolism.)[9]

The third movement, a Minuet and Trio, might be described as a perfect example of a Masonic triad: Order, Symmetry and Harmony.

The phrases in the Trio are perfectly balanced; in the second part we hear the theme which opens the *Finale*, C D F E. This four-note theme, which may be derived from plainsong, has been frequently used by composers from the sixteenth to the nineteenth century, often in a religious context. Mozart used it for the *Credo* of an early mass (K.192) and it also occurs in the *Sanctus* of the so-called "Credo" Mass (K.257). In the "Jupiter" Symphony it may be intended as a statement of belief.

In the *Finale* sonata form and fugue are combined. Its structure may be compared to a well-proportioned piece of architecture. E. J. Dent suggested that there might be Masonic significance in the structure itself. While it is impossible for the uninitiated to understand all its secrets, the architectural analogy can perhaps provide a clue to its meaning.

The column played an important part in Masonic ritual. Musical ensembles, as we have seen, were called "columns of harmony". Every temple was upheld by three pillars, such as Strength, Beauty and Wisdom. This triad is frequently referred to in Masonic songs. In the last scene of *The Magic Flute*, as Tamino and Pamina are received among the initiates the chorus sing: "Strength has conquered and attained the everlasting crown of Beauty and Wisdom." Sarastro's temple was the Temple of Wisdom, upheld by the three pillars of Strength, Beauty and Wisdom. May not the *Finale* of the "Jupiter" Symphony represent that temple?

The *Finale* is a synthesis of polyphony and harmony, illustrating in musical form the doctrine of the Pythagoreans already referred to, the fusion of opposites in the mean. This doctrine was taken over by the Freemasons because it was in accord with their ideas on democracy. In Masonic music counterpoint illustrates these ideas, through the equality of the various themes. In the coda of the *Finale* of the "Jupiter" Symphony all its five themes are stated at once. We have here a superb example of a fusion of contrasting elements.

The second theme of the *Finale* contains the dotted rhythm,

which may represent the "three knocks". (We may compare it with the opening of the scene of the Men in Armour in *The Magic Flute*.) In the first movement, the same rhythm is heard, played by trumpets and timpani (bar 9). It assumes great importance in the *Finale*. When it is stated in unison by the whole orchestra in the coda, it may be taken as an affirmation of unity.

The last five bars are almost identical with the last five bars of *The Magic Flute* (see p. 167). They consist of a fanfare of brass on the tonic chord, with three chords on strings and woodwind, repeated once. This is a conventional ending, it is true, but in the context of the whole work it assumes a new significance. In the *Finale* of the "Jupiter" Symphony aspiration and struggle are combined with confidence and hope of victory. It represents a summing-up of past experience, present struggle and hope of future triumph. We may quote the words of the Masonic cantata (K.623), written a few weeks before Mozart's death — words which reflect the ideas of the Illuminati: "Sweet is the remembrance of that former place, where every brother's heart shows what he was, and what he is, and what he may become" (see p. 173).

Can we not say that in the "Jupiter" Symphony Mozart expressed some of his profoundest beliefs, in perfect form?

NOTES

1 Robbins Landon, H., *The Collected Correspondence of Joseph Haydn*, London, 1959, p. 73.
2 Jahn, II, p. 276.
3 Anderson, p. 916.
4 ibid., p. 917.
5 Einstein, p. 245.
6 Cooke, p. 78.
7 Reti, Rudolph, *The Thematic Process in Music*, London, 1961, p. 134.
8 Massin, p. 1081.
9 Chailley, p. 255.

15

YEARS OF CRISIS

In March 1789 Mozart wrote to his friend Franz Hofdemel, begging for a loan of 100 gulden "until the 20th of next month". Hofdemel had recently joined the Order of Freemasons, and Mozart ended his letter with the words: "Well, we shall soon be able to call one another by *a more delightful name*! For your novitiate is very nearly at an end!"[1]

During the next two years, Mozart had to turn to his fellow-Masons many times for help, especially to Puchberg, for his financial difficulties had greatly increased. Constanze's health had been affected by frequent pregnancies; there were doctors' bills to be met, and payment of cures at Baden. His own health was not good, and his hopes of success with the Viennese public were fading. If one looks at the catalogue of his compositions between the autumn of 1788 and the end of 1790 one is struck by the predominance of lesser works – dance-music for his court duties; vocal canons for his friends; arrangements of Handel's oratorios for Baron van Swieten.

It is true that this period includes masterpieces like the Eb Divertimento for String Trio (K.563) and the Clarinet Quintet (K.581), composed respectively for Puchberg and another Mason, Anton Stadler. It also includes the Italian *opera buffa*, *Così fan tutte*, commissioned by Joseph II at the end of 1789. But he wrote no symphonies or concertos during this period, and although the King of Prussia ordered a series of six string quartets, as well as three piano sonatas for his daughter, Mozart found himself unable to complete more than three quartets and one sonata. Compared with the astonishing output of earlier years, we may say that this period was relatively unproductive. In the last year of his life a new period of intense creativity was to begin, during which he wrote some of his greatest masterpieces, including *The Magic Flute*.

We are reminded of a similar period in the life of Beethoven. Between 1815 and 1818 he wrote little, but after 1818 he produced some of his greatest works, such as the Ninth Symphony and the Mass in D. His increasing deafness, his general ill-health, worries about his nephew Karl – these are the reasons usually given for his comparative silence during those years. Frida Knight has put forward another suggestion.

"The silence of the unproductive years 1816, 1817 and 1818, can, I suggest, be explained by social and economic factors hinted at in several letters of those years."[2]

It is not impossible that Mozart's depression during 1789 and 1790 may also have been partly due to the economic and political conditions of that time. Joseph's wars against the Turks had caused distress through high taxation and rising prices, and there was considerable unrest throughout the Austrian dominions. Years later Constanze recalled the bad economic conditions of those days, when a loaf of bread formerly costing 3 kreuzer cost 12 kreuzer, rolls were unobtainable, and the 3-kreuzer loaf was "truck und schluck" (rubbish). In July 1788 there were bread riots in Vienna, and in lower Austria, where peasants were protesting against the war, detachments of cavalry were sent to put down the disturbances. In Bohemia peasants refused to pay their dues, and after 1789 they were "loud in their praise of the men of their own rank in France".[3]

The French Revolution had far-reaching effects throughout Europe. Albert Soboul writes: "Beyond the frontiers of France the popularity of the ideas of the Age of Reason among both the nobility and the middle classes made Germany and Britain especially vulnerable to the spread of revolution."[4] On 12 May 1789 an editorial in the *Wiener Zeitung* proclaimed: "In France a light is beginning to shine which will benefit the whole of humanity."[5]

Austrian intellectuals were eager for news of events in France, which were discussed in clubs and cafés. Many young writers and students wrote and spoke in favour of civil liberties and the rights of man. The authorities, becoming increasingly nervous, introduced new measures, such as a stamp duty on newspapers, "in order to hold back the rising flood of pamphlets and newspapers which ... exercise a harmful influence on public opinion and civil disobedience".[6] The censors were instructed "never to pass any books or pamphlets which cast ridicule upon the teachings of religion, the constitution, the Church, and the Clergy".[7] Under the new laws the writings of Ignaz von Born, for example, would certainly have been prohibited.

Count Pergen, the much-hated Chief of Police, advised the banning of all digests from foreign newspapers, and the censors were told to give prominence to all news items illustrating "the dire consequences of political fanaticism in all their enormity" and "the blessings of the monarchical constitution".[8]

Many of Joseph's progressive reforms were rescinded during the latter part of his reign, and after his death in 1790 Leopold II introduced further oppressive measures, instructing the censors "to cut out all references to the French principles, so fraught with danger at the present time, as well as all expositions of, or favourable comments on, the French system, which, in the present state of public opinion, might well create a most mischievous and pernicious impression on the people".[9]

One event which caused a sensation in Vienna is worth recording. In January 1791 a bookseller named Wucherer, who had sold a number of books and pamphlets critical of the government, was arrested, through an *agent provocateur*. His whole stock of books was seized and destroyed; he was fined 1,000 florins, and, since he was not of Austrian origin, he was expelled from the country.

Such actions were not justified by law, and were opposed by Mozart's friend Baron van Swieten, who was in charge of the censorship and who had fought against the restrictive measures introduced by the police. The authorities justified their action against Wucherer by saying that he was "a thoroughly dangerous and obnoxious man in every respect", and that "the state of public opinion made the complete suppression of these books absolutely necessary".[10] Pergen wrote to his superior, Count Kollowrat: "I have the honour to inform Your Excellency that Georg Philipp Wucherer has been banished from all His Majesty's hereditary dominions on the order of His Majesty personally, for selling prohibited and even uncensored books, and for another extremely important secret reason known to His Majesty."[11] The "extremely important secret reason" was that Wucherer was suspected of being one of the leading members of the German Union, a newly-formed organisation which was thought to be a cover for the Illuminati.

Among the books published by Wucherer was a collection of poems by Blumauer, a member of Born's former lodge, *True Harmony*. Mozart knew Blumauer, who was one of the Illuminati; he owned a copy of his poems, and had set one of them to music (see p. 66).

For a whole decade after 1789 rumours were current in Vienna that the Freemasons, and in particular the Illuminati, were responsible for the French Revolution. In August 1790 Marie Antoinette warned her brother, Leopold II, to "Take great care over any associations of Freemasons . . . it's by means of Masonry that the monsters in this country count on succeeding elsewhere. May God keep you and my native land from such miseries."[12]

It is impossible to give here a detailed account of the legend of the

Illuminists and the French Revolution. Today the idea seems fantastic, but it was taken seriously enough by the ruling-classes at the end of the eighteenth century. Some of the rumours spread at the time can be traced to the activities of Leopold Aloys Hoffmann, who has already been mentioned as secretary of Mozart's lodge *Beneficence* (p. 76). Hoffmann edited a journal, the *Wiener Zeitschrift*, the main purpose of which was to attack the Illuminati. "Germans, and not the French, were responsible for the French Revolution, the project of changing the world", this journal announced. "The French had the honour of pursuing it to its final consequences – guillotine, intrigues, incendiarism, assassination, cannibalism."[13]

The journal attacked Knigge, who was living in Hamburg at the time, as "the main spreader of these doctrines, liberty and equality".[14]

Knigge had written a pamphlet in which he stated that the violence of revolution, though undesirable in itself, was insignificant compared with the sufferings of the people oppressed by war and tyranny. In 1795 he issued an "Appeal to the Enemies of Tyranny", protesting against the use of espionage and oppressive measures "which must inevitably lead to a revolution as bloody as that of France", ending with an appeal "to all friends of truth to unite", and a statement that an association had already been formed, with branches in twenty-four cities.[15]

This leaflet gave Hoffmann, and another renegade named Zimmermann, the pretext for an act of provocation against Knigge. With the connivance of the Viennese police, he sent a letter purporting to come from the poet Blumauer, asking for details of the plans for a revival of Illuminism. Knigge fell into the trap, and sent the "pseudo-Blumauer" details of the proposed new society, together with a list of members in various cities, and a request to organise the movement in Vienna.

The publication of this material by the police enabled the authorities to take further action against secret societies, and virtually put an end to attempts to revive the Illuminati. But Hoffmann's attacks continued until 1799, and were taken up by others, such as the Abbé Barruel, a French émigré living in London, and Professor John Robison in Edinburgh, who was a member of a Masonic sect opposed to the Illuminati.

Thus it is mainly from Hoffmann that the legend of Illuminist responsibility for the French Revolution springs. He has been thought to be the prototype of Monostatos in *The Magic Flute* – symbol of treachery and cunning.

The atmosphere of tension in Vienna in the years immediately after the Revolution must have been similar in many ways to the Metternich period, during which Beethoven endured "suffocation of freedom, stagnation of the economy, decadence of culture".[16] But there is one notable difference between the two periods. The Metternich epoch was one of disillusionment and hopelessness, after the triumph of reaction. But in 1789 there were many who looked with hope towards the infant French republic, eagerly awaiting developments.

There is no direct evidence of Mozart's attitude to the events in France. But it is not hard to guess which side he was on. We know that one of his favourite books was by a French revolutionary writer (see p. 98). Most of his friends were Freemasons, including a number of Illuminati, whose ideas on liberty and equality were similar to those which inspired the Revolution. The fact that Mozart himself selected *The Marriage of Figaro* as a libretto for his opera is in itself an indication of where his sympathies lay in 1789.

Mozart greatly admired the English, calling himself "an out-and-out Englishman". No doubt he would have been glad to escape from the repressive atmosphere of Vienna to a country where there was relative freedom. Although invited several times, he was never able to visit England. But in the spring of 1789 he did escape from Vienna, when he accompanied his friend and pupil, Count Lichnowsky, to northern Germany. Lichnowsky, who is best known to us through his patronage of Beethoven, was a Freemason, and son-in-law of the enlightened Countess Thun. Mozart hoped for an introduction to Frederick William II of Prussia, and for fresh openings in Saxony and Prussia.

The journey took him through Prague, where he met some of his Masonic friends again, and Dresden, where he was introduced to another musician who was a Freemason, J. G. Naumann, Kapellmeister to the court. The two composers had a poor opinion of each other; Mozart thought that a mass by Naumann was "wretched stuff", while Naumann described Mozart as "a musical sansculotte", implying that his music was vulgar and plebeian.[17]

The tour was not a financial success. Mozart wrote to Constanze: "The Queen wants to hear me play on Tuesday, *but I shan't make much money*."[18] After playing his piano concerto in D major (K.537), he was presented with "a handsome gold snuff-box". Evidently the aristocracy were no more generous than they had been twenty years earlier, when the Mozart family first set out on their travels.

In Leipzig Mozart was again disappointed. "From the point of view of applause and glory this concert was absolutely magnificent, but the profits were wretchedly meagre."[19] Meanwhile Count Lichnowsky had proved a broken reed; he had borrowed money from Mozart and left him in Potsdam, "which is an expensive place" . . . "I had to lend him a hundred gulden, as his purse was getting empty. I could not well refuse him: you will know why."[20]

One result of this journey was a commission for six quartets and three sonatas for the King of Prussia.

By the end of May Wolfgang was back in Vienna, even more deep in debt as a result of his travels. Constanze was still in bad health, and that summer he fell seriously ill again himself. Debts continued to accumulate, and his letters to Puchberg are even more pathetic than those of the previous year. In spite of illness and depression, he planned to give some subscription concerts, but when he sent round a list for subscribers the only name on it was that of Baron van Swieten. Mozart seemed indeed to have been deserted by his friends. Yet he did not give up hope completely. "The bad is temporary; the good will certainly persist", he wrote to Puchberg.[21]

Perhaps it was this conviction that good would ultimately prevail, based on his Masonic beliefs, that enabled him to compose the serenely beautiful Clarinet Quintet (K.581) in the autumn of 1789. This work, written for a brother-Mason, the clarinettist Anton Stadler, may be considered Masonic in character. The instrument itself is associated with lodge ceremonies, and the key signature of three sharps may also have Masonic significance. Einstein has pointed out the "fraternal" character of the relationship between the clarinet and the strings, using the word "fraternal" advisedly on account of its Masonic implications.[22] The tender *Larghetto* is a characteristic example of Mozart's humanist style, anticipating the Clarinet Concerto.

The work contains Masonic symbols such as suspensions, pairs of slurred notes, and parallel thirds and sixths. We have already pointed out that one phrase in the first movement is identical with a phrase in *The Magic Flute* (see p. 72). The message of the Clarinet Quintet is one of hope and consolation in a period of loneliness and depression.

At the end of 1789 Mozart was asked by the Emperor to compose an Italian opera, with da Ponte as librettist. He must have felt that his hopes of achieving success were justified and that a turning-point in his fortunes had been reached at last.

The theme of *Così fan tutte*, which is said to be based on a true story of a scandal in Viennese society, was suggested by Joseph himself. This opera, like *Don Giovanni*, has aroused controversy. Beethoven thought the plot immoral, and wondered how Mozart could have composed music for such a libretto. This view was held by many people in the nineteenth century, while more recently certain critics have condemned the opera for its "elegant superficiality" and "rococo artificiality". It has even been suggested that in writing music for this opera Mozart was simply carrying out a commission which he dared not refuse. It is true that it might have been unwise to turn down the royal request, or to suggest an alternative theme, but the quality of the music is such that we cannot accept an explanation which implies that the work was entirely distasteful to him.

Some critics think that in *Così* Mozart was giving vent to his feelings of jealousy about Constanze, or denouncing the fickleness of women in revenge for the faithlessness of Aloysia. Wolfgang certainly understood the human passion of jealousy, to which he had already given powerful expression in Figaro's aria, "Yes, fools you are, and will be" ("Aprite un po'que gl'occhi"). It may be that some of Constanze's characteristics are portrayed in the flighty Dorabella. In the summer of 1789, while his wife was taking a cure at Baden, he had reproached her for being "too free and easy with N . . . N . . ." [the name was erased later by Constanze], and had begged her "not to torment yourself and me with unnecessary jealousy".[23] Such an interpretation merely takes *Così* at its face value, ignoring the fact that the satire is directed equally at the men, whose cruel trick is responsible for the women's behaviour.

In an illuminating broadcast on *Così fan tutte*, Professor Bernard Williams suggested that, had the opera been set to music by Rossini, it would have been brilliant, superficial and completely cynical. Mozart's music, he points out, transformed it into something else – something disturbing. "It is disturbing because of what we see and feel happening to the characters, when they are brutally returned to the conventional world, after their emotions have been aroused. . . . What is sad in that opera is that all that dimension of feeling exists, but the world rumbles on as though it didn't." Did Mozart approve of the attitude of the world, he asks, as expressed in "that somewhat hollow-sounding *Finale*?". His own opinion is that "Mozart was more concerned to *display* the demands of the world than to *justify* them".[24]

To understand *Così* it should be considered in relation to Mozart's other operas, to the circumstances of his life, and to the political events which we have outlined. *Così* was the last of the three Italian operas for which da Ponte wrote the libretto. Professor Dent described it as "a last jest at the departing age, for those who understood the humour of it. . . ." *Figaro* was "a prologue to the Revolution, *Don Giovanni* an opera for heedless pleasure-loving aristocrats dancing on the crust of a volcano".[25] The metaphor is appropriate, for the opera is set in Naples, under the shadow of Vesuvius, which the 14-year-old Wolfgang had seen and described to his sister in 1770: "Vesuvius is smoking furiously today. Thunder and lightning and all the rest."[26] As János Liebner writes: "the six characters in *Così fan tutte* – on the eve of the French Revolution – play their frivolous games at the very foot of the volcano".[27]

Così is full of contradictions. It is both cynical and tender, light-hearted and serious, satirical, yet imbued with sympathy for the victims of the satire. The characters at first appear to be mere puppets, but they end by becoming real human beings, one of whom, Fiordiligi, develops into a genuine Mozartean heroine, courageous and capable of deep emotion.

To Mozart, and to other artists of the Enlightenment, the expression of feeling was of supreme importance. But his audiences in the shallow aristocratic society of his day preferred superficial brilliance. A contemporary critic, who was a Freemason, defined the purpose of art as being "to imitate nature, and through that imitation to touch our hearts and our sentiments". The same critic stated that "Mozart's works affect these infallibly, provided that one does possess a heart and sentiments".[28]

The music of *Così* transforms a flippant and cynical theme into a profound statement on human relations within the society of the time. In 1789 that society, with all its artificiality and cruelty, was about to disappear. When Mozart portrayed characters like Count Almaviva and Don Giovanni, he attacked the aristocracy openly. In 1789 he had to be more subtle. *Figaro* had been considered "too outspoken"; *Don Giovanni* had "failed to please". But *Così* achieved instant success with the Viennese audience. Even Count Zinzendorf expressed approval: "26th January. Before 7 o'clock to the new opera, *Così fan tutte*, osia *La Scuogla degli amanti*. The music by Mozart is charming, the subject rather amusing."[29]

It is doubtful whether the Count understood the message of *Così*, but there must have been others who did. In that opera, Mozart and da Ponte satirised the Ancien Régime for the last time, using one of the forms typical of that régime – the *opera buffa*. Less than two years later, Mozart made a more profound and optimistic statement on human relations, presenting a vision of a new and better society. But *The Magic Flute* was addressed to a different audience, and it was in a different form.

The success of *Così* was short-lived, for Joseph died in February 1790 and all theatres were closed for a period of court mourning. Although the opera was revived during the summer, only nine performances were given. Leopold II was less interested in music than Joseph; it was rumoured that the new court theatre was to be built with boxes for card-playing. Several individuals who had enjoyed Joseph's patronage fell into disfavour, including da Ponte, who was expelled from Vienna – chiefly for political reasons.

During the remainder of 1790 Mozart composed very little. The only works entered in his catalogue between *Così fan tutte* in January and the String Quintet in D (K.593) in December were two quartets for the King of Prussia (K.589 and 590) and arrangements of Handel's *Ode on St. Cecilia's Day* and *Alexander's Feast* for Baron van Swieten (K.591 and 592).

As a performer he was almost completely ignored. When the King of Naples visited Vienna for the wedding of two of his daughters, music by Salieri, Weigl and Haydn was performed, but there was nothing by Mozart, who was not even asked to play. Later in the same year he played before the King of Naples in Munich, at the request of the Elector. He commented ironically: "It is greatly to the credit of the Viennese court that the King has to hear me in a foreign country."[30]

Early in May Mozart drafted a petition to the Archduke Francis, asking him to use his influence to obtain for him the post of second Kapellmeister at court, "since Salieri, that very gifted Kapellmeister, has never devoted himself to church music, whereas from my youth up I have made myself completely familiar with this style. The slight reputation which I have acquired in the world by my pianoforte playing, has encouraged me to ask His Majesty for the favour of being entrusted with the musical education of the Royal Family."[31] It is not known what reply, if any, Mozart received to this petition, but it was certainly not successful.

By this time he was in desperate financial straits, writing to Puchberg on 17 May: "I am obliged to resort to money-lenders; . . . to seek out the most Christian among this un-Christian class of people."[32] The number of his pupils had dwindled to two, and he asked Puchberg "to spread the news that I am willing to give lessons",[33] so that he might increase the number to eight. The publication of his works brought in little money, since there was virtually no demand for them. "I have now been obliged to give away my quartets (those very difficult works) for a mere song, merely to have cash in hand to meet my present difficulties."[34]

These difficulties included the expenses of Constanze's cure at Baden, and of his own illness in August, when he described himself as "ill and consumed by worries and anxieties".[35]

In a desperate attempt to find work elsewhere, he undertook another journey that autumn. Leopold II was to be crowned as Holy Roman Emperor at Frankfurt in October, and most of the leading musicians had been engaged to take part in the festivities. Mozart was not invited, but he decided to go there all the same, although he had to pawn his silver plate to raise money for the journey.

In Frankfurt he met friends, including Böhm, leader of a travelling theatre troupe, whom he had known from Salzburg days, and with whom he stayed. Böhm's company gave a performance of *Lanassa*, with music adapted from *Thamos*, which Mozart was able to see.

But in spite of the friends he met there, Wolfgang was deeply depressed in Frankfurt. He wrote to Constanze: "If people could see into my heart, I should feel almost ashamed. To me everything is cold — cold as ice. Perhaps if you were with me I might possibly take more pleasure in the kindness of those I meet here. But, as it is, everything seems so empty."[36]

In Frankfurt he gave only one concert, at which he played two piano concertos, the F major (K.459) and the D major (K.537), often called the "Coronation" concerto because it was played on that occasion. The concert was "a splendid success from the point of view of honour and glory, but a failure as far as money is concerned."[37] He wrote that he was "famous, admired and popular here; on the other hand the Frankfurt people are even more stingy than the Viennese."[38]

From Frankfurt he proceeded to Mainz, travelling by market-boat; after spending a few days there, he went on to Mannheim, where he met many friends and attended a performance of *Figaro*. The intendant of the theatre was still his old friend Dalberg — a former member of the Illuminati — who had done a great deal to develop German national opera in Mannheim. *Figaro* had not previously been performed there as an opera, though it appears that the audience were familiar with Beaumarchais's play. In a contemporary account of the opera we read: "It is Mozart's music alone that can make this caponised (*kombabisirten*) 'Figaro' tolerable, so much has he suffered from this mutilation; it suits the characters and sentiments of the singing personages, and for ear and heart alike is full of expression and truth. These qualities are characteristic of Mozart's works, and of him himself as a thoughtful artist."[39]

Evidently Mannheim music-lovers had more understanding for Mozart than the Viennese, and it was partly for this reason, no doubt, that his mood of depression changed into one of hope. On his way home he wrote to Constanze: "I am thinking of taking this very same journey with you, my love, at the end of next summer, so that you may try some other waters. At the same time the company, the exercise, and the change of air will do you good, for it has agreed very well with me. I am greatly looking forward to this, and so are all my friends."[40]

The proposed journey never took place, but Mozart certainly returned from his travels in an optimistic frame of mind. Jean and Brigitte Massin have put forward an interesting theory in connection with this change of mood. They suggest that on this journey Mozart met friends, both old and new, who were able to give him information about the French Revolution, which would not have been available in Vienna, and that this gave him fresh hope for the future. While there is insufficient evidence to prove this theory (as the Massins admit) it is worth examining the facts.

A good deal of Mozart's correspondence for this period is missing, and Constanze destroyed material which might be incriminating. Among the missing letters is one from Mainz, dated 17 October, of which only the postscript remains, starting with the words: "While I was writing the last page, tear after tear fell on the paper."[41] The Massins suggest that in that letter Mozart gave an account of his experiences in Frankfurt and Mainz, of the people he had met there, and of what he had learned about the events in France. The tears, they believe, were tears of anger and frustration at the thought that Vienna was so far away, and conditions there so different.[42]

Before dismissing this theory, we should consider what the impact of the French Revolution had been in many parts of Germany, especially in the Free City of Hamburg, and in the Rhineland and Palatinate, which were near the French frontier.

On 14 July 1790 the first anniversary of the fall of the Bastille was celebrated in Hamburg at a public ball, at which all the guests wore tricolor ribbons, a choir of girls sang in praise of liberty, and Klopstock recited one of his odes on the achievements of the Revolution. Among those who helped to organise the event were Adolf von Knigge, and a merchant called Sieveking, who had written a song for the occasion, beginning with the words: "Free Germans! sing of the hour in which the chains of slavery are broken!"[43]

From Hamburg, too, came a call from a group of writers, addressed to "the peoples of Europe", containing militant phrases such as "Arise! arise! you people, oppressed by harsh despotism under slavery's yoke! Arise! be free! now is the time!"[44]

This manifesto caused the authorities in Hamburg to impose stricter censorship; there were repercussions in other parts of Germany, too, particularly in the Rhineland, where peasants were refusing to pay their seigneurial dues.

Many Germans flocked to Paris as "pilgrims in search of liberty"; on their return, the events in France were eagerly discussed in clubs and reading-societies, many of which had been founded by Freemasons.

Among those who visited France at this time was Georg Forster, University librarian at Mainz, whom Mozart had met at the house of Countess Thun. Forster was "a passionate disciple of the Revolution". Later he became one of the leaders of the revolutionary group which welcomed the French invading troops in 1792, and helped to overthrow the government and to set up the short-lived Mainz republic. Although we have no direct evidence that Mozart met Forster in October 1790, we know that the latter was in Mainz at the time, and that he had just returned from Paris.

There is further evidence of the enthusiasm for the Revolution in the Rhineland in the fact that, at the Frankfurt fair of 1790, handkerchiefs inscribed "Rights of Man" were sold, and also brochures containing the slogan "Live free or die!" Fairs were suspected by the authorities of being used for gatherings of subversive organisations. In a letter to the Duke of Saxony in 1789, Frederick William II of Prussia warned that "there will be a gathering of the Illuminati from all districts at the Leipzig fair, to hold secret consultations, so it would be possible to make a good catch there".[45]

Mozart was in Frankfurt at the time of the fair, and it would be surprising if he had not met some of the Freemasons from other cities during his visit. In the following year he composed music for a cantata written by a merchant from Hamburg, F. H. Ziegenhagen (K.619). The ideas expressed in this cantata are similar to those of the Illuminati. No correspondence relating to this work is extant, but it is possible that contact between Mozart and Ziegenhagen was established through a Masonic intermediary in Frankfurt in October 1790.

The cantata and its author, which are of great importance in a study of Mozart's Masonic ideas, will be discussed in the next chapter.

NOTES

1 Anderson, p. 919.
2 Knight, Frida, *Beethoven and the Age of Revolution*, London, 1973, p. 108.
3 Wangermann, *From Joseph II to the Jacobin Trials*, p. 33.
4 Soboul, Albert, *The French Revolution*, London, 1974, p. 217.
5 Wangermann, p. 24.
6 ibid., p. 45.
7 ibid., p. 59.
8 ibid., p. 60.
9 ibid., p. 61.
10 ibid., p. 55.
11 ibid., p. 43.
12 Roberts, pp. 181 f.
13 Le Forestier, p. 649.
14 ibid., p. 651.
15 ibid., p. 645.
16 Knight, p. 109.
17 Dent, p. 393.
18 Anderson, p. 928.
19 ibid., p. 925.
20 ibid., p. 928.
21 ibid., p. 931.
22 Einstein, p. 204.
23 Anderson, p. 933.
24 Williams, Bernard, *Passion and Cynicism* (Radio 3, 17.6.72) (published in *Musical Times*, April 1973).
25 Dent, p. 307.
26 Anderson, p. 142.
27 Liebner, J., *Mozart on the Stage*, London, 1972, p. 199.
28 Deutsch, p. 355.
29 ibid., p. 362.
30 Anderson, pp. 947 f.
31 ibid., pp. 938 f.
32 ibid., p. 939.
33 ibid., p. 939.
34 ibid., p. 940.
35 ibid., p. 941.

36 ibid., p. 943.
37 ibid., p. 946.
38 ibid., p. 945.
39 Deutsch, p. 377.
40 Anderson, p. 948.
41 ibid., p. 946.
42 Massin, pp. 530 ff.
43 Steiner, G., *Franz Heinrich Ziegenhagen und seine Verhältnislehre*, Berlin, 1962, p. 137.
44 ibid., p. 137.
45 Engel, p. 247.

16

NEW HOPE

Franz Heinrich Ziegenhagen was born at Strasburg in 1753. His father was a surgeon; the family was Protestant, and the children were educated by a pastor named Oberlin, who had progressive views on education. Ziegenhagen became a merchant in the textile trade, and travelled widely throughout Europe. In 1775 he joined a Masonic lodge in Regensburg, *Zu den drei Schlüsseln* (The Three Keys), where he may have met Schikaneder, who was a member of the same lodge.

In 1780 Ziegenhagen settled in Hamburg; at that time business was flourishing, and he was able to make enough money to purchase an estate near the city, where he intended to found a colony, to be run on socialistic lines, based on the ideas of Rousseau and the French Encyclopaedists.

In 1792 he published his book on *The Right Relationship to the Works of Nature*. According to its teachings the laws of nature are irrevocable, depending ultimately on a higher power – a creator, or "supreme architect". But these laws are not followed by man, owing to his mistakes in ordering society. The chief fault in society is the oppression and poverty of the masses. Religion is used as a political weapon, to prevent the laws of nature from being applied correctly. Changes in society can be made through education and enlightenment, but these alone are not enough: economic changes are also necessary. Private property should be abolished; all property should be communally owned and divided among the members of the community, according to the level of production at a given stage. The right to perform socially useful work must be guaranteed to all. There must be an end to all social differences, and to the gap between town and country, and between mental and manual labour. Industry and trade should be encouraged, but they must serve the needs of the community. Social production and trade should be organised by democratically elected leaders.

The concepts of freedom and property are closely linked, so Ziegenhagen went on to explain. Real freedom can only be attained when all men have the right to share in the good things of the earth. Under the new conditions of equality and common ownership a worthy and progressive culture would flourish. Art and science would serve to produce an enduring improvement in the conditions of society and the state of mankind, by continually broadening and deepening man's knowledge of nature.

Ziegenhagen believed that a better society could be attained by the application of his theories. In a society based on collective property and collective work, it would, he thought, be possible "to transform deserts and mountains into fruitful plains, so that the earth would become a big garden, full of gay, healthy dwellings, green meadows, purling streams, shady streets, etc . . ., and where health, strength, skill and endurance would be joined together by love, harmony, and sincerity".[1]

Ziegenhagen differed from Rousseau and the French Utopians, such as Mably and Morelly, in that he saw the need to advance beyond the stage of primitive society by developing trade and manufacture in order to raise the productive resources of society. Primitive men were not entirely happy, because they were backward and ignorant; primitive society was not a "Golden Age" but an age of superstition.

His views on education were in advance of the progressive educationalists of his day, such as Basedow, because he believed in complete equality for all sections of the community, including peasants, artisans and craftsmen. Basedow thought that children should be taught to obey orders and to be satisfied with their station in life.

Ziegenhagen believed that, once private property had been abolished, society could be transformed through education. He thought that the rich could be taught to understand the advantages of a society based on equality and that they would surrender their privileges willingly. He may be classed among the utopian socialists, of whom Marx wrote: "They reject all political, especially all revolutionary action; they wish to achieve their end by peaceful means, and endeavour, by small experiments, to pave the way for a new social gospel. Such fantastic pictures of future society, painted at a time when the proletariat is still in a very undeveloped state and has but a fantastic conception of its own position, correspond with the first instinctive yearnings of that class for a general reconstruction of society."[2]

Unlike Morelly's Utopia, which was set on an imaginary island, Ziegenhagen's plan for an ideal community was a concrete one. The colony was to be situated near a town, so that artisans and craftsmen could teach the children skills of handicraft and industry, combining manual with mental labour. The main purpose of education, he thought, was to establish complete harmony within the community. "As in a concert general harmony can only result if every individual plays his allotted part exactly in time, and discord results if any single person introduces a wrong note, so the happiness of society depends on the correct relationship of the individual, and the happiness of the individual depends on the harmony within society."[3]

Music was an important subject in the scheme of education. It was to be developed through work rhythms, and through listening to the songs of birds. Language was of great importance in helping to develop clarity of thought. Speech should be based on truth, instead of on the repetition of meaningless phrases, like those used in religion. "Most religious poems, paintings, engravings, pictures and musical works spread superstitious beliefs instead of useful and beneficial truths. The poorer sections of the people have no refined religious literature, but are brought up on books of family prayer, which often feed their minds with poison instead of nourishment."[4]

Unlike Rousseau, Ziegenhagen advocated identical training for boys and girls. He believed in complete equality for women, and in this respect he was in advance of his time.

In 1788 Ziegenhagen started to carry out his educational experiments on an estate near Hamburg, with a few pupils, including his own two children. Meanwhile he was working on his book, which was finally published in 1792. The work contained a frontispiece and eight engravings by the progressive painter Chodowiecki, and a hymn set to music by Mozart, which was to be sung at meetings in the colony. Six thousand copies of the book were printed, and Ziegenhagen made great efforts to publicise his work. He hoped to find support for his ideas in France, and made several approaches to the National Assembly, requesting that his book be introduced into schools and colleges. Although he received no reply from the National Assembly, some of the ideas which he put forward were similar to those later adopted by the French government – for example, the statements on religion made by the Jacobins in the autumn of 1793.

The book was not well received in Germany. In Saxony the reactionary government imposed a ban on Ziegenhagen's works, accusing him of seeking the overthrow of all Christian religion. In Hamburg the authorities were more tolerant; they refused to ban his book. But he received little encouragement, because the rich merchants of Hamburg did not agree with his ideas about equality for all sections of the community, even the poorest. In 1795 fresh attempts to win support from the French National Assembly failed, because the government was concerned with developing production, and was therefore not opposed to private property. As Gerhard Steiner points out, in asking the French government to abolish private property, Ziegenhagen was asking the bourgeoisie to dig its own grave.

By 1800 Ziegenhagen's economic and political problems had become so acute that he was forced to abandon all his plans. He returned to Strasburg, where he still hoped that his friend and former teacher, Pastor Oberlin, might help him to found a socialist colony. However, these plans failed to materialise, and in 1806 he came to a tragic end by committing suicide.

Ziegenhagen's work has had little influence, and he is scarcely known, except as the author of the text of Mozart's cantata (K.619). His ideas were completely unrealisable in the society of his time. Yet his criticism of that society, and his vision of a future classless society, may have lessons for us even today. He believed in the possibility of establishing a society where there would be no more exploitation, and no more war. "Happy, thrice happy time when all the inhabitants of this beautiful earth live in the right relationship to each other and in harmony. . . . Then will all buying and selling of weaker fellow-men cease; avarice will not drive African nations to war; no one will covet land outside his homeland. No more will ambition destroy the natural bonds of friendship; no more will children fear their parents, or parents their children; no more will married couples, or brothers and sisters and relatives fear each other, as though they were dealers in men; no more will half-deserted areas be left for wild beasts to dwell in; no more shall we hear echoing the dreaded whip of the overseer on the backs of our weak black brothers in the sugar plantations, in the rice and tobacco fields, in the gold and diamond mines, in the coffee and spice plantations, and in the pearl fisheries. . . . No more will punishments be carried out, the mere description of which makes one shudder. Through our well-tested teaching on the correct relationship of mankind, all people will be ennobled and refined, and will attain fulfilment."[5]

We do not know whether Mozart ever met Ziegenhagen, although one of Leopold Mozart's letters to his son mentions a certain Herr Ziegenhagen, residing in Sedan, who was connected with the textile trade, and who may well have been the same individual.[6] Mozart cannot have seen the book, which was not published until 1792, but it is clear from the content of the cantata that he understood Ziegenhagen's ideas. We must therefore examine this work in some detail.

The cantata is in the key of C major; it is set for solo voice (soprano or tenor) with piano accompaniment. A short prelude, in dotted-quaver rhythm, is like a call to attention; it resembles the chorus "All hail to Sarastro" in *The Magic Flute*. The words of the first recitative bid men listen to their Creator, to whatever religion they may belong. This is an illustration of belief in the "Supreme Architect", and in the unity of all religions. The recitative leads into an *Andante* section in triple time, with broad melodies and wide intervals, typical of Mozart's humanist style. The words relate to two Masonic triads: Order, Symmetry and Harmony, and Beauty, Strength and Wisdom. In the music we may note the *gruppetto* in the accompaniment, the interrupted cadence at the word "harmony", and a phrase identical with one in Sarastro's aria "O Isis and Osiris".

An *Allegro* section follows, in A minor, 4–4 time. The words bid men "throw off the madmen's chains that bind you", to banish the strife which divides men into opposing sects, and to turn their swords into ploughshares. This represents an attack on religious superstition as one of the chief causes of war. The music contains chromatic phrases, discords, sforzandos and diminished sevenths. In *The Magic Flute* the Queen of Night is the representative of the forces of darkness and superstition. The music in this section of the cantata resembles that of the Queen's second aria (*The Magic Flute*, 14).

There follows an *Andante* in 6–8, tender and persuasive, to the words: "Be sure that evil has no place in my Creation; science will explain this and guide you to better actions, helping men to go forward, instead of rushing backwards in a state of strife."

The belief that the many scientific discoveries of the age would be used for the benefit of the whole of humanity was shared by most enlightened thinkers at the end of the eighteenth century.

This section is followed by two bars of recitative, which lead to another *Andante*, in 4–4 time. "Be wise, be strong, be brothers. My benediction then will fall upon you. Then tears of joy will flow instead of sorrow. Then will your grief be turned to great rejoicing. Deserts shall bloom like Eden's fairest garden; Nature will greet you smiling everywhere. Then you will know the truest joy of life."

The words "Be wise, be strong, be brothers" are set to music which evokes an atmosphere of mystery, like the dialogue between Tamino and the priest in the *Finale* of Act I of *The Magic Flute*. Mozart paid special attention to this passage in the cantata, as we know from sketches for the work. The words "be brothers" were originally repeated four times, and the section was introduced by a series of 6–3 chords.

The final version is more concise. The words "be wise" are set to a rising minor sixth, which is changed to a major sixth at the words "Then tears of joy will flow instead of sorrow", transforming a phrase of solemn admonition into one of hope and joy. In its major form, the phrase anticipates Tamino's expression of joy when he sees Pamina's portrait (*The Magic Flute*, No. 3), which is later echoed by Pamina and Tamino when they are reunited (*The Magic Flute, Finale* of Act II).

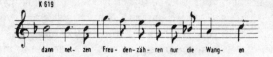

The music has modulated from D minor to F major, returning to C major, the main key of the cantata, at the word "then", which is repeated three times. The dotted-quaver rhythm of the opening is introduced again (on a dominant seventh chord), and the final *Allegro* is an expression of pure joy, reaching a climax with the rise of a major sixth to A'.

Here Ziegenhagen expresses his conviction that Paradise can be attained on earth, through the liberation of mankind, which he believed could be achieved by means of education and enlightenment. Is it not clear from the music itself that Mozart shared this belief?

This cantata was composed in July 1791, while Mozart was still working at *The Magic Flute*. In the instrumental compositions of his last year a style emerges of which the chief characteristics are simplicity and serenity. These qualities were demanded of artists by the Freemasons; they are to be found in most of Mozart's Masonic works. The compositions of 1791 are perhaps lacking in the brilliance and virtuosity of some of his earlier works, but simplicity of style is combined with depth of content.

The string quintet in D major (K.593) represents a turning-point in Mozart's creative life. Written "for a Hungarian amateur", who has been identified as Joseph Tost, Freemason and friend of Haydn, in December 1790, this was Mozart's first composition after his return from the Rhineland. Its Masonic character, as Massin points out, provides further evidence for the theory that his new mood of optimism was connected with his experiences on that journey. The work cannot be analysed in detail here, but certain features may be noted.

The dialogue form of the opening *Larghetto*, and the way in which the phrases are punctuated by silences, suggest the "question and answer" ritual of the candidate for initiation. The opening theme is identical with that of the Masonic *Adagio* (K.411) (p. 65), and the ensuing *Allegro* contains parallel thirds and threefold repetitions in its opening sentence. The return of the *Larghetto* near the end of the movement, followed by eight bars of the *Allegro*, underlines the Masonic significance of the work.

The theme of the *Adagio* is also Masonic in character, containing pairs of slurred notes, which are varied later by the introduction of dotted-quaver rhythm and a series of 6–3 chords. In the central section (which may be compared to that of the *Andante* of the "Jupiter" Symphony) the opening figure of the first movement is heard again, altered by modulation and diminution of note-values. These two themes, the one representing the ties of brotherhood, the other conveying the idea of struggle, provide most of the material for the movement.

Thus we may say that, both in form and content, this quintet is Masonic.

In January 1791 Mozart composed his last piano concerto, in B♭ (K.595). It was written for a concert given by the clarinettist Joseph Bähr; according to the *Wiener Zeitung* for 12 March the concert was enthusiastically received by an audience consisting chiefly of amateurs. Mozart had written only one piano concerto since 1786, the D major (K.537), composed in 1788, which he had played at Frankfurt in 1790. Unlike its predecessor, the B♭ concerto makes no concessions to popular taste. There are no displays of virtuosity; the orchestra contains no drums or trumpets, and the prevailing mood is one of serenity and resignation, tinged with a certain melancholy.

The theme of the first movement consists of a gentle, flowing melody, rather like the song "Gesellenreise" (K.468) which Mozart wrote for his father's admission to the second grade of Freemasonry. This movement contains some remarkable modulations; perhaps this "tonal" journey is intended to suggest the journey of the candidate for initiation. The opening melody is interrupted by a figure in dotted-quaver rhythm; a few bars later a motif recalling the second theme in the *Finale* of the "Jupiter" Symphony is heard (see p. 129). The second movement, a *Larghetto* in E♭, is like a Masonic processional. The opening theme contains both dotted-quaver rhythm and a series of descending 6–3 chords.

The serenity of this movement is disturbed in the central section by modulations to the minor and chromaticism. But when the theme is finally restated (bar 103), flute and violins play in unison with the piano. Once again, two passages in *The Magic Flute* come to mind. In the *Finale* of Act I, Tamino asks the priest "When wilt thou break the bond of silence?", to which the priest replies

> "When friendship leads thee by the hand
> To join the temple's holy band."

He is accompanied by cellos, playing the melody in unison with the voice.

In Sarastro's second aria, the words "He wanders, led by hand of friend" are accompanied by the first violins, which play the same melody two octaves higher (see p. 161). We suggest that the passage in the concerto to which we have referred may also illustrate the apprentice being "led by the hand of friendship".

For the *Finale* of this concerto Mozart used the theme of a song, "Sehnsucht nach dem Frühlinge" ("Longing for Spring") (K.596), composed at about the same time for a collection of children's songs. The tune is derived from a folk song.

("Come, lovely May, and make the branches green again.")

Evidently Mozart attached considerable importance to the education of children, as we know from references in his letters to that of his own son, Karl. He wrote several songs for a supplement to a journal published by two teachers at the Deaf and Dumb Institute in Vienna, to which both he and Ignaz von Born subscribed. The texts of several of these songs were by enlightened writers, such as Campe, Sturm and Overbeck, who believed that children should be taught to learn from nature, to serve the community, and to regard all men as brothers. Songs such as these were designed to counteract the teachings of the Catholic church, which supporters of the Enlightenment regarded as superstitious.

Freemasons looked on primitive people as "children of nature". Many of them, following Rousseau, believed that the childhood of the human race was a state of bliss, to which mankind might hope to return. Some of them, like Ziegenhagen, saw the need for the human race to advance towards a higher stage of society, in which all men would be equal, but at a higher level than that of primitive man. But he too believed that men should learn from the example of nature, and from the innocence of children and primitive people.

The choice of the same theme as "Sehnsucht nach dem Frühlinge" for the *Finale* of Mozart's last piano concerto is significant. The song expresses the innocent joy of children at the return of spring. The melodic line of this theme has been compared to "the soaring and dipping of a bird in flight".[7] Is there not some connection between this melody and Papageno, the bird-man, who called himself "a child of nature"? Even when the gaiety of the tune changes to pathos, in the minor modulations, we are reminded of Papageno, when he tries to hang himself.

Papageno is the representative of the human race in its infancy, the "natural man", whose simplicity is to be admired, though he will never attain a state of enlightenment. In using a theme from a song about a child's delight in nature, Mozart, consciously or unconsciously, was expressing one of the fundamental beliefs of the Enlightenment. Later in the same year he expressed these ideas more explicitly in some of his vocal works – in the Masonic cantatas, K.619 and 623, and, above all, in *The Magic Flute*.

NOTES

1 Steiner, p. 61.
2 Marx and Engels, *Manifesto of the Communist Party*.
3 Steiner, p. 14.
4 ibid., p. 18.
5 ibid., pp. 133 f.
6 ibid., p. 85.
7 Hyatt King, A., in *The Concerto* (ed. Ralph Hill), London, 1952, p. 107.

17

THE MAGIC FLUTE

Goethe once wrote of *Faust* that "the majority of spectators will enjoy it; the initiated will understand its higher meaning, as with *The Magic Flute*".[1]

Although the uninitiated may indeed be unable to understand all the Masonic allusions in this opera, its general meaning is clear. It is an allegory, in which Mozart clearly stated his Masonic beliefs, disguised as a fairy story. And the fact that Mozart dared to present them to the public at a time when Freemasonry – and Illuminated Freemasonry in particular – was under a cloud of suspicion, is an indication of his courage and of the strength of his convictions. After his death there were rumours that the opera might be banned.

There are many theories about the authorship of the libretto, which need not be discussed here.[2] From the available evidence it seems that the idea of a fairy opera came from Emanuel Schikaneder, the actor-manager, who produced plays for his theatre on the outskirts of Vienna. He probably wrote most of the scenes for Papageno and Papagena. Giesecke, an actor in the company who became a famous mineralogist, later claimed to have written the libretto; it is likely that he wrote some of the Masonic scenes in the opera. The influence of Ignaz von Born is reflected in the ritual scenes; but it is almost certain that it was Mozart himself who suggested that the opera should be a Masonic allegory, and that he had a considerable share in shaping the libretto.

There is insufficient evidence to support the once widely-held theory of a change of plot during the composition of the opera; apparent inconsistencies have been explained by Chailley and others. What is certain is that, in spite of all its varied elements – magic, pantomime, solemn ritual – *The Magic Flute* is a complete unity, and its unity is essentially due to the music.

The libretto is derived from a number of sources, one of which was a collection of oriental fairy-stories called *Dschinnistan*. The Masonic elements are partly derived from Terrasson's novel *Sethos*, and partly from Born's book on the Egyptian mysteries. Other possible sources are two operas by Naumann. *Osiris*, composed in 1781, portrays the sun-worship of the Egyptians; its hero undergoes various ordeals before winning the virtuous Aretea, and the opera ends with the destruction of the powers of darkness in the temple of the sun. Naumann's Swedish opera, *Cora och Alonzo*, composed in 1782, is based on Marmontel's novel *The Incas*, which was widely read in the eighteenth century. The choruses of Peruvian priests resemble Naumann's Masonic choruses, and foreshadow the priests' choruses in *The Magic Flute*, Mozart may have known this work, since a piano score made by his Dresden friend J. L. Neumann was popular in Germany.

Marmontel's book portrays the Inca state as an ideal one, based on equality and justice. "Their whole way of life was regulated by law; as in Athens, idleness was a punishable offence; but the laws that insisted on work also prevented poverty; forced to be useful, mankind could at least hope to be happy. Modesty was protected as something inviolable and holy; liberty, as the most sacred of nature's rights; innocence, honour and domestic peace, as heavenly gifts to be revered."[3]*

The idea of the "noble savage", which occurs in two of Mozart's early operas, *Zaide* and *Die Entführung*, was afterwards commented on by Marx. "According to a fiction current in the eighteenth century, the natural state was considered the true state of human nature. People wanted to see the idea of man through the eyes of the body and created *men of nature, Papagenos*, the naïvety of which idea extended even to covering the skin with feathers. During the last decades of the eighteenth century, it was supposed that *peoples in a state of nature* possessed primeval wisdom and everywhere one could hear bird-catchers imitating the twittering method of singing of the Iroquois, the Indians, etc. . . . , in the belief that by these arts the birds themselves could be enticed into a trap. All these eccentricities were based on the correct idea that the *primitive* state was a naïve Dutch picture of the *true* state."[4]

As we saw in the last chapter, Ziegenhagen's ideas about a utopian society were more concrete than those of his French predecessors. When Mozart set his cantata to music, he was assisting a project which aimed at creating an ideal society in a real, contemporary situation. In *The Magic Flute* he presented a vision of that society, founded on truth, justice and equality. The opera is an allegory about man's struggle to

---

* The suggestion that there might be a connection between Marmontel's novel and *The Magic Flute* was made by the late D. M. Garman. In Garcilaso's *History of the Incas* there is a picture of "the Noble Savage", with plumed headdress, which is strangely reminiscent of Papageno.

achieve such a society through enlightenment, and so to raise himself to a higher level of happiness than that of primitive man.

The Magic Flute embodies many of the ideas of the Illuminati and of Ziegenhagen. We may refer to the speech made to the Illuminati Dirigentes (see p. 81), according to which man can learn to order society by the study of nature, and of the history of the human race, which is a history of his struggle to satisfy his material needs. In primitive society men were free and equal; their needs were few, and easily satisfied. As the human race increased in number, men's needs increased, and there was not enough to satisfy them. Men began to enslave each other; equality disappeared, and property was established. Classes and nations arose; despotism reduced men to the level of beasts. Only through moral training in secret schools of wisdom will man become enlightened, and so achieve universal freedom and equality. Then he will regain the Paradise which he had lost.

The speech includes the following words: "Enlightenment means knowing what I am, what others are, and what others may become . . . it means helping others, sharing their joys."[5]

The similarity of these ideas, and even of these words, to those of the Masonic cantata (K.623), written shortly after *The Magic Flute*, suggests that Mozart may have been familiar with this speech (see p. 173). It is even possible that he had met Knigge, who had visited Vienna on his travels and who knew some of Mozart's Masonic friends, such as Blumauer. Knigge and his daughter had translated *Figaro* into German, and Mozart possessed a copy of one of his books (*Dramaturgische Blätter*). In view of the lack of documentary evidence, however, this must remain a matter for conjecture.

The earliest interpretation of *The Magic Flute* appeared in the *Journal der Luxus und der Moden* in 1794. The author of the article, Ludwig von Batzko, was a Freemason; he described the allegory as depicting "the age-old struggle between light and darkness, good and evil, enlightenment and superstition".[6] According to his interpretation, the Queen of Night represents Superstition; Pamina, Enlightenment, the child of the Queen and of Patriarchal Reason; Tamino, Spirituality not yet perfected; Papageno, Folly; the Three Boys, the Powers of the Mind; the Flute, the Single Voice of Nature; the Bells, Flattery; the Sevenfold Shield of the Sun, True Knowledge.

If Pamina represents Enlightenment, the struggle for her custody may be explained in the light of the speech to the Illuminati Dirigentes: "The despots, fearing revolution, encouraged enlightenment for their own ends. It was to stop such abuses of enlightenment and to prevent a relapse into the former state of oppression, that the secret schools of wisdom were developed."[7]

The Illuminati condemned patriotism and family pride. "Once it became permissible or was even considered a virtue to look on the inhabitants of other countries as inferior and to injure them, the next step was to restrict one's love of fellow-men still further to the inhabitants of a particular town, or to members of one's family, or even to oneself. So patriotism developed into parochialism, family pride, and finally egotism."[8]

In *The Magic Flute* Sarastro's wide love for humanity is contrasted with the Queen of Night's narrow selfish love and family pride, reflected in her grief at the loss of her daughter and of the Sevenfold Shield of the Sun. Monostatos, as his name suggests ("standing alone"), represents the selfish individualist.

Tamino is the symbol of man trying to perfect himself and to achieve wisdom by his courage, endurance and love for his fellow-men. "Will he be able to endure the trials?" asks the priest. "Remember, he is a prince." "He is more, he is a man", replies Sarastro.[9]

Pamina is the central character of the opera. She is the object of strife between the Queen of Night and Sarastro, the forces of Superstition and those of Reason. In the trials, it is she who leads Tamino, giving him the magic flute to guide them through the fire and water. In the final scene she is elevated to the company of the enlightened at Tamino's side.

Papageno represents man in the primitive stage of society. He calls himself "a child of Nature". In working for the Queen of Night he has become a slave – one of the men who "did not work for themselves, but only for others, entirely subordinate to the will of their conquerors, without inheritance, without property".[10] "I catch birds for the Queen of Night and her ladies; they give me food and drink in exchange."[11]

Papageno will never attain a state of enlightenment. But through music, love and friendship he can begin to perceive the higher things in life. He may also be said to represent the peasantry, seen through the eyes of the bourgeoisie.

The central theme of the opera is love for humanity, which embraces both a general love for one's fellow-men and the particular love of one human being for another. Pamina and Papageno sing of the power of love in their duet (No. 7); it is love which enables Tamino and Pamina to overcome in their ordeals, aided by music.

Throughout the opera there are allusions to the influence of music.

"Yes, 'tis only music
That has the power to weave the spell,
Jarring souls so to attune
That all in harmony may dwell."[12]

Tamino charms the wild beasts with his flute. (It is interesting to note that in one of the contemporary illustrations for the opera the wild beasts are depicted as primitive men.) Papageno's magic bells enchant Monostatos and his slaves; they save Papageno from suicide and bring Papagena to him. Above all, the magic flute guides Tamino and Pamina through their trial by fire and water.

Mozart hoped to change men's hearts through his music, to win them for an understanding of the ideas of the Enlightenment. "Can we have a higher object, or a more noble one, than to extend our knowledge by mutual instruction, and to show all those who join our ranks the way to virtue and the path of wisdom?"[13] These words, from an article by Born in the journal of the lodge *True Harmony*, are echoed in Sarastro's first aria:

"O hear us, Isis and Osiris,
For these that seek your light we pray;
In all their perils grant them patience,
And lead them safe in wisdom's way."[14]

The Magic Flute embodies the ideals of enlightened thinkers of the time, such as Born, Knigge and Ziegenhagen – ideals which were shared by Mozart himself. In this opera we find the quintessence of his humanist style, which has even been described as his "Magic Flute style". Jahn wrote that in works such as the cantata K.619 and parts of *The Magic Flute* "something is expressed of the essence of the Masonic character, of *moral convictions* (I had almost said *virtue* but fear to be misunderstood), which appears to be outside the province of music, but which has sometimes been made very effective, especially by Beethoven".[15]

Thus *The Magic Flute* may be taken as a key to the understanding of Mozart's music. The opera has been described as "a pot-pourri", because in it Mozart used a number of phrases found in some of his other works, and in those of other composers. Wyzewa wrote: "It is most desirable that musical writers should finally turn from enlightening us about the so-called 'Masonic' intentions of Mozart, and instead endeavour to set up for us an inventory of those 'sources' from which he drew the varied materials for his last opera."[16]

It is certainly interesting to trace these sources, but it is surely more important to try to reveal the significance of the ideas which are given musical expression in the opera.

It is impossible here to give a detailed account of all the musical symbolism in *The Magic Flute*,* but a few general points may be made, and an analysis given of one or two examples.

Firstly, the predominant tonality of the opera is E♭ major. C major is frequently used in Masonic scenes, like the *Finale* of Act I. C minor is associated with darkness; D minor with superstition, as in the Queen of Night's second aria. Sarastro's two arias are in F major and E major.

Secondly, certain rhythms recur throughout the opera, such as the stylised form of the "three knocks", first heard in the middle of the overture (see p. 42). Dotted rhythms are frequent in the Masonic scenes, such as the *Finale* of Act I.

Thirdly, certain harmonic progressions occur at moments of particular significance. The progression Tonic (I) Dominant (V) Submediant (VI), and the use of parallel thirds and sixths (6–3 chords) are the most notable examples.

Fourthly, a certain type of cadence, with feminine ending, may be associated with ideas of love and brotherhood.

Fifthly, the orchestration of the ritual scenes, using trombones and basset horns, imparts an atmosphere of solemnity. Clarinets are usually employed in numbers which have special Masonic significance, as at the first mention of the Three Boys (No. 5).

The *March of the Priests*, at the beginning of Act II, contains examples of many of the Masonic musical symbols. It is in the key of F major, scored for strings, flute, two basset horns, two bassoons, two horns and three trombones. The opening chords consist of the progression I V₇ VI. The next two bars contain a series of ascending 6–3 chords.

Bars 5–8: dotted-crotchet and dotted-quaver rhythm, ending with a feminine cadence.

Bars 22–28: rhythm

repeated six times.

The march is immediately followed by the "three knocks" played by flutes, oboes, basset horns, bassoons, horns and trombones. In the

* For a full account of the Masonic symbolism in *The Magic Flute* see Chailley, op. cit.

dialogue which follows Sarastro is asked by the priests whether Tamino is worthy to be accepted as a candidate for initiation. They ask if he possesses the qualities of virtue, silence and benevolence. The "three knocks" are repeated three times as the priests indicate their acceptance of Tamino as a candidate. The dialogue is followed by a prayer to Isis and Osiris, a hymn in antiphonal style. This is scored in sombre tones, for basset horns, bassoons, trombones, violas and cellos.

Sarastro's two arias in *The Magic Flute* provide us with the finest examples of Mozart's humanist style. In the second one, in E major (which follows the Queen of Night's D minor aria of vengeance) the central theme of the opera is stated: the idea of fraternity.

> "Within this sacred dwelling
> No vengeance shall be known;
> He who neglects his duty
> Through love his duty learns.
> He wanders, led by hand of friend,
> With joy to find a better land.
>
> Within this sacred building
> Where man his brother loves,
> No traitor can lie hidden,
> For each his foe forgives.
> He that delights not in our teaching
> Does not deserve to be a Man."[17]

The two-bar introduction expresses both tenderness and strength – tenderness in the soft opening phrase of the violins in thirds, strength in the two emphatic chords of the second bar, in which the strings are supported by flutes, bassoons and horns. When the words refer to the "hand of friend", the violins play the melody two octaves above the voice. The threefold repetition of the last couplet underlines the message of the song – and of the opera – while the tender phrase played by violins and flute in the closing bars (with an interrupted cadence) expresses the humanity of Masonic teaching.

The *Finale* of Act II is in the Masonic key of E♭, the main tonality of the opera. It opens with an *Andante*, in gentle march rhythm, scored for woodwind: two clarinets, two bassoons, two horns. These were the instruments most frequently used in lodge ceremonies; the number six is significant.

MAGIC FLUTE

The first bar is in the rhythm

In bar 3 slurred notes remind us of the ties of brotherhood. Bars 4 and 5 contain the rhythm

Bars 7 and 9 repeat the dotted-quaver rhythm of bar 1. Bar 10 concludes the introduction with a feminine cadence.

Thus these ten bars contain, in concentrated form, a number of Masonic musical symbols. The words sung by the Three Boys give the key to the meaning of the music. "Soon the dawn will bring us light; the golden sun will rise; soon superstition will disappear; soon the wise man will conquer."[18] The significance of the sunrise will be examined later. The words "wise man will conquer" are set to slurred notes.

"Come down, O peace, return into men's hearts. Then earth will be a paradise again, and mortals will be like gods."[19] We recognise here the thoughts of Ziegenhagen and Knigge – thoughts which have already been expressed in the *Finale* of Act I, when the chorus sang: "When Virtue and Righteousness strew the path of the great with glory then earth will be a paradise, and mortal men will be like gods."[20] (This idea is illustrated musically by a rise to a high G in Act I, and to A♭' in Act II; similarly when Pamina sings with Papageno that the power of love can make men equal to the gods, her voice soars to the dominant B♭'.)[21]

In the *Finale* of Act II, the rhythm becomes agitated at Pamina's entry; the music modulates to minor keys; chromatic phrases and discords express her anguish, as she threatens to commit suicide. The Three Boys intervene to save her. (Note the interrupted cadence, and the dotted-quaver rhythm). The music changes to triple time, and we hear a series of 6–3 chords. The words [the gods] "will protect you" are repeated three times. In the postlude, flowing quavers anticipate the theme associated with "wandering through danger" in the next scene. This section ends with the rhythm denoting courage and resolution.

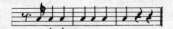

The stage directions for the next scene describe "Two mountains, one containing a rushing waterfall, the other spitting out fire. Before them there is an iron gateway, guarded by two Men in Armour."[22] Tamino is led in, "lightly clad, with sandals on his feet", to begin his ordeals. We hear the sombre sound of trombones and strings, playing the note C, in the rhythm

reminding us of the "three knocks". In the second bar, six woodwind instruments establish clearly that the key is C minor; the phrase ends on a diminished seventh. The triple rhythm is repeated on G (the dominant); once more the woodwind reply, leading back to C minor. Then the *fugato* commences: first the second violins, then the first, then the violas, cellos and basses. The theme begins with a rising scale of C minor, played very softly, staccato, like someone tiptoeing through the darkness. The countersubject contains suspensions and slurred notes, symbolising brotherhood, but in the minor and chromatic, suggesting arduous and dangerous struggle, which intensifies until the voices enter with their chorale – tenor and bass in unison, accompanied by woodwind.

The words of the chorale are taken directly from *Sethos*. "He who will wander down this path with his burden must be purified by Fire, Water, Air and Earth; if he can overcome the fear of death, he will raise himself from earth to heaven. Then he will be in a state of illumination, fit to be dedicated to the mysteries of Isis."[23]

The melody is that of a Protestant chorale, whose original words are a literal translation of a Hebrew psalm. In uniting a Christian melody, whose words are of Hebrew origin, with a pagan text, Mozart was again illustrating the Masonic belief in the unity of all religions. He had already expressed this idea in the *Masonic Funeral Music*. It is the opening thought in Ziegenhagen's cantata. The climax of the fugue is reached with the word "illumined" (German = *erleuchtet*), which must surely be taken as a reference to the Illuminati.

In the next section, the terrors of death are depicted by *tremolandos* and *sforzando* chords in F minor. Tamino declares that he is not afraid; then Pamina's voice is heard, and he gains fresh courage, declaring that no fate can part them now. The Men in Armour join to encourage the couple, and we hear the slurs of brotherhood again. In an ecstatic phrase which echoes his first aria, Tamino expresses his joy at meeting Pamina again; the woodwind punctuates the string accompaniment with three soft chords.

"A woman who does not fear death or night is worthy, and will be initiated."[24] These words, sung by Tamino and the Men in Armour, express a thought which is almost revolutionary. Freemasons were opposed to initiation for women, although there were female "Lodges of Adoption". Jacques Chailley argues that in *The Magic Flute* Mozart was asserting the right of women to be admitted to the lodges on the same terms as men – that is to say, if they were found worthy. (Naturally such women as the Queen of Night and her Three Ladies would be excluded.) Ziegenhagen, in advance of his time, advocated identical training for boys and girls, and complete equality for women. Did Mozart share those views? We cannot tell; but several of his heroines, such as Ilia, Constanze and Susanna, are at least equal, or even superior to their male counterparts in courage, intelligence and sensitivity. The essential message of *Figaro* is one of equality of sex, even though some of Beaumarchais's outspokenly feminist dialogue had to be omitted from the opera.

The words "night" and "death" are accompanied by *tremolandos*, *sforzandos* and chromaticism; the phrase "is worthy and will be initiated" (*ist würdig und wird eingeweiht*) is set to the following rhythm, with an interrupted cadence at the word "initiated":

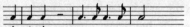

The stage directions tell us that "the doors open; Tamino and Pamina embrace". The section which follows is the musical climax of the whole opera. A phrase consisting of six quavers, soft and staccato, is repeated three times, modulating to F major. Then, after a pause, the next eight bars express the love and perfect harmony of the couple. "Tamino mine! O what joy!" "Pamina mine! O what joy!" The idea of love and joy is illustrated by the rise of a major sixth, followed by a descending scale. The phrase is related to Tamino's "portrait" aria (see p. 151). Harmony is expressed by the perfect balance of the two phrases, and the basic simplicity of the chords.

In the section which follows, it is Pamina who leads the way. She tells the story of the magic flute, carved by her father from a thousand-year-old oak, "in lightning, thunder, pelting storm" (tremolandos and diminished sevenths). She bids Tamino "take the magic flute and play"; the Men in Armour join the couple in singing:

> "By the power of the flute's sound
> We wander joyfully through death's dark night".[25]

The "wandering" is illustrated by the interweaving of the parts in a perfect blending of harmony and counterpoint. The effect is indescribably moving. A single chord modulates from F major to C major – the key of light. Tamino and Pamina enter through the gates and pass through the fire, then through the water, to the mysterious and awe-inspiring sound of flute, accompanied by chords on horns and trombones, with drum-beats (note the "three knocks" on the timpani). The first bar contains a *gruppetto*, while the second bar contains a rising sixth (interval of love and joy), followed by a descending scale (p. 151). When they emerge in safety, the couple sing in tenths, accompanied by the warm tone of the strings. After their second ordeal, Tamino and Pamina sing: "O gods! what a moment! We are granted the happiness of Isis!"[26] The mysterious chord on the submediant (VI) at the word "moment" indicates that this is the moment of initiation. The chorus take up the song of joy as the pair enter the temple, in a triumphant assertion of C major.

In the next scene Papageno, lonely and disconsolate, tries to summon Papagena. Throughout the opera, Papageno sings in the accents of the people, with the melodies of German and Austrian popular song. He carries on the tradition of Harlequin and Hanswurst. In this *Finale*, his music is in the style of a folk waltz.* Like Pamina, he tries to commit suicide, but is saved by the Three Boys, who tell him to play his magic bells. The music for the duet with Papagena, in the "profane" key of G major, contains no Masonic symbolism, but when the pair sing of their "beloved children" they sing in tenths, in a phrase resembling Tamino's "portrait" aria. The music changes to C minor, as the Queen of Night enters, with her Three Ladies and Monostatos, on tiptoe, bent on destroying the Temple of Wisdom. (It has been suggested that this is an allusion to a raid by Maria Theresia on the lodges in 1743.) Thunder and lightning, with *tremolando* strings, *sforzandos* and diminished sevenths, illustrate vividly the struggle against the forces of darkness. As Sarastro and his priests appear, there is a transition from C minor to Bb major, from agitated rhythms to calm, majestic chords, expressing the change from darkness to light. A series of suspensions (ties of fraternity) leads to the Masonic dotted-quaver rhythm

with three chords on wind and basses, as Sarastro proclaims: "The rays of the sun have banished the night; they have destroyed the stealthy power of the hypocrites."[27]

To the contemporaries of the French Revolution, it seemed that the Age of Reason had been established in France, and that a new dawn had broken. Henning had written in similar terms: "The sun which has risen over the ruins of the Bastille has dispersed the clouds of folly and superstition, and made it possible to return to the Age of Saturn."[28]

The opening phrase of the final chorus ("Hail! ye souls enlightened!"), in Eb, is similar to the first phrase in the last chorus of *Thamos*, which is a Hymn to the Sun. Similar phrases in *Idomeneo* and *Figaro* are associated with the idea of reconciliation.

Magic Flute

Heil sei euch Ge- weih— ten!   Heil sei euch Ge- weih— ten!

---

* Compare K.516 (see p. 120).

"Thanks, thanks, thanks to thee, Osiris!" sing the chorus, and the strings express the idea of brotherhood once more, with a series of slurred notes in semiquavers.

The final *Allegro* section is like a joyous dance. The chorus sing of Strength, Beauty and Wisdom – the three pillars of the Temple of Wisdom. In the orchestral introduction to this section, we hear the three chords I, V and VI (compare the opening of the *March of the Priests*), followed by a joyful descending scale.

These eight bars are repeated at the end of the opera, with the addition of a brilliant fanfare of trumpets, whose sound strikes a note of triumphant reality, as though Mozart were asserting his belief that the Brotherhood of Man might soon be attained on earth.

NOTES

1 Endres, F. C., *Goethe und die Freimaurerei*, Basel, 1949, p. 91.
2 See Chailley, pp. 11 ff.
3 Métraux, A., *The Incas* (tr. Garman), London, 1965, p. 12.
4 Marx, Karl, *Collected Works*, London, 1975, Vol. I, p. 203.
5 Engel, p. 156.
6 Nettl, p. 82.
7 Engel, p. 155.
8 ibid., p. 154.
9 *The Magic Flute* (tr. Dent), Act II scene 1.
10 Engel, p. 154.
11 *The Magic Flute*, Act I scene 1 (tr. Dent).
12 ibid., No. 5. (tr. Dent).
13 Bradley, H., *Brother Mozart and some of his Masonic Friends*, (transactions Quatuor Coronati Lodge, xxvi, London, 1913, p. 11).
14 *The Magic Flute*, No. 10 (tr. Dent).
15 Jahn II, p. 410.
16 Hyatt King, A., *Mozart in Retrospect*, Oxford, 1955, p. 141.
17 *The Magic Flute*, No. 15.
18 ibid., No. 21.
19 ibid., No. 21.
20 ibid., No. 8.
21 ibid., No. 7.
22 ibid., No. 21.
23 ibid., No. 21 (see Dent, *Mozart's Operas*, p. 227).
24 *The Magic Flute*, No. 21.
25 ibid., No. 21.
26 ibid., No. 21.
27 ibid., No. 21.
28 Le Forestier, p. 633.

18

SWAN-SONG

In the summer of 1791, while he was still working on *The Magic Flute*, Mozart received two important commissions, which must have been very welcome in view of the precarious state of his finances. One was for a *Requiem*, the other for an *opera seria* to be given in Prague for the coronation of Leopold II as King of Bohemia.

Recent research has shown that *La Clemenza di Tito* was not as hastily-written as suggested in many biographies of Mozart; it had probably been planned some time before the commission was received.[1]

Leopold II did not have a reputation for tolerance, and Mozart's choice of theme for an opera for his coronation – that of an enlightened ruler who forgives all his enemies – might be regarded as an appeal to the new emperor. Mozart had already composed music on a similar subject in *Thamos*. In many respects Tito resembles Thamos in character. "If I cannot govern except through harshness, take my empire from me, ye gods! or else give me another heart",[2] he declares, just as Thamos had stated that he could not govern "without friends or the love of my people".

Tito's goodness and wisdom remind us of Sarastro, too. "I know all, I forgive all, I forget all", he says, when he learns that his best friend has betrayed him.[3]

Masonic ideas about forgiveness, tolerance and friendship, already expressed in *Zaide* and *Die Entführung*, are the central theme of *La Clemenza di Tito*. These sentiments are reflected in the Masonic character of much of the music, which a discerning contemporary critic praised for its "Grecian simplicity", and for the "quiet majesty throughout the music which touches the sensitive heart lightly, but the more deeply."[4]

But the aristocratic audience at the coronation festivities did not care for it. The Italian-born Empress called it "una porcheria tedesca" (a piece of German filth), while the ubiquitous Count Zinzendorf, who of course was present, described it as "the most tedious spectacle."[5] Performances were not well attended; one report stated that "at court there was moreover a certain prejudice against Mozart's composition".[6] But later the people of Prague showed their appreciation of their beloved Mozart, for he wrote to Constanze on 7 October: "And the strangest thing of all is that on the very evening when my new opera [*The Magic Flute*] was performed for the first time with such success, *Tito* was given in Prague for the last time with tremendous applause. . . . The little duet in A major which the two maidens sing had to be repeated; and had not the audience wished to spare Madame Marchetti, a repetition of the rondo would have been very welcome."[7]

The "little duet", "Ah perdono!" ("Ah! forgive me!") is in the style typical of Mozart's last year: simplicity, serenity and tenderness are the predominant qualities. (The melodic line of the opening of this duet is the same as that of the *March of the Priests*, and the harmonic progression is identical with that in the final chorus of *The Magic Flute*, quoted on p. 167).

Meanwhile the "new opera" was immensely popular with the general public at the small suburban *Theater auf der Wieden* in Vienna, where it continued to play to full houses until long after Mozart's death. It was also well received by the "connoisseurs". Mozart wrote that Salieri, his former rival, had "listened and watched most attentively and from the overture to the last chorus there was not a single number that did not call forth from him a 'bravo' or 'bello'".[8]

On 7 October he wrote to Constanze: "But what always gives me most pleasure is the *silent approval*! You can see how this opera is becoming more and more esteemed."[9] On the following day he took his mother-in-law and his little son Karl to the opera, writing: "In her case what will probably happen will be that she will *see* the opera but not *hear* it".[10] He went on to relate how one of his acquaintances "applauded *everything* most heartily. But he, the know-all, showed himself to be such a thorough *Bavarian* that I could not remain or I should have had to call him an ass. Unfortunately I was there just when the second act began, that is, at the solemn scene. At first I was patient enough to draw his attention to a few passages. But he made fun of everything. Well, I could stand it no longer. I called him a *Papageno* and cleared out. But I don't think that the idiot understood my remark".[11]

This letter shows how much importance Mozart attached to the Masonic content of the opera, for the scene referred to contains little music, consisting chiefly of Masonic dialogue.

Another member of the audience who showed little understanding for the content of the opera, was, not surprisingly, Count Zinzendorf. His comment was "The music and the stage-designs are pretty, the rest an incredible farce. A huge audience."[12]

The success of *The Magic Flute* brought Mozart little financial benefit. When he died on 5 December he left many debts, and was buried in a pauper's grave.

He left also the unfinished score of the *Requiem* (K.626), a work which has been the subject of numerous legends and speculations. It had been commissioned by Count Walsegg, in memory of his wife. Since he intended to pass it off as his own composition, he sent his agent Leutgeb to Mozart in July 1791, without revealing his identity. There was thus a certain mystery about the commission, and Mozart, who was already ill at the time, became obsessed with the idea that he was composing his own requiem. He commenced work on it immediately, but set it aside in order to complete *The Magic Flute* and to write *La Clemenza di Tito*, which had to be ready for the coronation festivities on 6 September.

Although Mozart composed two more works that autumn – the Clarinet concerto (K.622) and a Masonic cantata (K.623) he did not finish the *Requiem*, which was completed after his death by his pupil Süssmayr. Only the opening *Requiem* and *Kyrie* are known to have been completed by Mozart, although he left sketches for the *Dies Irae*, and instructions to Süssmayr for the remaining numbers.

There are certain similarities between the *Requiem* and *The Magic Flute*. Einstein suggests that Masonic elements may have infiltrated into the funeral rites of the Church.[13] The sombre scoring of the opening *Requiem*, with basset horns and trombones, reminds us of the solemn scenes in the opera, and certain phrases in the *Tuba mirum* resemble phrases in *The Magic Flute*. But, as Dent points out: "The difference is at once apparent; the words of the *Requiem* insist constantly on just that fear of death which Freemasonry had taught Mozart to overcome. It is to *Die Zauberflöte* [*The Magic Flute*] that we turn to know Mozart's religious feelings at their sanest and most exalted moment."[14]

The question whether the composition of a work for the liturgy of the Catholic church conflicted with Mozart's Masonic beliefs deserves consideration. Mozart had written scarcely any sacred music since the unfinished Mass in C minor (K.427), begun in 1782.* He had made a vow to write a mass if Constanze recovered from an illness, just before their marriage. When Leopold reproached him for not fulfilling his vow, Wolfgang replied: "I made the promise in my heart of hearts and hope to be able to keep it. . . . The score of half a mass, which is still lying here

---

* In the summer of 1791 he composed the short motet *Ave verum* for his friend Anton Stoll, the choirmaster at Baden.

waiting to be finished, is the best proof that I really made the promise."[15]

Mozart later used parts of this work for an oratorio, *Davidde penitente* (K.469). One of the reasons for his failure to complete the Mass may have been his growing interest in rationalist ideas at that time, through his contact with men like Ignaz von Born.

Mozart certainly never formally renounced the Catholic faith. But when he was dying, it was with difficulty that a priest was found willing to administer the last rites. His sister-in-law, Sophie Haibl, described how "For a long time they refused to come, and I had a great deal of trouble to persuade one of those clerical brutes to go to him."[16]

Mozart's views were clearly regarded as unorthodox; his association with members of the Illuminati would be enough to condemn him in the eyes of the priests.

It was not inconsistent, however, for a Freemason to be a Christian. The Funeral Oration delivered at a Masonic lodge in memory of Mozart in 1792 contains the following passage: "The ability courageously to conquer such repugnant thoughts on death, and to take the great and important step into the unknown fields of eternity with a calm smile, can only be attained by him who has learned in this very place the great art of living in virtue that he may die as a Mason, as a Christian."[17]

The Illuminati believed in a Divine Creator, or Supreme Architect of the Universe, as did Ziegenhagen. Knigge wrote that "the secret meaning of the teaching of Jesus was to lead men without revolution to universal liberty and equality".[18] No doubt Mozart also held such views, but it is clear that the Masonic ideals of human love and brotherhood meant far more to him than the teachings of the Catholic church. This is confirmed by a comparison between the music of the *Requiem* and that of *The Magic Flute*, but if further evidence is required it may be found in the *Kleine Freimaurer-Kantate (Little Masonic Cantata)* (K.623), which was his last completed work.*

In January 1792 the following publisher's advertisement appeared in the *Wiener Zeitung*:

Announcement of a cantata by the late distinguished composer Mozart.

It is a work which it is fitting to call his swan-song, fashioned with

---

* The hymn "For the Closing of the Lodge" (K.623a) (now the Austrian National Anthem), is considered by many scholars to be of doubtful authenticity. Both words and melody are typical of the best Masonic songs, and even if it is not by Mozart himself it is a worthy example of the music of the Order.

Swan-song 173

his usual artistry, and the first performance of which he himself directed among a circle of his best friends two days before his last illness. It is a Cantata for the inauguration of a Masonic Lodge in Vienna and the text is by one of the members of the same.[19]

The new temple was for the lodge *Newly-crowned Hope*, of which both Mozart and Giesecke were members. The authorship of the text has been attributed to Schikaneder, but, since he had been expelled from his Regensburg lodge for some misdemeanour, and had never been admitted to a lodge in Vienna, it is more likely that Giesecke was the author. Mozart's first biographer, Niemetschek, recorded that "The happy completion of this work, and the great applause with which it was received, revived his spirits".[20] Mozart himself said: "How madly they have gone on about my cantata! If I did not know that I had written better things, I should have thought my best composition."[21]

The cantata expresses joy in life, unity in work, love of humanity, and hope for the future of mankind. It has been aptly described by Massin as "a song of fraternity joined to work".[22] It is set for three-part male-voice chorus, with tenor and bass soloists, accompanied by strings, flute, oboes and horns. The jubilant opening chorus in C major recalls the chorus "All hail to Sarastro" in the *Finale* of Act I of *The Magic Flute*. The instrumental prelude contains dotted-quaver rhythm and a descending series of 6–3 chords, while the words "golden chains of brothers" are set to slurred notes, in a short contrapuntal section for three solo voices.

A recitative follows, for tenor voice, the words of which express ideas similar to those of the Illuminati (p. 130). "Sweet are the feelings of a Mason on such an auspicious occasion, when the chains of brotherhood which bind us are forged anew: sweet is the feeling that humanity has come to dwell with mankind again; sweet is the remembrance of that former place, where every brother's heart shows what he was, and what he may become; where truest love and brotherhood are found, and where the Queen of all the virtues, Beneficence, is enthroned in quiet radiance."

There follows an aria in praise of the goddess Beneficence (an allusion to Mozart's former lodge). Slurred notes, parallel thirds, and the rise of a major sixth express unity and joy. The aria leads into a recitative, in which the tenor is joined by a bass, to the words: "Let harmony unite this dearest band, woven together in purest brotherhood."

In this passage the word "harmony" is illustrated by the following
chords: Tonic (I), Subdominant (IV), Supertonic (II), Dominant (V)
Tonic (I). An augmented fifth adds mystery to the word "purest", and a
"modal" chord (II) is used for the word "dearest". After a short passage
in imitation, the two voices join together to illustrate the word
"Brotherhood". The dotted-quaver rhythm of the voices suggests
firmness; the accompaniment consists of detached quaver beats on the
lower strings, with a semiquaver figure on the violins. These five bars,
combining harmony and counterpoint, contain the essence of Masonic
ideas, as symbolised by the triad Harmony, Beauty, Strength.

The duet which follows, for tenor and bass, is a beautiful example of
Mozart's humanist style. It is in F major, in 3–4 time, simple, tender and
serene. "May our voices and our instruments proclaim our love and

brotherhood. Then will envy's voice be silent, then our wishes will be granted with the crowning of our hopes."

The idea of a crowning as symbolic of man's final achievement of his goal was an essential part of Masonic ritual, derived from the Eleusinian mysteries, together with other features, such as the blindfolding, the sudden illumination, the trials, journeys and questions.

Here the words "the crowning of our hopes" are set to music resembling a passage in the last chorus of *The Magic Flute*, in which the words proclaim that "Strength, Beauty and Wisdom have attained the crown of victory." In both passages, the interweaving of the parts suggests the weaving of the crown itself – an idea already referred to in the recitative preceding the duet. The music echoes a phrase from the scene of the Men in Armour, in which the words describe a journey through ordeals, guided by music.

The four concluding bars of the duet contain the rhythm associated with courage and resolution. The cantata ends with a repetition of the opening chorus, like a triumphant reaffirmation of Masonic joy and confidence. The repetition is all the more significant when we recall that this was Mozart's swan-song.

Just before the performance of this cantata, Mozart had composed his last instrumental work, the Clarinet concerto (K.622), written for his friend and fellow-Mason, Anton Stadler. The *Adagio* of this work evokes an atmosphere similar to the ritual scenes in *The Magic Flute*. The melody of the solo instrument is repeated by the *tutti* in the manner of an antiphonal hymn, like the solo and chorus "O Isis and Osiris (*The Magic Flute*, 10). In the cadences we hear echoes of Sarastro's E major aria, and of the second chorus of priests (*The Magic Flute*, 18).

In this movement, which is surely one of the most serene and beautiful that he ever wrote, Mozart seems to assert once more, without words, his belief in the Masonic ideals of fraternity and love for humanity, as expressed in the triad Beauty, Strength, Wisdom.

These ideals run like a thread all through Mozart's life, and through his music. Some of his early songs, like "An die Freude" (K.53) ("To Joy") and "O heiliges Band" (K.148) ("O sacred band") are already imbued with Masonic thought, and they are simple and serene.

The noble choruses of *Thamos* and the tender melodies of *Zaide* foreshadow *The Magic Flute*. Even in the music of his *galant* period, there are examples of the humanist style, especially in the slow movements of some of his most brilliant piano concertos. In the great symphonies, concertos and chamber music of his maturity, complete mastery of form is combined with depth of feeling, and a wide range of emotions. Many of these works, as we have indicated, are unmistakably Masonic both in form and content.

During the last year of his life, Mozart's music reached a higher level of simplicity and serenity, expressing a profound love for humanity in a form which could be readily understood by ordinary people.

As a young man, Mozart had said: "I cannot write in verse, for I am no poet. I cannot arrange the parts of speech with such art as to produce effects of light and shade, for I am no painter. Even by signs and gestures I cannot express my thoughts and feelings, for I am no dancer. But I can do so by means of sounds, for I am a musician."[23] The nature of these "thoughts and feelings" is revealed in the Masonic Oration, which we have already quoted at the beginning of this book. "He was a husband, a father, a friend to his friends, a Brother to his Brethren; he lacked only the riches which would have enabled him to make hundreds as happy as he would have wished."[24]

To the great artists of the Enlightenment the purpose of music, as defined by a Freemason, J. F. Schink, was "to imitate nature, and through that imitation to touch our hearts and sentiments".[25] It is only in comparatively recent times that music has come to be regarded primarily as entertainment, or as an escape from reality. Handel, when praised for a performance of his *Messiah*, replied: "I should be sorry if I only entertained them; I wish to make them better."[26] The young Beethoven declared: "I will only use my art for the benefit of the poor."[27] Later he wrote: "In the world of art, as in our great creation, *freedom* and *progress* are the main objectives."[28]

Thus Mozart was far from unique among great composers in his desire to use his art for the benefit of humanity. But his active membership of the Masonic Order makes it possible to illustrate concretely how he was able to achieve his aim. For Mozart himself the value of his art lay, not merely in the music itself, but in the ideas which it conveyed.

> "He that delights not in our teaching
> Does not deserve to be a Man."

NOTES

1 Moberly, R. and Raeburn, C., "The Mozart Version of La Clemenza di Tito", in *Music Review*, xxxi, London, 1970.
2 *La Clemenza di Tito*, No. 20.
3 ibid., No. 25.
4 Raeburn, C., Talk on Radio 3, 31.8.74 (quoted in "Mozarts Opern in Prag,", article in *Musica*, March 1959).
5 Deutsch, p. 404.
6 Raeburn, talk on Radio 3, 31.8.74.

7 Anderson, p. 967.

8 ibid., p. 970.

9 ibid., p. 967.

10 ibid., p. 969.

11 ibid., p. 969.

12 Deutsch, p. 412.

13 Einstein, p. 95.

14 Dent, pp. 252 f.

15 Anderson, p. 834.

16 ibid., p. 976.

17 Deutsch, p. 449.

18 Engel, p. 132.

19 Deutsch, p. 440.

20 ibid., p. 511.

21 Holmes, p. 276.

22 Massin, p. 1169.

23 Anderson, p. 363.

24 Deutsch, p. 448.

25 ibid., p. 355.

26 Ballantine, C., *Music and Society, the forgotten relationship*, University of Natal, Durban, 1974, p. 10.

27 Finkelstein, p. 80.

28 Knight, pp. 109 f.

APPENDIX I

MELODRAMA IN *THAMOS**

"The third Act closes with the treacherous dialogue between Mirza and Pheron."

Bars 1–23. *Allegro* in G minor, 3–4 time. Strongly accented chords, dotted rhythms, chromatic scales and diminished sevenths express the determination of the traitors to pursue their villainous plans.

"Sais comes from the house of the Sun maidens; she looks about to see if she is alone."

Bars 24–29. Soft staccato chords; modulation to B♭. Pause. "The temple doors are closed. Nothing hinders their resolution."

Bars 30–35. *Allegretto* in B♭, 2–4 time. Rising thirds, soft and staccato. She tiptoes to the door of the temple. A falling seventh recalls Thamos's "noble character". "She begins to doubt".

Bars 35–42. *Andante* in B♭ minor; slurred semitones and throbbing semiquavers express her anxiety. "Menes, is it true that thy blood runs in my veins? Then cast a glance upon thy daughter from the dwellings of the immortals! Dispel the darkness which surrounds me! Show thy daughter what is required of her for Egypt's good."

Bars 43–56 F minor. Sais is torn between her love for Thamos and her loyalty to her father and her country. The music of this section reminds us of other Mozartean heroines, like Constanze and Pamina. Descending chromatic scales and diminished sevenths, syncopated minor chords, like sighs, and a Neapolitan sixth (bar 55) express her sorrow. "Yes, now thou hearest me. My resolution has revived. Thou art inspiring me."

Bars 56–63. F major. A tender phrase, related to Thamos's "noble" theme. Repeated cadences express quiet determination. "Shall I be the instrument of traitors? Shall the sceptre be wrested from the hand of the best of princes through me?"

* For a discussion of the view that the music to this Entr'acte is not a Melodrama, and that it was in fact composed before Mozart knew Benda's work, see N.M.A. II, 6. In any case, the music can only be fully understood by studying the text.

Bars 63–68. Staccato semiquavers on diminished seventh chords; chromatic scales. *Sforzando* chords and strongly-marked rhythms denote resolution. Modulation to G minor. "No! it shall remain in his hands!"

Bars 69–73. *Più vivo.* G minor. Rhythmic figure denoting courage and resolution. (p. 42) Dotted quaver rhythm; *forte* cadence in G minor. Pause. Sais has resolved on a course of action which she believes to be the right one, although it will bring suffering upon herself. "If the daughter of Menes cannot share the throne with Thamos, no other hand shall raise her to it."

Bars 73–79. *Più Adagio.* Agitated semiquavers on the strings. (She is still torn by her feelings for Thamos.) Pathetic drop of a diminished fifth. The music hovers between B♭ major and B♭ minor. Syncopated minor thirds express her grief. (79) Another pause. "Yes, it shall be so! I will take the solemn vow." She has decided to dedicate herself as a priestess of the Sun.

Bars 79–85. *Allegretto* in B♭ major, 2–4 time. Repetition of bars 30–35. The melodrama is in free form, but the repetition of this section serves a similar function to that of the recapitulation in sonata form. We see Sais in a new light, after the emotional conflict expressed in her monologue. "She kneels to take the solemn vow of dedication to the Sun-god."

Bars 85–90. "The vow". *Adagio.* In the coda we hear again the theme which recalls Thamos, with the fall of a diminished fifth expressing pathos (bars 86 and 88). Semiquavers persist in the accompaniment, but there are no more minor or chromatic chords; the music is calmer. In the last bar, the quiet repetition of the tonic chord of B♭, in sixths, anticipates the close of the Trio in *The Magic Flute* (No. 19). The effect is one of calm resignation to fate.

APPENDIX II

LETTER FROM MEGGENHOFEN TO ADAM WEISHAUPT*

Munich, in the Franciscan
Monastery, 29th Nov. 1785.

My teacher, my friend,

Here am I sitting in this lonely cell, my dear friend, to which superstition and fanaticism have condemned me, and my first thought is for you; my desire is to inform you of the amazing story of my inquisition. Could you, my teacher, ever have supposed, a few years ago, when we were rejoicing among ourselves at the progress made in our Institute, and at the tremendous advances which our country was making in enlightenment and culture – could you ever have believed that the reward for our labours would be, for you, banishment to a foreign country with your wife and children, and for me, imprisonment in a monastery, by way of punishment because we attempted to enlighten our fellow-countrymen and to dam the strongly-flowing stream of spiritual despotism? – But a weak government allowed the evil against which we fought to grow strong roots, and we were defeated.

O friend! I should like to lament, like Jeremiah, about the destruction of our country, and to shed bitter tears over the ruins of our fine work. – But why ruins? – The oak still stands firmly rooted. – The lightning of fanaticism has struck down a few branches, divided them, and enabled them to be planted in other districts, where they may grow more peacefully into trees.

But now for my story, which goes back to the September before last. Under the Elector's proclamation, all officers who belonged to the Illuminati were obliged to make a declaration within six weeks, stating that they were no longer members of this society. Three weeks after that time the commandant of the regiment at Burghausen received a special

---

* The contents of this letter were published in 1786 by Meggenhofen as *Meine Geschichte und Apologie* (My story and my defence), see Engel, *Geschichte des Illuminaten Ordens*.

order to hand to me a statement which must be added to my declaration, and which must be completed within three days. The document comprised twenty-six questions to which I must reply; thus it was a veritable cross-examination. I weighed up my own and my ruler's rights and limitations, and at first wavered in doubt as to whether I should answer the questions. Eventually I found more reasons in favour of answering them than against, . . . so I answered the questions, I think, with freedom and warmth, declaring that I had left the Order. I was extremely curious to see the effect of my declaration . . . , but I heard and noticed nothing more, except that the commanding officers were instructed to keep a watchful eye on me.

Meanwhile it so happened that I wrote to young Baron von Leiden, introducing him to a clever young man named Kapfinger, and telling him about the dismissal of this young man from an administrative post at Armenstorf. In this letter I used the following expressions: "During your absence (he was then in Switzerland) scenes and events have taken place which will surprise you – marvellous stories – I would never have believed them possible. But in spite of everything my conviction remains firm that all that is happening will be for the best, and that it will bring great trouble to those who persecute virtue and enlightenment."

The letter arrived on Baron Leiden's wedding-day at Elbkofen (Baron Daxberg's castle), at supper-time. As fate would have it, Baron Leiden was ill and did not arrive at the castle on the day appointed for the wedding. The letter was handed to Baron Daxberg, who was pleased to open it and send it to the Inquisitor in Munich. This treachery of Daxberg's deserves contempt and pity from me and from all the world. – And yet I cannot harbour any grudge against him, for he has compelled me to put my philosophy into practice, whereas up till now it has been purely theoretical. In general. . . . I find that my spiritual condition has been a strange one for some time. Through a deep feeling for goodness and beauty I can look at the unpleasant events which have occurred with the greatest indifference. Nothing can provoke me – all is well.

Am I indebted to our Order for this blessed indifference? I believe so.

Soon after these events the commander at Burghausen received an order to take immediate possession of my apartment and of my papers; this he did. A week later the regiment was informed that I had been relieved of my commission and would be sent to Munich to answer certain questions. . . . This news did not cause me to change my attitude, and I am perfectly satisfied with my behaviour at that time. . . .

The hardest task lay before me: that of informing my parents. At the end of the court-martial I went to see them, and eventually, after many devious approaches, I informed them of my suspension and dismissal. – O friend! never did I have greater need of my philosophy than at that moment. Let us draw a veil over that cruel scene or my heart will break and I shall go mad. Then I went on parade.

The lieutenant on duty seemed afraid to say anything about the order he had received. I saw that I must make the first approach, and I asked him if he had received any order about me. Relieved from his embarrassment he replied that he had, and handed me the order. I took my leave as soon as I had bid farewell to the officers, who loved me. I said goodbye to my parents, prepared myself for the journey, and came here.

The day after my arrival I reported to my superiors and to Herr Geheimrat Hunsch, who ordered me to attend the trial at 10 o'clock. During the next two days I spent fifteen hours in court. Never have I wished more ardently that I could draw than during this trial. My examiner was Dr. Stanzius, a fat, rotund fellow, dressed in black from head to foot, who sat in a large professorial chair. Sometimes when my replies were rather long my examiner fell quietly asleep. The busiest person was the recorder, a saucy rascal who took a malicious delight in reminding my friend Stanzius of what he had to ask. O for the masterly pencil of a Hogarth or Chodowiecki, with which to expose such objects of ridicule!

First they set before me letters from my friends, and made me answerable for certain expressions. . . . I explained the passages in question in such a way as to do no harm to my correspondents, without denying the truth. . . . O despotic suspicion! how petty, ridiculous and cruel can you be? In your blind eyes the slightest expression of friendship, and the free utterances of a blameless heart signify treachery and insult. . . .

. . . The second charge against me consists of a few visits that Drexel and Schelle paid me at various times. His Lordship the examiner could not understand how two people could spend a couple of hours chatting together without being Illuminati and conspiring to overthrow the state. He asked me what we talked about; so I replied that as far as I could remember our conversation had been scientific; we also laughed about a lampoon which had appeared against us. This answer did not please Dr. Stanzius at all, and he shook his head at it.

My third crime was that I had corresponded with Schelle on Drexel's behalf; he had written to ask me if I could find somewhere for him to stay in the Salzburg district.

"So", I said, "it is a crime in your eyes to concern oneself for one's friends? I would not refuse my worst enemies if they were in such need; how much more should I stand by someone whom I loved and help him in word and deed? Nature and duty teach me this."

. . . But to go on with the ridiculous crimes of which they accused me. The fourth was that they had found among my papers two speeches and a protocol dated 1783, although according to my declaration I had given up all papers connected with the Order. In answer I showed them a package lying under the papers, on which it was written that I had received these papers three weeks after I had signed the declaration. . . . "Moreover", I added, "you may judge from these papers whether our teaching is dangerous and whether we deserved this persecution. You should first read them and study them, and then judge, if you are willing to do so."

Then my examiner had the effrontery to ask why I had not handed in all my friends' letters in which the Order was mentioned. "Because", I answered, with a look of supreme contempt, "His Excellency cannot possibly suppose that I would betray my friends and act against all obligations of honour and righteousness."

Finally, last of all, came the passage already quoted from my letter to Leiden; my examiner asked me whether I had written this passage. . . . I replied that I had written not only that passage but the whole letter, and that moreover I was not embarrassed by them. That I held the deep conviction that the aims of the Order of Illuminati were good and necessary in the interests of mankind's search for truth . . . , that the society encouraged its members to pursue virtue and true enlightenment; that I naturally thought that the result of the enquiry ordered by the ruler would prove that the supposed treachery of the Illuminati was an invention by wicked and prejudiced men, who were doing great harm to our ruler's reputation in foreign countries, and that as soon as the matter had been investigated these liars and bad counsellors would be dismissed with contempt. And in addition I believed that these liars and slanderers would be pricked by bad consciences, and that this would be revenge enough. All this therefore had caused me to say that what had happened would bring trouble to the enemies of virtue and truth.

While I was dictating all this, my examiner flew into a rage, saying that all this was treasonous, that it had nothing to do with him, since he had no jurisdiction over such matters.

The next question was: were the "events which would have surprised

Baron Leiden" connected with the Elector's command, and, if so, whether I had criticized that command? I answered that this had never entered my head. . . .

Now came the really tricky question: whether the Elector would be to blame if he tolerated such an unlawful, revolutionary society, even if it had the best of aims. I replied that the Elector had the right to do anything he pleased; consequently I hoped no one would accuse me of trying to dispute that right.

This was the essence of my long trial. As regards my conduct, I am aware that I played my role honourably. . . . I know well that I might often have answered the questions better and more freely . . . I was restrained by the thought that a greater degree of vehemence and freedom of speech might harm my friends; this, combined with the maxim that a wise man should not speak when it is better to be silent, made me keep my finger on my mouth. . . . Finally, I pictured myself as a subject protected by his innocence and clear conscience, who does not cringe, nor offend his judge, even though he may be biased – but who keeps calm and continues to justify himself.

A week after my last hearing I was called before the Military Court. I expected nothing less than dismissal, which would certainly have followed, had not certain noblemen in the town begun to agitate on my behalf. Hansler read me the sentence, which was as follows: – "The letters and papers revealed that I had renounced the Illuminati only in words and not in deeds; moreover in secret correspondence I had tried to promote this sect under pretext of spreading virtue and enlightenment. In order to lead me, an impertinent philosopher and Illuminist, away from such a treacherous sect, which had not succeeded in improving me or my fellow-members, in morals or enlightenment, and in order to bring me to the true path of virtue and enlightenment, I was condemned to be shut up in a Franciscan monastery for an indefinite period, and to receive there instruction in the Catholic faith and morality."

I merely replied that I understood the laws on insubordination; I went quietly up to the local captain, handed him my sword, and placed myself under arrest.

The Father Superior received me politely and showed me into a cell. The first thing that met my eyes was the works of Father Merz and Schoenberg in the bookcase. This was to be my reading material – a punishment cleverly designed by my judge. Soon afterwards the Reverend Lector came along, then the Father Superior, offering me consolation. I told them that they would see that I needed none, since I was in good spirits. On the next day the Lector assured me that he did not intend to give me religious instruction, and that the whole library would be at my disposal. Later I became intimate with these monks, and they showed me great consideration.

Apart from this, I am happy and peaceful, and why not? Even here there are people, human beings, with whom I can sympathize; wherever I might be, in the Libyan desert or in cold Siberia, I could still find nourishment for my feelings. Moreover, when one can purify a monk from all the dust and darkness in which his prejudices, his education and his position have enveloped him – underneath his cowl one can still find a human being capable of feeling, and, even more important, of suffering.

I see myself as a missionary, who finds himself in a strange, barbarian country. I preach our doctrine to the monks. My way of life (I eat nothing but eggs at midday, and at night I drink cold milk), my quiet manner and cheerfulness, all that I say and do, seems new and paradoxical to the good fathers; they are beginning to speak in defence of the Illuminati in the town. If matters continue in this way I shall soon be in a position to convert the whole monastery.

That is my story up till now. It is as I would wish it to be. I intend to wait until the judge gives me my freedom; then, in accordance with military orders, I shall write to my regiment, saying that I am convinced that I have proved myself an obedient subject, that I have played my part, and ask permission to take my leave.

I await your reply eagerly about the whole affair. I am anxious to know whether you are satisfied with my behaviour; also whether, when I leave the monastery, I may find somewhere far away, a room where I can continue to have my daily meal of milk and eggs – for I have no money and I am no craftsman.

Farewell – consider me worthy to be called your pupil.

J. Meggenhofen

[Note: After his release Meggenhofen kept his resolve to live quietly and humbly. On 26 October 1790 he was drowned in the river Inn, when a boat in which he was travelling was overturned. Since his body was not immediately found a priest declared that he had been carried straight to hell as a member of the Illuminati. (His body was eventually found over a year later, thus dispelling the legend.)]

APPENDIX III

SYNOPSIS OF *THE MAGIC FLUTE*

Pamina, daughter of the Queen of Night, has been taken from her mother by Sarastro, High Priest of Isis and Osiris. The Queen sends her three ladies-in-waiting to rescue Prince Tamino from a serpent, giving him a portrait of Pamina, and telling him that Sarastro is a wicked magician. Tamino, accompanied by Papageno, the Queen's birdcatcher, sets out to find Pamina. The ladies give him a magic flute, and Papageno magic bells, and tell them that three boys will guide them.

Pamina has been pursued by Monostatos, Sarastro's Moorish servant, who attempts to seduce her. Papageno saves her by playing his magic bells.

The Three Boys lead Tamino to the Temple of Wisdom, where he is met by a priest, from whom he learns that Sarastro is wise and good, and that Pamina has been taken from her mother, who is an evil woman, for her own good. Tamino is told that he may win Pamina for his bride if he can successfully pass through various ordeals, after which he may become one of the initiates.

In Act II, Tamino is questioned by Sarastro and the priests, and accepted as a candidate for initiation. Monostatos again attempts to seduce Pamina, but is prevented by the Queen of Night, who gives Pamina a dagger with which to kill Sarastro.

Tamino must pass the test of silence: he may see Pamina but must not speak to her. Pamina, thinking that he does not love her, tries to kill herself with the dagger, but is saved by the Three Boys, and brought to Tamino. Together the couple go through the final tests of fire and water, aided by the magic flute.

Papageno is unable to pass the tests; he tries to hang himself, but is rescued by the Three Boys, who tell him to play his magic bells, and bring him a wife, Papagena.

The Queen and her ladies, with Monostatos, attack the Temple of Wisdom, but are defeated by Sarastro. The opera ends with a chorus of rejoicing, as Tamino and Pamina enter the Temple of Wisdom to join the Enlightened.

GLOSSARY

Adagio. (It.) Slow.

Allegretto. (It.) A little slower than Allegro.

Allegro. (It.) Quick, lively.

Anapaestic. Rhythm consisting of two short syllables followed by a long one.

Andante. (It.) Walking pace, moderate tempo.

Andantino. (It.) A little faster than Andante.

Antiphonal. Sung in the manner of responses between two groups or between solo and chorus.

Appoggiatura. (It.) Ornament; auxiliary note added above or below the main note.

Aria. (It.) Vocal piece with orchestral accompaniment.

Arietta (It.), or *Ariette* (Fr.). Short aria.

Arpeggio. (It.) Playing of chords in a broken manner.

Assai. (It.) Very.

Augmentation. Lengthening of note-values.

Augmented interval. Interval made wider by a semitone. (e.g. C–G♯ =augmented fifth)

Basset horn. Type of tenor clarinet.

Bridge passage. Transitional passage, especially between first and second subjects in sonata form.

Cadence. Closing phrase at end of composition or section.

Cantabile. (It.) Song-like style.

Cantata. (It.) Short vocal work for solo or chorus with orchestral accompaniment.

Canon. Exact imitation of a melody by another voice, either in unison or at different pitch.

Cantus Firmus. (Lat.) Fixed melody treated contrapuntally, usually placed in tenor part.

Chorale. German hymn.

Chromatic scale. Scale proceeding by semitones. Chromatic music is the antithesis of diatonic, i.e. using notes not included in major or minor key.

Clavier. (Ger.) General term for keyboard instruments; in Mozart's time usually piano.

Coda. (It.) Tail-piece; section at end of movement.

Coloratura. (It.) Florid style of singing.

Common chord. Major or minor triad consisting of note with major or minor third and perfect fifth, usually that which determines key of a piece.

Common time. $(C = \frac{4}{4})$ Four crotchets in a bar.

Concerto. (It.) Composition for one or more solo instruments with orchestra.

Con moto. (It.) With movement.

Con sordini. (It.) With mutes.

Contrabass. (It.) Double bass.

Contredanse. (Fr.) Country dance.

Counterpoint. (Adj. contrapuntal.) Art of combining two or more melodies according to strict rules. (Antithesis of harmony; music composed horizontally.)

Countersubject. Theme in a Fugue which continues in 1st voice when 2nd voice enters.

Coup d'archet. (Fr.) Bow attack in string playing.

Credo. (Lat.) Section of Mass. ("I believe")

Crescendo (It.) Getting louder.

Crotchet $\frac{1}{4}$ of a semibreve; unit of time signature of which lower figure is 4 (black-headed note with stem).

Da capo aria. (It.) Vocal piece in three sections of which the third is a repetition of the first.

Development. Second section of a movement in sonata form, during course of which thematic material is developed. (Sometimes called Working-out section.)

Diatonic. Using notes proper to major or minor key without chromatic alteration.

Dies Irae. (Lat.) Section of Mass ("Day of Judgment").

Diminished interval. Interval made narrower by a semitone (e.g. C–G♭ = diminished fifth).

Diminished seventh, chord of. Chord of three superimposed minor thirds (e.g. C♯ E G B♭).

Diminution. Shortening of note-values.

Divertimento. (It.) Instrumental work in several movements, usually containing several minuets (cf. *Serenade*, usually in *galant* style).

Dominant. Fifth note of scale of any key (V).

Dominant seventh, chord of. Common chord on the dominant of any scale with minor seventh added (e.g. G B D F in key of C). This chord calls for resolution on the tonic (V 7).

Dotted-crotchet, dotted-quaver. Notes prolonged by half their value by dot placed after them.

Duodrama. Musical stage work for two solo singers.

Duple time. Two beats to a bar.

Entr'acte. Interlude between acts of a drama.

Ensemble. Concerted singing or playing.

Episode. Section between two recurrences of the subject.

Fantasia. (It.) Instrumental composition in free form.

Faux bourdon. (Fr.) (Fa-burden) Forerunner of descant, with melody in tenor, often consisting of a series of first inversions (6–3 chords).

Feminine cadence. Cadence in which conclusive tonic is on a weak beat.

Fifth. See *Interval.*

Figured bass. Indication of harmonies by figures placed under bass.

Finale. (It.) Last movement of instrumental work in several movements, or last number in act of an opera.

First inversion. See *Six-three chord.*

First subject. First main thematic material in sonata form.

Flat. Sign (♭) which lowers a note by a semitone.

Forte. (It.) Loud.

Fortepiano. (It.) Early Italian name for piano.

Fröhlich. (Ger.) Joyfully.

Fugato. (It.) In the manner of a fugue.

Fugue. Composition in which a definite number of parts or voices combine in stating and developing a single theme.

Galant. (Fr.) Courtly style which came into favour in middle of eighteenth century. (Main characteristics elegance and formality.)

Gruppetto. (It.) Ornament; turn consisting of four notes connecting two adjacent notes, i.e., note above, note itself, note below, note itself.

Hanswurst. (Ger., "Hans Sausage") Stock character in popular German or Austrian comedy; type of comedy with stock characters (cf. Commedia dell'Arte).

Harmonic progression. Movement from one chord to another according to rules of harmony.

Homophony. Music in plain harmony, in which all parts move together, as opposed to *Polyphony.*

Imitation. Repetition of a musical figure in another part.

Interrupted cadence. Evasion of tonic chord by substituting another chord, usually Submediant (V–VI).

Interval. Distance between two notes. (C–E = a third, C–G = a fifth).

Kammermusikus. (Ger.) Musician in charge of chamber music.

Kapellmeister. (Ger.) Conductor or musical director.

Key. System of notes related to each other and based on a particular note (see *Tonality*).

Key signature. Indication of key by placing sharps or flats at beginning of a piece.

Köchel. German musicologist who compiled index of Mozart's works, based on his own catalogue (K or K V).

Konzertmeister. (Ger.) Leader of orchestra.

Larghetto. (It.) A little faster than *Largo.*

Largo. (It.) Slow movement, broad style.

Legato. (It.) Smoothly.

Libretto. (It.) Text of an opera.

Lied. (Ger.) Song.

Liederbuch. (Ger.) Song-book.

Maestoso. (It.) Majestic, rather slow.

Major. Interval greater than minor by a semitone (C–E = major 3rd, C–E♭ = minor 3rd).

Major scale. Scale in which third and sixth are major.

Major triad. Common chord of three notes in major key.

Mannheim crescendo. Orchestral crescendo introduced into symphonic works by members of Mannheim school in eighteenth century.

Ma non troppo. (It.) But not too much.

Mass. Musical setting of Catholic celebration of Eucharist.

Mediant. Third degree of scale (III).

Melodrama. Dramatic composition or part of work in which actor speaks while orchestra plays a commentary.

Minor. Interval one semitone less than *Major.*

Minor scale. Scale in which third and sixth are minor. (In melodic minor scales sixth and seventh are major ascending.)

Minor triad. Common chord of three notes in minor key.

Minuet. (It. *Minuetto*, Fr. *Menuet*) Dance-form in $\frac{3}{4}$ time.

Modal chords. Term used for degrees of scale which differ in major and minor scales, especially Mediant (III) and Submediant (VI).

Modulation. Passing from one key to another.

Molto. (It.) Much, very.

Monodrama. Musical stage work for a single singer.

Monothematic. Based on a single main theme (as in a fugue).

Motif. Short theme.

Movement. Separate piece in composition of several detached parts, such as a symphony or sonata.

Neapolitan sixth. Chord consisting of a minor sixth and minor third on subdominant. (In C minor, F, A♭, D♭).

Obbligato. (It.) An essential instrumental part in a composition.

Octave. Interval of eight notes of diatonic scale.

Opera buffa. (It.) Type of comic opera, with recitative accompanied on harpsichord.

Opera seria. (It.) Serious opera with recitatives and arias, usually on heroic or mythological themes.

Oratorio. (It.) Vocal work for solo voices and chorus with orchestral accompaniment, usually on sacred theme.

Overture. Orchestral piece opening an opera, oratorio, etc.,

Parallel thirds and sixths. Series of chords consisting of a third with a fourth above it (6–3) (also called first inversions).

Pedal, dominant. Single note, usually in bass, which is held or repeated while the other parts move.

Piano. (It.) Soft.

Piano concerto. (It.) Work for solo piano and orchestra.

Piano sonata. (It.) Work for solo piano in sonata form.

Pizzicato. (It.) Method of playing stringed instruments by plucking the strings.

Plainsong. Medieval church music sung in unison, without measured beat.

Polyphony. Antithesis of *Homophony*: part-music distinguished by linear or horizontal aspects.

Postlude. Short instrumental section at end of a piece.

Prelude. Introductory piece.

Presto. (It.) Very fast.

Premier coup d'archet. (Fr.) Opening of an orchestral piece by playing in unison.

Programme music. Instrumental music based on descriptive subject.

Quartet. Instrumental or vocal work for four players or singers.

Quaver. Half a crotchet (q.v.).

Quintet. Instrumental or vocal work for five players or singers.

Recapitulation. Section in sonata form where first subject returns.

Recitative. Declamation in singing, with fixed notes but without definite metre or time.

Relative major, minor. Connection between major and minor keys with same key signature (A minor is rel. mi. of C).

Requiem. Mass for the dead.

Ritornello. (It.) Orchestral *tutti* in a concerto.

Rondo. (It.) Musical form consisting of refrain or main theme with several episodes (A B A C A D A, etc.).

Scale. Succession of adjoining notes in special order.

Scale, chromatic. Scale proceeding by semitones.

Scale, diatonic. Major or minor scales.

Second subject. Second main thematic material in sonata form.

Second inversion. See six-four chord.

Semiquaver. Half a quaver, quarter of a crotchet (q.v.).

Semitone. Half a tone. Smallest interval in western classical music.

Sequence. Melodic figure repeated rising or falling at least twice in succession.

Serenade. (Evening song) Instrumental work in several movements, of which the first is in sonata form, containing one or more minuets. Often performed in open air.

Seventh, chord of the. See *Dominant seventh.*

Sforzando. (It.) Sudden strong accent.

Sharp. Sign (♯) which raises a note by a semitone.

Sinfonia concertante. (It.) Work in symphonic form for one or more solo instruments, with orchestra.

Singspiel. (Ger.) Dramatic work with spoken dialogue interspersed with songs.

Six-four chord. (6–4) Chord with fifth in bass, or second inversion. This chord often precedes the cadence chord, and is used before the cadenza in a concerto.

Six-three chord. (6–3 or 6) Chord with third in bass, or first inversion.

Slurred notes. Notes grouped under a curved line, or slur, indicating legato playing or singing.

Sonata. Instrumental piece in three or four movements, of which the first is usually in sonata form.

Sonata form. Single movement consisting of Exposition, with two main thematic groups (First and Second Subject), Development, or Working-out section, in which themes are developed, and Recapitulation, in which themes of opening section are repeated. A Coda, or tail-piece, may be added.

Sonata rondo. A form of rondo in which one of the episodes appears a second time, like a second subject in sonata form.

Sostenuto. (It.) With sustained tone.

Sotto voce. (It.) Music sung or played very softly.

Staccato. Detached. Indicated by dots placed over the notes.

Subdominant. Fourth degree of scale (IV).

Submediant. Sixth degree of scale (VI).

Supertonic. Second degree of scale (II).

Suspension. Note anticipated or retarded so as to appear before or after the chord to which it belongs.

Symphony. Orchestral work in three or four movements, of which the first is in sonata form, sometimes with a slow introduction.

Syncopation. Displacement of an accent to weak beats of bar.

Tonality. Feeling of a definite key suggested in a composition or passage.

Tonic. Keynote. First degree of scale, which determines key (I).

Transition. See *Bridge passage.*

Tremolando. (It.) Rapid alternation of two notes.

Triad. Common chord of three notes.

Trio. (a) Instrumental or vocal work for three players or singers. (b) Alternative section in a Minuet, after which the first part is repeated.

Triplet. Group of three notes, indicated by curved line over the notes with the figure 3 placed under it.

Triple time. Three beats in a bar.

Tutti. (It.) Orchestral passage in a concerto where the soloist is silent.

Variation form. Theme (usually in two eight-bar phrases) followed by varied treatment.

Vivace. (It.) Lively, fast.

Vivo. (It.) Animated.

Vocal score. Arrangement of operas, oratorios, etc., for voices with piano accompaniment condensed from orchestral score.

Volkslieder. (Ger.) Folk songs.

Well-tempered Clavier. Title of Bach's Forty-eight Preludes and Fugues (well-tuned, with equal tuning in semitones).

SELECT BIBLIOGRAPHY

Anderson, E., *The Letters of Mozart and his Family* (2nd ed.), New York, 1966.

Ballin, E. M., *Der Dichter von Mozarts Freimaurerlied "O heiliges Band"*, Tutzing, 1960.

Banner, H. S., *These Men were Masons*, London, 1934.

Batley, E. M., *A Preface to The Magic Flute*. London, 1969.

Bauer, W. A., and Deutsch, O. E., *Mozart, Briefe und Aufzeichnungen*, Kassel, 1962–3.

Beaumarchais, P.-A. de, *Le Mariage de Figaro* (ed. Arnould), Oxford, 1952.

Brophy, B., *Mozart the Dramatist*, London, 1964.

Chailley, J., *The Magic Flute, Masonic Opera* (tr. Weinstock), London, 1972.

Cohen, A., *Lessing's Masonic Dialogues*, London, 1927.

Cooke, D., *The Language of Music*, London, 1959.

Da Ponte, L., *Memoirs* (ed. and tr. Sheppard), London, 1929.

Dent, E. J., *Mozart's Operas* (1913), 2nd ed. London, 1947.

Deutsch, O. E., *Mozart, A Documentary Biography*, London, 1965.

Deutsch, O. E., *Mozart und die Wiener Logen*, Vienna, 1932.

Einstein, A., *Mozart* (1946), London, 1971.

Engel, L., *Geschichte des Illuminaten-Ordens*, Berlin, 1906.

Farmer, H. G., *New Mozartiana*, Glasgow, 1935.

Finkelstein, S., *Composer and Nation*, London, 1960.

Forman, D., *Mozart's Concerto Form*, London, 1971.

Frost, T., *Secret Societies of the European Revolution*, London, 1876.

Girdlestone, C. M., *Mozart's Piano Concertos*, London, 1948.

Hill, R., *The Concerto*, London, 1952.

Hobsbawm, E., *The Age of Revolution*, London, 1962.

Holmes, E., *Life of Mozart* (1845), 2nd ed. London, 1921.

Hyatt King, A., *Mozart Chamber Music*, London, 1968.

Hyatt King, A., *Mozart in Retrospect*, London, 1955.

Jahn, O., *Life of Mozart* (1856–9) (3 vols.) (tr. Townsend), London, 1882.

Jacob, H. E., *Joseph Haydn, His Art, Times and Glory*, London, 1950.

Kelly, C., *Conspiracy against God and Man*, Western Islands, 1974.

Kelly, M., *Reminiscences* (1826) (ed. Fiske), London, 1974.

Knepler, G., *Musikgeschichte des 19. Jahrhunderts*, Berlin, 1961.

Knight, F., *Beethoven and the Age of Revolution*, London, 1973.

Koch, R., *Br. Mozart, Freimaurer und Illuminat*, Bad Reichenhall, 1911.

Köchel, L. von, *Chronologisch-thematisches Verzeichnis sämtlicher Tonwerke Wolfgang Amadé Mozart* (1862) (ed. Einstein, 3rd ed.), Leipzig, 1937.

Le Forestier, R., *Les Illuminés de Bavière*, Paris, 1913.

Levey, M., *The Life and Death of Mozart*, London, 1972.

Lewis, L., *Geschichte der Freimaurerei in Oesterriech und Ungarn*, Leipzig, 1872.

Liebner, J., *Mozart on the Stage*, London, 1972.

Marx, Karl, and Engels, Frederick, *The Communist Manifesto* (in Marx–Engels Selected Works), London, 1968.

Massin, J. and B., *W. A. Mozart*, Paris, 1959.

Métraux, A., *The Incas* (tr. D. Garman), London, 1965.

Moberly, R. D., *Three Mozart Operas*, London, 1967.

Naumann, J. G., *Vierzig Freymaurer-Lieder* (1782), 2nd ed. Berlin, 1784.

Nettl, P., *Mozart and Masonry*, New York, 1970.

Neue Mozart Ausgabe [N.M.A.], Kassel, 1957–.

Novello, V. and M., *A Mozart Pilgrimage* (ed. Medici and Hughes), London, 1955.

Pusch, E., *Letters of an Empress*, London, 1939.

Reti, R., *The Thematic Process in Music*, London, 1961.

Robbins Landon, H. C., *The Collected Correspondence of Joseph Haydn*, London, 1959.

Robbins Landon, H. C., and Mitchell, D., *The Mozart Companion*, London, 1956.

Roberts, J. M., *The Mythology of the Secret Societies*, London, 1974.

Robison, J., *Proofs of a Conspiracy*, Edinburgh, 1797 (repr. U.S. 1967).

Scheibe, J. A. *Vollständiges Liederbuch für Freymaurer*, Copenhagen and Leipzig, 1776.

Schenk, E., *Mozart and his Times* (ed. and tr. Winston), London, 1960.

Schneider, H., *Quest for Mysteries*, New York, 1947.

Soboul, A., *The French Revolution, 1787–1799* (tr. Forrest and Jones), London, 1974.

Stadtlaender, C., *Joseph Haydn of Eisenstadt*, London, 1968.

Stauffer, V., *New England and the Bavarian Illuminati*, New York, 1918 (repr. 1967).

Steiner, G., *Franz Heinrich Ziegenhagen und seine Verhältnislehre*, Berlin, 1962.

Valentin, E., *Mozart, A Pictorial Biography*, London, 1962.

Van Dülmen, R., *Der Geheimbund der Illuminaten*, Stuttgart, 1975.

Wangermann, E., *The Austrian Achievement*, London, 1973.

Wangermann, E., *From Joseph II to the Jacobin Trials*, Oxford, 1969.

Webster, N., *Secret Societies and Subversive Movements*, London, 1924.

Wyzewa, T. von, and Saint-Foix, G. de, *Wolfgang Amadée Mozart*, Paris, 1912–46.

SELECT LIST OF RECORDINGS

MASONIC WORKS

Music for Masonic Occasions (Maag). Turnabout (2 records) TV34213/4.

Masonic Music (Kertesz) (L.S.O.). Decca SXL 6409.

Masonic Music (Cotte) (Musicians of Paris). Arion 30 A 100.

Mozart Lieder Recital (Fischer-Dieskau and Barenboim). E.M.I. ASD 2824.

Thamos King of Egypt (Klee). Philips 6500 840.

OPERAS

Die Zauberflöte (Karajan). E.M.I. SLS 5052.
(Also excerpts.)
Le Nozze di Figaro (Davis). Philips 6707014.
(Also excerpts.)
Don Giovanni (Fricsay). D.G. 2728003.
(Also excerpts) (Krips). E.M.I. SDD 382.
Cosi fan Tutte (Boehm). E.M.I. SLS 5028.
(Also excerpts.)
Die Entführung (Böhm). D.G. 2740102.
+ *Impresario (Der Schauspieldirektor).*
La Clemenza di Tito (Excerpts) (Kertesz). Decca SET 357–9.
Zaide (Klee). Philips 6500 983–4.

SYMPHONIES

No. 38 (Prague) (Maag). Decca SDD 331.
+ *Clarinet Concerto* (Peyer).
No. 39 (E♭)
+ *No. 40 (G mi.)*   (Barenboim). H.M.V. ASD 2424.
No. 41 (Jupiter)
+ *No. 31 (Paris)*   (Barenboim). H.M.V. ASD 2379.

Sinfonia Concertante (Oistrakh). E.M.I. SDD 445.

STRING QUARTETS

Nos. 14–19 (Haydn) (Quartetto Italiano). Philips SAL 3632–4.
Nos. 20 and 21 (Hoffmeister and King of Prussia, K.499 and 575).
  Philips 6500241.

STRING QUINTETS

Complete (Grumaux Trio augmented). Philips 6747107.
Nos. 4 and 5 (G mi. and D ma.) (Amadeus). D.G. 138057.

Piano Trio (K.542)
  + *K.502 and 564)*   (Beaux Arts). Phonogram SAL 3681/2.
Clar. Quintet
  + *Trio for Pf. Clar. and Vla.*   (Melos Ensemble). H.M.V. ASD 605.
Piano sonata in C mi. (K.457)
  + *Fantasia in C mi.* (K.475)   (Klien). Turnabout TV 37005.
Adagio in B mi. (Piano)
  + *Rondo in A mi.* (Piano)   (Klien). Turnabout TV 37011.

PIANO CONCERTOS

Complete (Barenboim). H.M.V. SLS 5031.
  (Anda). D.G. 2720030.
Nos. 12 and 19 (Barenboim). H.M.V. ASD 2956.
Nos. 9 and 14 (Brendel). Vanguard HM 30.
Nos. 20 and 17 (Anda). D.G. 138853.
Nos. 21 and 24 (Badura Skoda). Supraphon 1101176.
Nos. 25 and 27 (Brendel). Turnabout TV 34129.
Nos. 20 and 23 (Fischer). H.M.V. SXLP 30148.
Nos. 24 and 18 (Barenboim). H.M.V. ASD 2887.
Nos. 21 and 22 (Fischer). H.M.V. SXLP 30124.

SACRED MUSIC

Mass in C minor (Leppard). E.M.I. ASD 2959.
Requiem Mass (Böhm). D.G. 2530 143
  or (Davis). SAL 3749.

GENERAL INDEX

Adamberger, Valentin: 54, 81, 91
d'Alembert, Jean: 12, 21, 41
Alxinger, Johann: 64, 76–7
Amann, Basilius von: 17
Anderson's Constitutions: 12
André, Johann: 45
Apponyi, Count Anton: 79
Arco, Count Georg von: 22, 51–2, 55
Artaria and Co.: 73

Bach, C. P. E.: 61
Bach, J. C.: 45
Bach, J. S.: 61, 67, 71
Bähr, Joseph: 152
Barisani, Dr. Sigmund: 17, 74, 118
Barruel, Abbé Augustin de: 134
Basedow, Johann: 146
Batzko, Ludwig von: 157
Bavaria, Elector of, see Karl Theodor
Beaumarchais, P. A. C. de: 96–8, 100,
    104, 140, 164
Beethoven, Karl van: 131
Beethoven, Ludwig van: 29, 52, 53, 54,
    62, 67, 74, 109, 112, 120, 131–2,
    135, 137, 159, 177
Benda, Georg: 29, 33, 179n.
Beneficence (Masonic lodge): 11, 61, 76,
    79, 84, 87, 116, 134, 173
Bichler (florist): 77
Blumauer, Alois: 63, 64, 66–7, 76,
    133–4, 157
Böhm, Johannes: 28, 45, 140
Born, Ignaz von: 16, 21, 63–4, 76–8, 79,
    80–3, 89, 91, 115–17, 121, 132–3,
    153, 155, 159, 172
Bretzner, C. F.: 53, 55
Brophy, Brigid: 122
Bullinger, Abbé Joseph: 47

Campe, J. C.: 119, 153

Canal von Malabaila, Count Joseph:
    99–100
Cavalieri, Madame Caterina: 54
Chabot, Duchesse de: 35
Chailley, Jacques: 7, 85n., 86–7, 128,
    155, 160n., 164
Chodowiecky, Daniel: 147, 183
Cicero: 78
Clement XII, Pope: 13
Cobenzl, Count Johann Philipp: 53,
    61–2, 64
Cobenzl, Count Ludwig: 62
Colloredo, Count Hieronymus, Arch-
    bishop of Salzburg: 7, 19, 22, 24,
    32–3, 39, 50–2, 55, 57, 73, 100
Condorcet, Marie-Jean: 12
Cooke, Deryck: 43n., 103, 127
Crowned Hope (Masonic lodge): 80–1,
    90, 95
Crux, Marianne: 17

Dalberg, Baron Wolfgang von: 34, 38,
    46, 60, 140
da Ponte, Lorenzo: 96–9, 120, 122,
    136–9
David, Anton: 90
Daxberg, Baron von: 182
Dent, Professor E. J.: 45n., 122, 129,
    137–8, 171
Diderot, Denis: 14, 21, 35
Diodorus Siculus: 26
Donaueschingen, Prince of: 107
Drexel, Anton: 183

Einstein, Alfred: 11, 17, 83, 110, 125–6,
    136, 171
Égalité, Philippe, see Orleans, Duke of
Engel (master tailor): 77
Engel, Ludwig: 181n.
Esterhazy, Count Franz: 70, 82
Esterhazy, Prince Paul Anton: 32

Stanzius, Dr.: 183
Steiner, Gerhard: 148
Stephanie, Gottlieb: 48, 53, 56, 106
Stoll, Anton: 171n.
Storace, Nancy and Stephen: 107
Storch (upholsterer): 77
Strinasacchi, Regina: 73
Sturm, Christian: 153
Süssmayr, Franz: 171
Swieten, Baron Gottfried van: 53, 61, 67, 68, 131, 133, 136, 139

Terrasson, Abbé Jean: 26, 155
Thun, Count Johann: 99
Thun, Countess Wilhelmine: 53, 64, 68, 135, 142
Thurn und Taxis, Count Johann Baptist von: 19
Tinti, Baron Anton: 79
Tinti, Baron Bartolomäus: 79
Torricella, Christoph: 73
Tost, Joseph: 151
Trattner, Johann Thomas von: 70, 74
Trattner, Therese von: 74
True Harmony (Masonic lodge): 17, 63, 76–7, 79, 80, 115–16, 133

Vaughan Williams, Ralph: 120
Vogler, Abbé Georg: 34

Voltaire, François Marie Arouet de: 12, 32, 35, 37–8, 98

Walsegg-Stupach, Count Franz: 171
Weber, Aloysia: 34, 38–9, 53, 137
Weber, Constanze, *see* Mozart, Constanze
Weber, Maria-Cäcilia: 170
Weber, Sophie, *see* Haibl, Sophie
Weigl, Joseph: 139
Weishaupt, Adam: 8, 14–16, 47, 61–3, 77–8, 122, 181–6
Wieland, Christoph Martin: 24, 27, 33, 34
Wieser, Siegfried: 77
Williams, Bernard: 137
Winter, Sebastian: 107
Wolff, Dr. Joseph: 20
Wucherer, Georg Philipp: 133
Wyzewa, Théodore de: 159

Ziegenhagen, Franz Heinrich: 38n., 142–3, 145–8, 151, 156–7, 159, 163–4, 172
Zimmermann, Johann Georg von: 134
Zinzendorf, Count Karl: 99, 106, 121, 138, 169, 170
Zwack, Franz Xaver von: 15, 77, 115

INDEX OF COMPOSITIONS
MENTIONED IN THE TEXT